Capitalism, Democracy, and Welfare

This book builds on new institutionalist theory in both economics and political science to offer a general political economy framework for the study of welfare capitalism. Based on the key idea that social protection in a modern economy, both inside and outside the state, can be understood as protection of specific investments in human capital, the book offers a systematic explanation of popular preferences for redistributive spending, the economic role of political parties and electoral systems, and labor market stratification (including gender inequality). Contrary to the popular idea that competition in the global economy undermines international differences in the level of social protection, the book argues that these differences are made possible by a high international division of labor. Such a division allows firms to specialize in production that requires an abundant supply of workers with specific skills, and hence high demand for protection. The rise of nontraded services undermines this specialization and increases demands for more flexible labor markets.

Torben Iversen is Professor of Government at Harvard University. He is the author of *Contested Economic Institutions: The Politics of Macroeconomics and Wage Bargaining* (Cambridge University Press, 1999) and coeditor of *Unions, Employers, and Central Bankers: Macroeconomic Coordination and Institutional Change in Social Market Economies* (Cambridge University Press, 1999). He is also the author or coauthor of articles in such journals as the *American Journal of Political Science, American Political Science Review, British Journal of Political Science, Comparative Politics, Comparative Political Studies, International Organization, Oxford Review of Economic Policy, Public Choice, Quarterly Journal of Economics,* and *World Politics,* as well as in numerous edited volumes.

Cambridge Studies in Comparative Politics

General Editor
Margaret Levi *University of Washington, Seattle*

Assistant General Editor
Stephen Hanson *University of Washington, Seattle*

Associate Editors
Robert H. Bates *Harvard University*
Peter Hall *Harvard University*
Peter Lange *Duke University*
Helen Milner *Columbia University*
Frances Rosenbluth *Yale University*
Susan Stokes *University of Chicago*
Sidney Tarrow *Cornell University*

Other Books in the Series

(*Continued after the index*)

Capitalism, Democracy, and Welfare

TORBEN IVERSEN

Harvard University

CAMBRIDGE
UNIVERSITY PRESS

CAMBRIDGE UNIVERSITY PRESS
Cambridge, New York, Melbourne, Madrid, Cape Town, Singapore, São Paulo

Cambridge University Press
40 West 20th Street, New York, NY 10011-4211, USA

www.cambridge.org
Information on this title: www.cambridge.org/9780521848619

First published 2005

Printed in the United States of America

A catalog record for this publication is available from the British Library.

Library of Congress Cataloging in Publication Data

Iversen, Torben.
Capitalism, democracy, and welfare / Torben Iversen.
   p. cm. – (Cambridge studies in comparative politics)
Includes bibliographical references.
ISBN 0-521-84861-X (hardback) – ISBN 0-521-61307-8 (pbk.)
1. Welfare economics. 2. Human capital. 3. Income distribution.
4. Social choice. I. Title. II. Series.
HB99.3.I94 2005
330.12′6–dc22   2004020247

ISBN-13 978-0-521-84861-9 hardback
ISBN-10 0-521-84861-X hardback

ISBN-13 978-0-521-61307-1 paperback
ISBN-10 0-521-61307-8 paperback

Til min mor og far

Contents

Tables

Tables

Figures

Acknowledgments

This manuscript is the result of more than half a decade of research into the causes and consequences of social policy, and it is in large measure the fruit of collaboration with numerous outstanding scholars and colleagues. I am particularly grateful to David Soskice who worked with me on every part of this book, especially Part II, which is mainly the result of joint work. David has been a constant source of inspiration, and the book would not have been possible without his ideas, insights, and encouragement – even as he remains a critic on parts of the argument in this book. In addition, parts of this book have benefited greatly from collaborative work with (in alphabetical order) Tom Cusack, Barry Eichengreen, Margarita Estevez-Abe, Frances Rosenbluth, and Anne Wren. My primary claim to authorship is that I am probably the only person prepared to assume responsibility for the manuscript in its entirety, including all the errors, omissions, and questionable arguments.

Three other people deserve special mention because they read and commented on the entire manuscript: Peter Lange, Margaret Levi, and Charla Rudisill. In addition to many helpful substantive comments, Peter Lange's advice on the organization and presentation of the materials, and especially his detailed comments on several iterations of Chapter 1, made this a much better book. Margaret Levi organized an extremely useful colloquium on a preliminary version of the book in the Department of Political Science at the University of Washington in May of 2002, where she and other participants (especially Terry Givens and Erik Wibbels) pushed me to be clearer about the argument and to make significant improvements to the analysis. I am grateful to two anonymous reviewers for the same reason. Last, but not least, Charla Rudisill read every word in this book to make sure it made at least some sense to people who do not spend most of their waking hours thinking about these issues. She also patiently put up with me while I did just that.

In addition, I have received many helpful comments on parts of this book from (in alphabetical order) Jim Alt, Uwe Becker, Pepper Culpepper, Robert Fannion, Jeff Frieden, Geoff Garrett, Robert Goodin, Peter Hall, Bob Hancké, Peter Katzenstein, Lane Kenworthy, Gary King, Herbert Kitschelt, Isabela Mares, Paul Pierson, Jonas Pontusson, Nirmala Ravishankar, Philipp Rehn, Ron Rogowski, Fritz Scharpf, Ken Scheve, Michael Shalev, Ken Shepsle, and Wolfgang Streeck. Of these, Robert Fannion and Nirmala Ravishankar also provided excellent research assistance.

Various segments of the manuscript have found their way into articles and papers. Some of the arguments and data found in Chapters 1 and 2 originate in a paper I coauthored with Margarita Estevez-Abe and David Soskice, published in Peter Hall and David Soskice (eds.), *Varieties of Capitalism: The Challenges Facing Contemporary Political Economies*, Oxford University Press (2001). Chapter 2 also draws on a paper with Barry Eichengreen that was previously published in *Oxford Review of Economic Policy* under the title of "Institutions and Economic Performance in the 20th Century: Evidence from the Labor Market." Chapter 3, which presents and tests the individual-level implications of the argument, is an expanded version of a paper I wrote with David Soskice for the 2000 Annual Meeting of the American Political Science Association (APSA) in Washington, DC, subsequently published in the *American Political Science Review* under the title "An Asset Theory of Social Policy Preferences." The parts in this chapter on gender preferences appear in a somewhat different form as a section in a 2003 APSA paper with Frances Rosenbluth called "The Political Economy of Gender: Explaining Cross-National Variation in Household Bargaining, Divorce, and the Gender Voting Gap." Chapter 4 is built on two unpublished papers with David Soskice. One was presented at the 2002 Annual Meeting of the Public Choice Society, San Diego, and is entitled "Political Parties and the Time Inconsistency Problem in Social Welfare Provision"; the other was first presented at the 2002 Annual Meeting of the American Political Science Association in Boston and is entitled "Electoral Systems and the Politics of Coalitions: Why Some Democracies Redistribute More Than Others." The two sections in Chapter 5 on the effects of major shifts in the occupational structure build on a paper that I wrote with Tom Cusack and presented at the 1998 Annual Meeting of the American Political Science Association in

Acknowledgments

Boston; it was later published in *World Politics* under the title "The Causes of Welfare State Expansion: Deindustrialization or Globalization?" (April 2000). Finally, sections of Chapter 6 draw from a paper written with Anne Wren that appeared in *World Politics* (July 1998) under the title "Equality, Employment, and Budgetary Restraint: The Trilemma of the Service Economy."

Capitalism, Democracy, and Welfare

PART I

Welfare Production Regimes

1

**A Political Economy Approach
to the Welfare State**

Printing is one of the world's oldest industries, and typography is one of the oldest occupations in the industrial economy. Typographers essentially transformed stacks of typed and handwritten manuscripts into a form that permitted the mass production of books, newspapers, and journals. Half technicians and half craftsmen, typographers were highly skilled, well paid, and proud harbingers of Gutenberg's revolutionary invention. However, the craft was radically transformed over time: first from "hot-metal" typesetting to "analog" typesetting and then to digital CRT (cathode ray tube) and laser image-setting. In the process of change, previous typesetting skills were swept aside in a matter of a decade or two, and large numbers of typesetters and other printing production workers lost their jobs – many by an invention that the printed word helped set in motion: the computer. Lead molds, printing plates, and all the other paraphernalia that went into the original printing processes were retired to the dusty shelves of industry museums. But retirement was not an option for the majority of typographers whose livelihood depended on using the skills they had acquired through long apprenticeships and years of learning by doing.

The depth of desperation these workers felt as their industry was transformed – manifested in bitter strikes across the developed world – can be loosely conceptualized as a product of the nontransferability of their skills and the speed with which their skills were rendered obsolete by new technology *minus* the availability of public policies such as unemployment insurance, public health insurance, pensions, retraining programs, and public job creation that all cushion the effects of skill redundancy. And this formula for desperation can, of course, be applied not just to typographers but to all workers – past, present, and future – who have skills that are limited in application and can be made obsolete by new technology and other forces of change. Social scientists are certainly no exception to this logic. If it were not for the institution of tenure, many Kremlinologists would have had little marketable expertise following the collapse of the Soviet Union.

The point of this story is to highlight a central theme of this book: the importance of political and economic institutions for protecting the human capital in which people have invested. Job protection, unemployment benefits, income protection, and a host of related policies such as public retraining programs and industry subsidies, all help to insure workers against the loss in asset values when external shocks in technology and labor market conditions shift the demand for skills. Indeed, having in place some form of protection is a precondition for people making investments in specific skills in the first place. High job security, wage protection backed by union power, and guaranteed health and pension benefits have encouraged generations of young people to follow in their parents footsteps and choose typography as their trade. And, needless to say, the health of the printing industry depended on people willing to invest in specific skills. Likewise, the acquisition of specialized knowledge in academia, including that represented by Kremlinologists, would be very risky without some form of job security, and specialized knowledge is the lifeblood of any major research institution. Even if the institution of tenure was invented as a response to the Red Scare in the 1920s, its persistence owes much to the fact that it is functional to the production of new knowledge.

But social protection is clearly not only about insurance, it is also about redistribution and political conflict. By this I mean that whereas insurance is an institutional device for workers to consensually pool their risks and reimburse each other for potential future losses, redistribution is a device wherein money is taken from some workers and given to others in the present, without prior consent to do so. When printers' unions went on strike across the industrialized world in the 1970s, it was to seek subsidization of their own jobs and income, not to collect an already agreed upon insurance or to guarantee the future reproduction of old typographical skills. Everyone understood that traditional typesetting as a trade was doomed and that protection of current workers served largely distributive purposes. For the unions, it was a matter of survival, and they fought bitter battles, sometimes violent, to delay the introduction of new technology and to force employers to retain their old typographical workers. It is no accident that the first publishing houses to introduce new technology, such as *LA Times* and *Oklahoma City Times*, were ones with the weakest unions.

4

A Political Economy Approach to the Welfare State

As the printing example highlights, the political economy of insurance and of redistribution are in fact closely intertwined. Policies adopted for insurance purposes have redistributive consequences, and, as I will argue in detail later in this chapter, redistribution can also sometimes serve insurance purposes. Indeed, a central contention of this book is that answers to many of the most pressing questions about the relationship between social protection and the economy can be found in the intersection of insurance and redistribution, or more specifically in the interplay of income, skills, and democratic politics. Close linkages exist between workers' investment in skills, the international product market strategies of firms, electoral politics, and social protection. As I have argued with Margarita Estevez-Abe and David Soskice (Estevez-Abe et al. 2001), these linkages have been organized into distinct "welfare production regimes" in different countries, each associated with its own political-economic dynamic and reinforced, not undermined as often presumed, by the international division of labor.

Standard approaches to the welfare state fail to account for the relationship between production and social protection, and they leave behind a number of key questions that any political economy approach to social protection needs to answer. For example, if social protection undermines markets, as commonly argued, why is there no apparent relationship between the generosity of such protection and economic growth? A related question is why globalization has not led to a competitive race to the bottom as many feared. Indeed, it seems to be the rise of sheltered, nontraded, services that has prompted some governments to embark on labor market deregulation. To understand why, we need to examine the intersection between welfare production regimes and the creation of comparative advantages in the international economy. The same is true if we want to understand why employers are not universally opposed to generous social protection, and why they continue to invest heavily in economies with high social spending despite the widely held view that such spending is detrimental to business interests.

Even traditional distributive politics, I submit, is not well understood in the existing literature. Though there is considerable evidence that class politics matters, why is distributive politics played out so differently in different countries? The fact that partisan politics is systematically biased to the left in some countries but to the right in others is not in any straightforward way related to the power of unions or the size of the traditional working class. For example, it is striking that the decline of the industrial

5

working class and their unions has been associated with a rise, not a collapse, in the political support for the welfare state. Also, countries with the most skewed distribution of income, where standard class arguments would predict the most radical redistribution, are in fact the least redistributive. The solution to these puzzles, I argue later, is to be found in the interplay of insurance and redistributive incentives to support the welfare state, as well as in the political institutions that translate these motives into policy. In turn, preferences for social protection are explained by the key assets, especially skills, that economic agents have invested in.

In the rest of this chapter, I first provide a more thorough critique of the existing literature and introduce the key concepts and causal mechanisms in the asset or welfare production regime argument (Section 1.1). I then spell out the implications of the argument for understanding the role of electoral politics (Section 1.2) and the relationship between the international economy, economic change, and the rise of social protection (Section 1.3). I finally explore how the approach can help explain cross-national variance in some of the key dimensions of inequality and redistribution (Section 1.4).

1.1. *Toward a New Approach to the Study of the Welfare State*

As the printing industry example suggests, the ability of management to introduce radical new technology is undermined by strong unions and labor market regulation. Indeed, the notion that these institutions, and the welfare state more generally, erode the market is a central theme among neoclassical economists and political sociologists alike. According to those who take this view, labor is an anonymous commodity, easily aggregated into a single factor L, where each constituent unit (worker) is "replaceable, easily redundant, and atomized" (Esping-Andersen 1990, p. 37). Logically, the opposite of market (or "commodification") is state (or "decommodification"). It means that "a person can maintain a livelihood without reliance on the market" (Esping-Andersen 1990, p. 22). The welfare state transforms L into not-L, and thereby set the worker free: free to organize, free to oppose capital, free to be an individual rather than a commodity. Again in the words of Esping-Andersen: "Decommodification strengthens the worker and weakens the absolute authority of the employer. It is for exactly this reason that employers have always opposed decommodification" (1990, p. 22). The welfare state is "politics against markets" (Esping-Andersen 1985), and the historical strength of the political left, mediated by alliances with the middle classes, determine how much welfare state and how much market

6

you end up with (Korpi 1983, 1989; Esping-Andersen 1990; Huber and Stephens 2001).

The power resources model of the welfare state as it is known is the dominant approach to the study of the welfare state. It suggests that the welfare state is built on the shoulders of an unwilling capitalist class, who will be looking for any opportunities to unburden itself. This is also a central theme in the burgeoning literature on globalization where the "exit option" for capital presents precisely such an opportunity. As Wolfgang Streeck explains in the case of Germany: "Globalization, by increasing the mobility of capital and labour across national borders, extricates the labour supply from national control and enables the financial sector to refuse doing service as a national utility" (Streeck 1997). In a similar vein, Dani Rodrik concludes that "integration into the world economy reduces the ability of governments to undertake redistributive taxation or implement generous social programs" (Rodrik 1997).

Indeed, if welfare capitalism is primarily about decommodification and exploitation of the rich, one should have expected capitalists to shun productive investment in large welfare states well in advance of the onset of globalization in the 1980s. Perhaps globalization has made the tradeoff between redistribution and investment steeper because of expanded menu options for capital, but as argued by Lindblom (1980), Przeworski (1986), and others, economic performance has always depended on the cooperation of capital. Yet, the remarkable fact about the observed relationship among levels of public spending, investment, and national income in advanced democracies is that there is none (Lindert 1996). Or if there is one, it is so weak that it does not appear to have imposed much of a constraint on governments' ability to spend and regulate labor markets. Among democracies, the countries with the largest welfare states are no poorer, or richer, than countries that spend much less.

In recent years, an alternative approach to the welfare state has emerged, which emphasizes the role of employers. Contrary to the power resources model, Peter Swenson (2002) shows through careful archival research that employers played a proactive role in the early formation of social policy. Swenson argues that in tight labor markets employers will seek to take social benefits out of competition by creating a uniform, national social insurance system. When labor markets are slack, on the other hand, high-cost producers may feel compelled to impose costs on low-cost producers through mandatory social insurance arrangements. Swenson argues that the first logic helps explain early welfare reforms in Sweden, while the latter helps explain salient features of the New Deal legislation in the United States.

In a similar vein, Isabela Mares (2003) has argued that companies and industries that are highly exposed to risks will favor a social insurance system where costs and risks are shared, leading these employers to push universalistic unemployment and accident insurance. This is remarkable because universalism is usually associated with strong unions and left governments. Mares also suggests, and this idea is emphasized in this book, that social protection may encourage the acquisition of skills in the labor force, which in turn enhances the ability of some firms to compete in international markets. Consequently, for example, some high-skill firms favor generous unemployment insurance.

In a recent dissertation on the German welfare state, Philip Manow (2002) has likewise advanced the thesis that the German system of social protection, through a process of institutional coevolution, emerged as an important complement to the collective bargaining system, which in turn underwrote union wage restraint and international competitiveness. By delegating much of the responsibility for social policy to the social partners, the institutional incapacity of the German state to guarantee full employment (as a result of federalism, an independent central bank, etc.) was compensated for by a social system that provided very high levels of insurance in the event of unemployment and other shocks to income. In earlier work, Peter Baldwin (1990) also challenges the notion that the welfare state was erected by the industrial working class alone, against the will of the middle classes. Much universalism in the "social democratic" welfare states of Scandinavia, for example, was the result of pressure by farmers and other nonworkers at the turn of the century to be included in social programs that served as instruments of insurance as much as tools of redistribution.

The evidence presented by Lindert, Mares, Swenson, Manow, and Baldwin strongly suggests that social protection cannot be conceived exclusively in terms of simple dichotomies between the state and the market, or between commodification and decommodification. We need a "politics *of* markets" rather than a "politics *against* markets," or, more precisely, a theory that acknowledges that social protection can improve the operation of markets as well as undermine them. Building on Estevez-Abe et al. (2001), this is precisely what this book aims to provide. It develops an approach to production and labor markets in which the role of social protection is explicitly modeled. The theory reconciles the controversy between the power resources perspective and the new employer-focused approaches, and it also links the study of the welfare state to recent work on the importance of democratic institutions for social policy.

At the heart of the difficulties in the standard view of the welfare state is a neoclassical conception of markets that largely ignores differentiated skills. Although unskilled day workers can sensibly be analyzed as an undifferentiated factor L, and although such labor can be exchanged efficiently in something that approximates spot markets, in Becker's (1964) seminal work and in new institutional economics, these conditions are considered the extreme of a continuum. At the other extreme, you find workers with highly asset-specific investments in skills – L_s, where $s = (1, 2, 3, \ldots, n)$ refers to differentiated skills – coupled with nonmarket institutions that protect and manage these investments.

Of course, workers are not the only ones who invest in specific assets; firms, merchants, and virtually any agent involved in economic exchange do also. And because economic agents are engaged in exchange, and because they sometimes own the assets jointly, most assets are cospecific in the sense that they tie together the welfare of people and make them dependent on one another. For every worker whose livelihood is tied to a specific skill, there is an employer who depends on the worker with those skills. As argued by Polanyi (1944), Williamson (1985), North (1990), and others, when an economy is characterized by heavy investment in such cospecific assets, economic agents are exposed to risks that make efficient market exchange problematic. A precondition for such an economy to work efficiently is a dense network of institutions that provide information, offer insurance against risk, and permit continuous and impartial enforcement of complex contracts. In the absence of such institutions, exchange is possible only at a small scale in local trading communities where people know each other well and engage in repeated face-to-face interactions.[1] At a larger scale, markets left to their own devices either will fail to produce much exchange, will be accompanied by costly and continuous haggling, or will involve only very homogeneous types of assets (L as opposed to L_s).

Nowhere is the importance of institutions more evident than in the labor market where the welfare state plays a key mediating role. Social protection is particularly important in solving market failures in the formation of skills. Without implicit agreements for long-term employment and real wage stability, investment in skills that are specific to particular jobs, firms, or

---

[1] Marshall's concept of industrial districts likewise emphasizes repeated interactions in localized settings as a precondition for efficient outcomes (Marshall 1922).

industries will be suboptimal. In the absence of insurance, workers shun such investments because unanticipated shocks to the economy, whether as a result of recessions or technological change, can prevent workers from reaping the returns on their investments. Employers will also be reluctant to invest in their employees' skills, or in equipment that requires those skills, unless they believe that institutions that prevent poaching and discourage unions from exploiting the potential holdup power that specific skills confer are in place.

The importance of asset specificity is already well understood for explaining other policy areas. For example, when there is little credible protection of property rights, property owners will be more inclined to hold their wealth in liquid assets that can be quickly moved from one jurisdiction to another (Bates, Brock, and Tiefenthaler 1991). Even when basic property rights are well protected, investments vary significantly in the degree of their asset specificity. When investors cannot trust suppliers or employees on whose cooperation they depend, they will shun investments in relation-specific assets and rely instead on anonymous market transactions where one supplier or employee can easily be replaced by another. Conversely, when investments in physical assets are specific to a particular location, supplier network, or employee relationship, firms are more prone to lobby the state for protection against uninsurable risks (Frieden 1991; Alt et al. 1999).[2] In the most general "varieties of capitalism" (VoC) formulation, national or regional institutions act as complements to the strategies of firms, allowing them to make better use of their assets (Hall and Soskice 2001).

A similar logic applies to human capital. When skills are specific to a particular firm, industry, or occupation, their owners are exposed to risks for which they will seek nonmarket protection such as protection of jobs, standardization of wages, or state-guaranteed benefits. Skills that are portable, by contrast, do not require extensive nonmarket protection, and when there is little protection, investing in such skills is the best insurance against adverse market conditions and technological change. Yet, despite its intuitive appeal, asset specificity plays virtually no role in existing explanations of the welfare state. Labor is L, and workers are "replacable, easily redundant, and atomized." Correspondingly, politics is labor against capital, L against C. By contrast, the approach offered in this book emphasizes the critical

---

[2] Alt et al. (1999) shows empirical evidence that lobbying rises with the asset specificity of industries. See also Alt et al. (1996) for a more theoretical treatment of this and related arguments concerning the importance of asset specificity.

importance of the *level* and *composition* of human capital (L_s) for explaining the character of the welfare state – the *level* because it determines income and hence workers' demand for redistribution; the *composition* because it determines workers' exposure to risk and hence their demand for insurance. It is natural to label this an asset theory of the welfare state, although political institutions are also important as we will see in a moment.

The link between assets and the welfare state explains the continued and even growing importance of social policy in advanced, and therefore human-capital-intensive, economies. In 1999, for example, American workers over the age of 25 with a four-year college degree earned an average of $47,400 compared to $26,500 earned by workers with a high school degree and $16,900 earned by workers who had less than a high school degree (U.S. Census Bureau 2000). Ignoring other group differences, having a college degree is equivalent to a 3 percent real return on a net fortune of about $925,000 (compared to someone with less than a high school degree). For comparison, the median net worth of an American household, most of which is tied up in real estate wealth, is $53,000 (Wolff 1998).[3] And, of course, some of this wealth reflects accumulated past returns on skills. Human capital is, thus, easily the most import asset for a majority of people.

Do ordinary people also worry about protecting the value of these assets? The answer obviously varies from individual to individual according to the level and mobility of her skills, but there is no question that many workers face a substantial risk that their training can be made partially or entirely redundant by new technology or other forces of change (as in the example of typographers). Taken as a whole, manufacturing employment in the OECD has been cut in half since the 1960s, and a large portion of the jobs that remain require substantially different skills. There is every reason for workers and their unions to concern themselves with insurance against income losses as a result of redundant skills, although it is hard to quantify.[4] And such insurance cannot be provided exclusively through the market as a result of well-known problems of moral hazard, adverse selection, and other market

---

[3] These are 1995 numbers expressed in 1999 dollars.

[4] One of the difficulties of quantifying the specificity of skills is that wage and social protection systems are set up to reduce the riskiness of specific skills. Skill certification and wage standardization by skill categories, for example, are ways for unions to prevent individual workers from experiencing large drops in income. Variability of wages is therefore not an indicator of asset specificity. Chapter 3 goes to considerable length in developing alternative measures of skill specificity and to tie such specificity to social policy preferences.

failures (Przeworski, 2003 Ch. 11). Writing complete contracts to cover all contingencies in a labor market characterized by incomplete information and highly specific investments is precisely what transaction cost economics rules out. Nearly all unemployment insurance, for example, is provided through public insurance; health insurance markets always produce limited coverage, and there is no effective private insurance against the adverse effects of technological change on earnings capacity. For the vast majority of people in advanced democracies, insurance against job and income loss comes from the state and, to a lesser extent, from individual savings.

1.2. Bringing Electoral Politics Back in

As implied earlier, employers who are pursuing product market strategies that require specific skills also have a vested interest in social policies that reduce the risk of acquiring those skills (Mares 1998, 2001; Estevez-Abe 1999a; Swenson 2002). The focus on employers, however, tends to leave the democratic state, electoral politics in particular, underexplored. The power of employers is primarily "structural" in nature, but governments must win elections to stay in power, and it cannot be assumed the electoral incentives of politicians are perfectly aligned with their economic incentives (Elkin 1985; Block 1994). In Swenson's (1997) account of the New Deal, for example, politicians are faithful representatives of employers' long-tem interests, yet they face an urgent need to accommodate popular demands for political action. Indeed, Swenson acknowledges that business often opposes such action, yet it somehow ends up benefiting from it.[5] But electoral politics operates according to its own dynamic, and more often than not this dynamic is powerfully affected by popular demands for redistribution. As Stephen Elkin explains, "the democratic impulse is egalitarian, because rule by all requires not only political equality but also economic equality sufficient not to vitiate the premise of equal participation" (1985).

One of the great strengths of the power resources model is that it has a credible account of electoral politics. But the role of democratic politics must be reconsidered in the context of a different understanding of the economy and of employer interests. The emphasis on class interests ignores the importance of insurance motives in people's demand for social protection, and, as noted earlier, it leaves us with the puzzle of why democracies

---

[5] See Hacker and Pierson (2002) for an extensive critique of Swenson and related work on the role of employers in the rise of the welfare state.

with high inequality are not more redistributive than democracies with low inequality. The key here is to understand that redistribution (the focus of the power resources model) and insurance (the focus of institutional economics and VoC approaches) are intimately related. Insurance against the loss of income not only is conducive to investment in risky assets but also has the effect of redistributing income. This is obviously the case of the unemployed, who have no income, but it applies much more widely to any social protection, such as health insurance or pensions, that is not completely dependent on current employment and income. Ex ante, or behind the veil of ignorance as Rawls would say, people may support policies for purely insurance reasons, which, ex post (after the veil is raised), will redistribute income. Conversely, policies that are deliberately redistributive will simultaneously serve insurance functions. Those who are unemployed, sick, old, and have low pre-tax income more generally, will rationally press for redistribution. But by doing so, many of those who are employed, healthy, young, and enjoying a high incomes will enjoy some measure of insurance against losing these goods.

This Janus-face of the welfare state means that it is unlikely to be understood simply as a tool of power as a complement to the economy. The welfare state is simultaneously an arena for distributive struggles *and* a source of comparative advantage. Those who see only the first face will tend to conclude that it is an impediment to market capitalism and that it can survive only if capital is held captive and labor is politically strong. Those who see only the second face tend to reduce democratic politics, and electoral politics in particular, to a symbolic game where the welfare state always mirrors the needs of the capitalist economy (or employers), trumping the pursuit of competing interests. To understand the welfare state, we must understand how popular preferences for social insurance and redistribution are rooted in peoples' position in the economy, how these preferences are aggregated into social policies, and how policies in turn affect individuals' investments into assets that shape economic performance and interests. Chapter 3 presents a theory of social policy preferences in which individuals who have made risky investments in skills demand insurance against the possible future loss of income from those investments. Modeling popular preferences for social protection as a function of the assets people own in the economy is the first departure from the power resources approach to mass politics.

The second departure is my attention to the specific design of democratic institutions. Consider, for example, that because social insurance may only be enjoyed by the current median voter *some time in the future*, the median voter has an incentive to support such insurance *only* if future median voters do the same. The current median voter, therefore, faces a problem of how to commit future median voters. This translates into a *time-inconsistency problem* for the government because it has an incentive to renege on its promise to the current median voter when it seeks to attract the support of the future median voter. Again, the reason is that the median voter at any given time, when choosing a policy for the present, does not have an interest in high transfers. This problem is addressed in Chapter 4.

One solution points to the role of institutions that can hold the government to its promises about future policy. The organization of political parties and their relation to private groups is particularly important in this respect. Another solution builds on the close relationship between redistribution and insurance. Because redistribution also serves insurance purposes, institutions that promote redistribution serve as (imperfect) solutions to the time-inconsistency problem. In Chapter 4, I use recent work on the economic effects of political institutions by Persson and Tabellini (2000, 2003) and others to show that redistribution is intimately related to the electoral system (and that the electoral system is also closely associated with the presence of responsible and programmatic parties).

1.3. Globalization, Deindustrialization, and the Expansion of Social Protection

As noted previously, it is a puzzle that globalization has not led to convergence in social protection. The coupling of social protection and skill systems helps us understand the puzzle by pointing to their effect on the international product market strategies of companies and the creation of comparative advantages in the global economy. Specifically, where there is a large pool of workers with advanced and highly portable skills and where social protection is low, companies enjoy considerable flexibility in attracting new workers, laying off old ones, or starting new production lines. This flexibility allows for high responsiveness to new business opportunities and facilitates the use of rapid product innovation strategies. Such capacities are lower for firms in economies that rely heavily on nontransferable skills and that protect these skills through restrictions on the ability of firms to hire and fire workers. On the other hand, the latter types of welfare-production regimes give a comparative advantage to companies that compete in markets where there is a premium on the ability to develop deep competencies

14

within established technologies and to upgrade and diversify existing product lines continuously – what Wolfgang Streeck in a seminal article has dubbed "diversified quality production" (Streeck 1991).

The international division of labor not only perpetuates particular product market strategies but is also likely to feed back into political support for existing social protection regimes. As countries specialize in production that uses abundant factors intensely, demand by the owners of those factors for protection of their value rises. Contrary to the popular notion of a social "race to the bottom," differences across countries, therefore, need not disappear with a deepening of the international division of labor – a proposition implied by Hall and Soskice's concept of comparative institutional advantage (Hall and Soskice 2001). Social spending in continental Europe continues to be much higher than in Ireland and the Anglo-Saxon countries, and in many areas the gap has increased. Moreover, whereas labor markets have become even more deregulated in the latter countries, employment protection for full-time employees has stayed high and largely unchanged in the former (OECD 1999b).[6]

The asset theory of social protection also suggests a different explanation of the expansion of the welfare state than is offered by either the power resources model or theories emphasizing the role of the international economy. One of the most remarkable facts about the welfare state is that public spending did not vastly differ between the United States, continental Europe, and Scandinavia in the early 1960s (Rothstein 1998). "In the 1960s," writes Rothstein, "the difference between these countries in total public spending was much smaller [than today] – the level in the United States was about 28 percent compared to a mean of 29 percent for the Scandinavian countries." This does not mean that basic differences in unemployment, employment, and wage protection through labor market institutions did not exist at that time. They did, but the role of the state in the social insurance system through taxes and transfers was not terribly dissimilar.

The tremendous expansion of social spending since then, and the increased variation across countries, can be gleaned from Table 1.1. It shows total government spending as a percentage of gross domestic product (GDP) across seventeen OECD countries, the standard deviation of spending in these countries, and the difference in spending between Sweden and

---

[6] There are however significant reforms in the regulation of part-time and temporary employment, as well as in a range of social transfer programs, which will be discussed in Chapter 6.

Table 1.1. *Government Spending and Variation in Spending across Seventeen OECD Countries, 1960–1993*

	Government Spending as Percentage of GDP	Standard Deviation of Spending	Difference between Swedish and U.S. Spending
1960	28.7	4.9	3.0
1965	31.8	5.2	8.1
1970	35.2	6.4	9.1
1975	42.2	6.9	13.1
1980	45.3	8.9	25.6
1985	48.0	9.1	27.1
1990	46.3	8.4	24.6
1995	49.0	9.0	31.0
Ratio of 1995 level to 1960 level	1.71	1.85	10.38

Notes: Government spending includes government consumption, includes government transfers, plus interest payments and subsidies.

Source: OECD, *National Accounts, Part II: Detailed Tables* (various years).

the United States from 1960 to 1995. Note that spending rose by about 70 percent during this period, from 29 percent in 1960 to 49 percent in 1995, but the variation in spending grew even faster. Thus, the standard deviation in spending increased by about 85 percent in this period, and the difference between Sweden and the United States ballooned from 3 percent to 26 percent of GDP – a tenfold increase.

The power resources model attributes this growing gap to differences in working class power. But as noted in the introduction to this chapter, it is awkward to emphasize the role of the industrial working class in the postwar rise of the welfare state because it has been on the decline everywhere. In Chapter 5, I show that there is also little empirical evidence for the other prominent argument that the growth of the welfare state is the result of increased exposure to risks in the international economy (Cameron 1978; Garrett 1998; Rodrik 1998). As I have argued with Thomas Cusack (Iversen and Cusack 2000), the asset theory points to a quite different force of change, one that is in some respects the opposite of globalization: the transition to a largely sheltered service economy. Because deindustrialization represents a serious threat to those workers who have made significant investments in firm- or industry-specific skills – a threat that cannot easily be addressed within the "private" system of protection in the labor market – it is associated with a rise in electoral demands for public compensation and risk sharing. Additionally, even though deindustrialization has occurred everywhere, the speed at which it has taken hold has varied considerably across countries.

More importantly, the effects of deindustrialization have been mediated by the skill regime, as well as by the institutional capacity of the political system for credible commitment. Building on recent work on unemployment by Blanchard and Wolfers (2000), I demonstrate this institutional conditioning of common shocks with a variety of empirical tests in Chapter 5.

The growing electoral pressure for government spending has also provided politicians and political parties with an opportunity to shape the structure of social protection according to ideological preferences. In this respect, I am entirely in line with scholars such as John Stephens and Geoffrey Garrett who underscore the importance of partisan politics. As Anne Wren and I have argued (Iversen and Wren 1998), a particularly contentious partisan issue has concerned the extent to which the state should expand publicly provided services. Because high-protection countries with extensive wage and employment regulation have created relatively few jobs in low-productivity services, and because this is where the potential for job growth (especially for women) is greatest, social democratic parties have favored an expansion of jobs in public services while Christian democratic parties have emphasized transfers and social services provided through the family. Liberal parties, by contrast, have advocated deregulation.

A critical issue examined in Chapter 6 is the relationship between social protection, especially a relatively flat wage structure, and employment. Although high-protection countries have been very successful in international markets, belying the notion that high protection reduce competitiveness, they have been poor employment performers in nontraded private services (Iversen and Wren 1998). At the same time, good employment performers such as the United States have paid a heavy price in the form of greater inequality. The underlying problem, I argue, is that lack of international trade in services has undermined the ability of countries to take advantage of their comparative advantage. High-protection countries, for example, have squeezed out low-skill jobs without an offsetting expansion of high-skill jobs. I call the emerging response "selective and shielded deregulation," which means that greater flexibility in parts the labor market (especially for part-time and temporary employment) is coupled with new tax and transfer policies to shield the inequalizing consequences. I assess the limits and possibilities of this strategy and compare it to the welfare reforms characterizing Anglo-Saxon countries.

1.4. Implications for Inequality and Redistribution

As pointed out earlier, there is a close affinity between the insurance and distributive aspects of the approach. Building on Estevez-Abe et al. (2001) in this section, I suggest how the asset argument can be extended to unravel three sets of previously neglected causes logics by which welfare production regimes affect distribution. These propositions help explain several of the remaining puzzles noted in the opening to this chapter. They are elaborated and tested more extensively in subsequent chapters.

First, general skill systems are more likely to generate wage inequality and "poverty traps" because they limit opportunities and incentives for skill acquisition at the low end of the academic ability distribution. The skill system is also related to the wage-setting system, which strongly affects the earnings distribution. This helps explain why welfare production regimes are linked to wage dispersion. Second, demand for insurance against social risks leads to significant redistribution of income through the welfare state, and redistributive pressures are accommodated by their insurance benefits. This helps explain why the welfare state is so broadly supported in some countries, despite modest levels of inequality. Finally, gender inequality in the labor market is intimately related to skill and social protection regimes, and such inequality, unlike wage inequality, tends to be higher in specific skills systems. The skill argument helps us understand why that is the case. All in all, specific skills systems tend to be notably more egalitarian and redistributive than general skills systems, but labor markets in these countries tend to be more gender segregated.

1.4.1. Skills and Wage Inequality

It is striking, though not surprising, that all countries with a strong emphasis on industry-specific skills have developed effective wage coordination at the industry level. Conversely, general skills countries, especially countries with a strong emphasis on firm-specific skills (Japan in particular), lack such coordination. Very extensive evidence has in turn been accumulated and verifies that the structure of the wage bargaining system has important consequences for the wage structure (see especially Rowthorn 1992; Freeman and Katz 1994; Iversen 1999; Wallerstein 1999; and Rueda

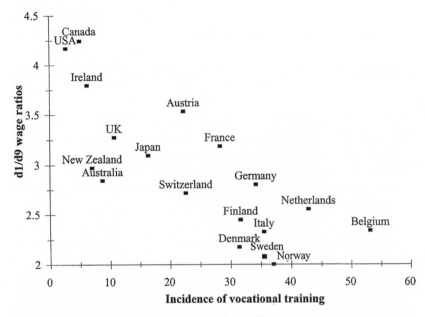

Figure 1.1 Vocational training and wage inequality.
Notes: The d1/d9 wage ratios are the earnings of workers in the top decile of the earnings distribution relative to a workers in the bottom decile of the earnings distribution. The incidence of vocational training is the share of an age cohort in either secondary or postsecondary (ISCED5) vocational training.
Sources: UNESCO (1999); OECD, *Electronic Data Base on Wage Dispersion* (undated).

and Pontusson 2000). As implied by the skill argument, intraoccupational compression of wages serves as a complement to employment and unemployment protection because it helps ensure against a big drop in income if a worker loses his or her job. Collective bargaining at the industry or higher levels also gives low-income groups influence over the distribution of wages that they lack in the market. Such influence tends to promote equality.[7]

But the skill system itself is also important as suggested in Figure 1.1. This graph uses the incidence of vocational training as an indicator of the extent to which workers are acquiring specific vocational skills as opposed

---

[7] This influence also reduces wage differentials between skills categories, which is contrary to the goal of maintaining high wage protection for the employed (i.e., maintaining stable wage differentials across occupations). The problem was particularly great in Sweden and led to a revolt against centralized (though not coordinated) bargaining among skilled workers and their employers (Iversen 1996; Pontusson and Swenson 1996).

to general academic skills.[8] Note the strong empirical association between skills and earnings equality. Because specific skills systems generate high demand for workers with good vocational training, young people who are not academically inclined enjoy career opportunities that are largely missing in general skills systems. Whereas a large proportion of early school leavers in the former acquire valuable skills through the vocational training system, in the latter most early school leavers end up as low-paid unskilled workers for most or all of their working lives.

This pattern also implies that young school goers in specific skills systems have strong incentive to work hard in school, whereas the same is not true for students in general skills systems who do not expect to go on to college.[9] Although there are clearly alternative interpretations, data from standardized international literacy tests are consistent with this idea as suggested in Figure 1.2. Countries are ranked by their share of poor performers, and the rough division between general and specific skills countries has been indicated with brackets.[10] Whereas the percentage with the lowest score averages 20 in Ireland and the Anglo-Saxon countries, the comparable figure in countries emphasizing more specific skills is 10. The correlation between vocational training intensity and the percentage with low test scores is .73. Likewise, those who leave school without an upper secondary education tend to have much higher test scores on job-relevant skills (here measured by document literacy) when they are in specific skills rather than in general skills systems: 46 percent of early school leavers in the former have high literacy scores compared to only 28 percent in the latter.

In combination, the wage bargaining system (i.e., whether it is industry coordinated or not) and the skill system (i.e., whether it is specific skills or general skills biased) provide a powerful explanation of earnings inequality. It points to the importance of paying attention to factors outside the welfare state that affect distribution. Much of the welfare state literature fails to do this, notwithstanding its almost exclusive focus on distribution. In the welfare production regime argument, nonstate institutions are integral parts

---

[8] Measures of skills will be discussed extensively in Chapters 2 and 3.

[9] This idea was suggested to me by David Soskice.

[10] Country coverage is limited. One country, Switzerland is excluded from Figure 1.2 because the test was administered in different areas using only one of the three official languages; consequently, many people took the test in a nonnative language. This practice appears to have significantly affected test scores (OECD and Statistics Canada 2000, 56). If included, Switzerland is positioned below Belgium, where a similar issue may be at play.

of the story even though the main functions of these institutions may be insurance and efficient management of cospecific assets.

1.4.2. Social Insurance and Redistribution

As I noted previously, workers who are behind Rawl's veil of ignorance do not know with certainty how they will fare in terms of future employment and income. In this situation, risk-averse people will demand insurance against loss of employment and income. If these preferences are translated into policy, *when* the future arrives, and some workers have experienced a drop in income, the distribution of income will be more egalitarian than without insurance. A generous tax and transfer system will therefore result in redistribution of income *even if* the system is solely intended for social insurance purposes. A related logic works from redistribution to insurance. If pressure for redistribution produces a more egalitarian after tax and transfer

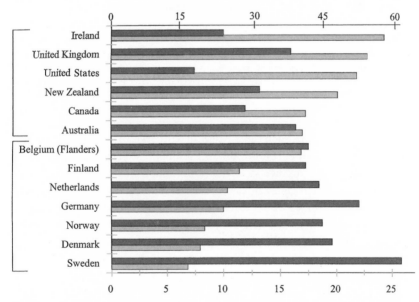

Figure 1.2 The percentage of adults with poor literacy scores (bottom scale) and the percentage of adults with low education and high scores (top scale): thirteen OECD countries, 1994–1998.

Notes: The top bars (using top scale) show the percentage of adults who have not completed an upper secondary education but have high scores on document literacy. The bottom bars (using bottom scale) show the percentage of adults taking the test who get the lowest score, averaged across three test categories.

Source: OECD and Statistics Canada (2000).

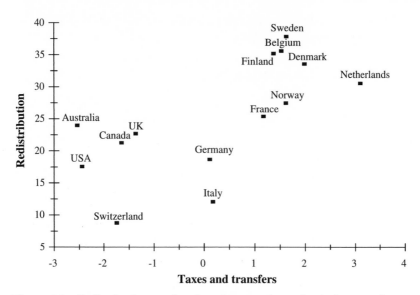

Figure 1.3 Redistribution as a function of taxes and transfers in fourteen democracies.
Notes: Redistribution is the percentage reduction in the Gini coefficient from pre- to posttax and transfer for households with working-age adults. Taxes and transfers is total taxes as a percent of GDP plus total transfers as percent of GDP, after both measures have been standardized. Both measures were developed by Bradley et al. (2003) based on LIS data and OECD national accounts data.

distribution of income, such redistribution will serve an insurance function. This is particularly important to understand because redistribution, unlike provision of social insurance, does not imply a time-inconsistency problem. Also it helps us understand why countries that redistribute income regularly perform better than we would expect from a standard neoclassical analysis.

Chapter 4 explores this interaction between redistribution, insurance, and the economy in detail. A key proposition is that much observed redistribution can be attributed to the political support for insurance. Here this basic idea can be illustrated with some data on pre- and posttax and transfer income from the Luxembourg Income Study (LIS; see Bradley et al. 2003 for details).[11] The inequality measure is the Gini coefficient, and redistribution is the percentage reduction in the Gini from the pre- to posttax

[11] I'm using the Bradley et al. (2003) data where pretax and transfer income consists of income from wages and salaries, self-employment income, property income, and private pension income, while posttax and transfer income is disposable personal income, including all market income, social transfers, and taxes.

and transfer distribution of income. To ensure that the measure is related to the concept of wage protection, the data only include the working age population. The data are available for fourteen advanced democracies and represent averages for a period starting in the late 1970s and ending in the mid-1990s (time coverage varies by country).

Figure 1.3 shows the reduction in pre- and posttax and transfer inequality as a function of the level of taxes and transfers. As expected, there is a positive relationship ($r = .68$), and, although we do not know from this relationship how much is the result of a deliberate attempt to produce redistribution as opposed to insurance, Huber, Stephens, and their associates have found a strong positive relationship between tax and transfers and redistribution after controlling for the partisan preferences of governments and a host of other factors (Bradley et al. 2003). In fact, their findings indicate that the level of taxes and transfers (what they term "welfare state generosity") is one of the most important determinants of both redistribution and poverty reduction. They do not, however, explain welfare state generosity itself. The asset theory implies that generosity is strongly affected by the structure of skills and the demand for insurance to which they give rise.

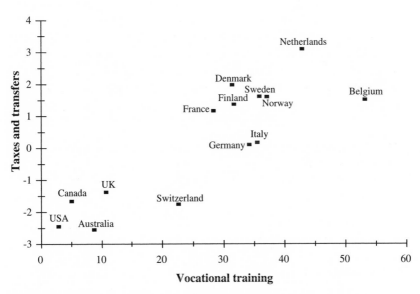

Figure 1.4 Taxes and transfers as a function of vocational training activity.
Notes: Same as in Figures 1.1 and 1.3.
Sources: Same as in Table 1.1 and Figure 1.3.

The second step in the argument, therefore, is to relate skill structure to the level of taxes and transfers. Again using vocational training rates as a rough indicator for national skill structure, Figure 1.4 shows that skills are indeed closely related to the magnitude of taxes and transfers ($r = .86$) and indirectly to redistribution ($r = .50$). Despite the emphasis on insurance over distribution, skill structure is, thus, important for explaining not only pretax/transfer income equality as shown previously) but also welfare state redistribution.

But this does not mean that the power resource story is irrelevant because, again, the causality also runs in the opposite direction. That is to say, if investment in specific skills is a function of the availability of income insurance, redistribution via the tax and transfer system will tend to produce, in equilibrium, a skill profile that is more specific. Without redistributive insurance, investment in general skills is the best defense again adverse changes in the labor market. And there is strong empirical evidence that countries dominated by politically left-leaning governments also redistribute more (Hibbs 1977; Korpi 1983, 1989; Boix 1998; Bradley et al. 2003; Pontusson and Kwon 2004).

This raises the question, however, why some countries are dominated by left-leaning governments while others are dominated by right governments. If the left and right took turns in government, it would provide no institutionalized support for investment in risky assets. But Chapter 4 argues that partisanship is determined by the differences in coalitional dynamics resulting from differences in electoral systems. Table 1.2 shows the strong empirical relationship between electoral system and partisanship using a new data set on parties and legislatures assembled by Cusack and Engelhardt (2002)

Table 1.2. *Electoral System and the Number of Years with Left- and Right-Leaning Governments, 1945–1998*

		Government Partisanship		Proportion of Right-Leaning Governments
		Left	Right	
Electoral system	Proportional	342 (8)	120 (1)	0.26
	Majoritarian	86 (0)	256 (8)	0.75

Note: Excludes centrist governments and PR cases with single-party majority governments.
Source: Cusack and Engelhardt (2002) and Cusack and Fuchs (2002).

and Cusack and Fuchs (2002). The figures are the total number of years with right- and left-leaning governments in seventeen advanced democracies between 1945 and 1998. Among majoritarian systems, 75 percent of governments were center-right, whereas in proportional representation (PR) systems 70 percent were center-left (excluding "pure" center governments). The numbers in parentheses convey a sense of the evidence at the level of countries, indicating the number of countries that have an overweight (more than 50 percent) of center-left or center-right governments during the 1945–98 period.

The importance of the pattern revealed in Table 1.2 for the argument in this book is that the electoral system is, in fact, related to the production system. Peter Katzenstein (1985) pointed out this association many years ago by linking social corporatism to PR. More recently, Hall and Soskice (2001) have argued that "coordinated market economies" are much more likely to have PR institutions than "liberal market economies." Here the association is explained by the equilibrium relationship between electoral institutions, redistribution, insurance, and investment in specific skills. In terms of the argument of this book, if the government is induced by the electoral system to engage in redistributive spending, the latter serves as insurance against the loss of income when specific skills are rendered obsolete by technological and other forms of change. Chapter 4 argues that PR is a key commitment mechanism in political economies that depend on workers making heavy investments in highly specific skills.

1.4.3. Skills and Gender Inequality

When we compare access to high-skilled and high-paid jobs, it is well documented that women are at a disadvantage. Economists usually ascribe this disadvantage to "statistical discrimination" by employers: If women are more likely to interrupt their careers for child birth and child rearing, and if individual women do not have access to effective commitment mechanisms, all women will be treated as a less valuable source of labor for employers. As argued by Estevez-Abe (1999b, 2002), however, this disadvantage clearly depends on the skills involved. If employers can easily find workers with the skills they need in the external labor market, career interruptions are of less consequence. Indeed, in a competitive neoclassical labor market, every employed worker has a perfect substitute willing to work for the same wage (it is labor L). Any employee is therefore readily replaceable. When employees bring skills that cannot be easily substituted (L_s), career

25

interruptions become critical to the employer. In terms of providing training and offering promotions, employers in this setting have an obvious incentive to discriminate against women. This is reinforced by women's own investment decisions because the returns on specific skills will be negatively related to the prospect of interrupted careers. This implies a heavily gendered structure of educational choices that is probably reinforced through socialization (Estevez-Abe 2002).

Let us look at the outcomes. Figure 1.5 relates a measure of the specialization of skills in different occupations to the percentage of women in these occupations using the International Labour Organization's (ILO's) International Standard Classification of Occupations (ISCO-88).[12] The numbers are averages for the thirteen countries where comparable ISCO-88 data are available. Bolded occupations are those that have disproportionately large numbers of low-skilled and low-paying jobs.

As expected, there is a strong negative relationship with men dominating occupations that, as implied by this measure, require highly specialized skills. This basic pattern is repeated in all thirteen cases. Not surprisingly occupations with specialized skills are found in agriculture and manufacturing rather than in services. Also note that because men on average participate more in the labor market than women do, most occupations have an underrepresentation of women. Women are also overrepresented in jobs that require relatively low general skills (and that tend to pay low wages), but women have at the same time achieved near-parity with men in professional occupations (in the United States there is complete gender parity among technicians and associate professionals).[13]

An important part of the gender story that is not captured by Figure 1.5 is the cross-national variance in the labor market position of women. Numerous studies document such cross-national variance (e.g., Melkas and

---

[12] Ignoring military personnel, ISCO-88 contains nine broad occupational groups, which are subdivided into numerous subgroups depending on the diversity of skills represented within each major group. At the most detailed level, there are 390 groups, each supposedly characterized by a high degree of skill homogeneity. By dividing the share of unit groups in a particular major group by the share of the labor force in that groups, we can get a rough measure of the degree of specificity of skills represented by each major group. See Chapter 3 for details.

[13] Within the professions, however, it is still the case that women tend to be in jobs and positions with lower pay and skills – for example, teachers in primary and secondary education rather than in higher education, nurses rather than doctors, and junior rather than senior associates – and they are notably underrepresented among senior officials and managers.

Anker 1997; Chang 2000; Breen and Garcia-Penalosa 2002; Porter 2002). The evidence suggests that specific skill systems exhibit high levels of occupational gender segregation (Estevez-Abe 2002). Comparative survey data from the International Social Survey Program (ISSP), for example, show that the correlation between vocational training activity and women's share of private sector employment is −.71 for twelve Organization for Economic Co-ordination and Development (OECD) countries in 1997 (ISSP 2000).

The weak position of women in the private labor market in specific skills countries is modified by public policies deliberately designed to counter them, especially public provision of social services and hence employment opportunities for women (Orloff 1993). These public policies enable the Scandinavian countries to have high female participation rates despite having a male-dominated private sector (Esping-Andersen 1990, 1999a; Iversen and Wren 1998). At the same time, however, women in countries with large service-oriented welfare states become "ghettoized" into the public sector instead of competing equally with men for the best private sector jobs.

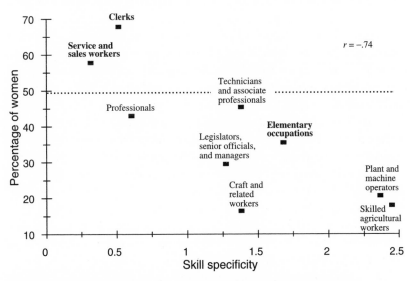

Figure 1.5 Skill specificity and occupational gender segregation, 2000.
Note: Percentage of women refers to the average percentage share of women in different major categories of ILO's International Standard Classification of Occupations across thirteen countries. The skill specificity measure is explained in footnote 12 and in Chapter 3.
Source: International Labour Organization, *Labour Statistics Database*. ILO 1998–2004.

The implication of this logic is that conflict over public sector service provision, parental leave policies, and education is likely to be gender related. Especially in specific skills countries, women will have a strong interest in an active state that provides daycare services and counters the disadvantages of women in the private job market. Also, women depend on generous leave policies to balance family and work; however, for such policies not to put women in a serious disadvantage in the competition for the best jobs, men must shoulder some of the burden of caring for infants (essentially forms of mandatory parental leave). Finally, because women have a comparative advantage in general skills, we should expect them to be more supportive of public spending on general education than men. I explore these hypotheses in Chapter 3.

1.5. Recap

This book builds on new institutionalist theory in both economics and political science (especially Hall and Soskice's VoC perspective) to offer a general political economy approach to the study of welfare capitalism. The book demonstrates that to a substantial extent social protection in a modern economy, both inside and outside the state, can be understood as protection of specific investments by both workers and firms in human capital. It then shows that such an understanding provides a systematic explanation for popular preferences for redistributive spending, the economic role of political parties and electoral systems, and labor market stratification (including gender inequality). In doing so, it helps resolve the debate between power resources theory and recent work on employers and the welfare state by systemically linking demand for redistribution and demand for social insurance and by tying social protection to the way firms compete in the international economy. Contrary to the popular idea that global competition undermines cross-national differences in the level of social protection, the book argues that these differences are made possible by a high international division of labor. Such a division is what allows firms to specialize in production that requires an abundant supply of workers with specific (or general) skills, and hence high (low) demand for protection.

The rise of nontraded services, however, undermines this specialization and leads to pressure for more flexible labor markets. The reason is that when specific skills countries can no longer achieve a complete specialization in production that uses such skills intensely, governments concerned about employment must create regulatory and institutional conditions that are conducive to the expansion of general skills jobs, especially at the low end of the wage scale. In turn, this raises the critical issue of how governments can deregulate a portion of the labor market without undermining the comparative advantages of generous social protection, and without causing a significant rise in inequality.

1.6. Outline of Book

The book is divided into three parts. This first part is an overview, which includes this chapter. Chapter 2 presents a comparative-historical analysis that traces the rise of the postwar social protection system to compromises between interests rooted in the industrial economy. It also provides much of the comparative data used throughout the book. Those who are familiar with these data and economic history can jump to the subsequent chapters. Part II focuses on the comparative statistics of the argument and explores cross-national differences and the microfoundations of these differences. Chapter 3 develops an asset-based theory of the sources of individual social policy preferences and shows how skills and gender are key in explaining these preferences. Chapter 4 considers the translation of these preferences into policies through the political system, emphasizing the role of political parties and electoral systems. Part III focuses on the dynamics of the argument. Chapter 5 explains the rise of the welfare state since the 1960s as a politically mediated outcome of the shift from industry to services. Chapter 6 explores the distributive and political consequences of this shift, as well as the recent reforms that can be attributed to it.

2

A Brief Analytical History of Modern Welfare Production Regimes

The introductory chapter outlined a broad theoretical approach to the study of social protection and hypothesized close linkages between social protection, skills, firm strategies, and the political-institutional foundations of the welfare state. This chapter ties national and international developments to the emergence of a few national institutional equilibria or ideal types. Although the chapter will discuss causal mechanisms, the main purpose is to put some empirical meat on the conceptual bones presented in Chapter 1. I will provide the reader with a range of background information, and I will show some striking interconnections between skill systems, social protection, and political institutions that cry out for explanation. Building on a joint paper with Barry Eichengreen, I argue that these interconnections metamorphosed into very distinct regime clusters in response to the challenges of postwar reconstruction and international economic integration, and each cluster is associated with distinct economic advantages that are reinforced through the international division of labor. Relative advantages have been shifting over time, however, and I discuss these forces of change with a view to developing the themes that are explored in greater depth, and with a sharper analytical knife, in subsequent chapters.

Much of the political-institutional divergence that occurred during the postwar period, I argue, reflects the structural-institutional potential for postwar growth in particular countries, the strength of organized labor and capital, and the inherited capacity for centralized collective action. In countries where the rewards for solving the distributive and collective action problems were high and where employers and workers were relatively well constituted as collective actors, solutions emerged that emphasized generous levels of social protection, responsible and programmatic parties, long-term investment in specific skills, and specialization in high-quality niche markets. In countries where the potential for economic growth was smaller and where distributive and collective action problems among unions and employers were intense, policies came to rely increasingly on market solutions. This divergent economic history is the focus of Section 2.1.

Over time these differences were magnified by economic crisis and international trade because intensified competition encouraged governments and economic actors to "specialize" in institutions and policies that were complementary to the production system and therefore reinforced comparative advantages. Section 2.2, which builds on a joint paper with Margarita Estevez-Abe and David Soskice (Estevez-Abe et al. 2001), provides a comparison of some key structural-institutional features of capitalist democracies – especially social protection, education and training, and position in the international division of labor – and how these features cluster to form distinct welfare production regimes. Part II of the book is designed to explain the differences identified between these regimes. Readers who are familiar with the main institutional differences across advanced capitalist democracies can skip this section.

Section 2.3 focuses on the tensions between the political-institutional frameworks that emerged in the first decades after the war and changes in technology and tastes that occurred subsequently. Because institutions and policies had been built around the economic and political conditions prevailing in the internationally integrated industrial sector, they were not well adjusted to cope with the decline of industry and the rise of a mostly sheltered sector of services. Much production in the rising services did not play to the strengths of the egalitarian and high-protection systems of continental Europe. In terms of private sector employment, this caused a rather remarkable reversal of fortunes when we compare continental Europe to the United States. Equally important, the transformation of the occupational structure generated new insecurities for workers with specific skills, and these could not easily be addressed through the existing employment protection system or through the collective wage bargaining system. The causes of these changes, and the responses of government to them, will be the focus of Part III of the book.

2.1. Postwar Reconstruction and Institutional Divergence[1]

2.1.1. The Shadow of History

The remarkable economic success of western Europe after World War II must be understood against the backdrop of prewar developments.[2] In an important sense, the industrial revolution spread beyond isolated pockets in northern Europe and North America only in the final decades of the nineteenth century. Only then can it be said that Marx and Engels's vision of large-scale manufacturing animated by centralized power, housed in large factories, and manned by an anonymous proletariat became a widespread reality. The challenge for the twentieth century was, thus, to solve the problems of efficiency and legitimacy posed by the spread of this new system, and this required the creation of institutions and structures through which the participation and cooperation of the rising industrial working class could be secured.

Nineteenth-century liberal capitalism in its post-1848 form had been predicated on limited-suffrage democracy, management control, and decentralized labor-market arrangements. By the end of the century, however, the rise of heavy industry, large corporations, and mega-banks had raised troubling questions about the prevailing distribution of economic power and the legitimacy of existing political institutions. Organized labor movements, socialist parties, and Catholic organizations (religious and political) challenged the legitimacy of both the electoral institutions and the existing social basis for production.

These were not problems on which Europe made much progress in the first half of the twentieth century. The extension of the franchise destroyed the inherited political equilibrium without substituting another. The creation of new states and the adoption of new electoral systems, leading to party proliferation, did not simplify reaching mutually acceptable decisions in a context of mass mobilization; indeed, the opposite was true. The volatility of party systems and a rapidly changing class structure constituted an unpredictable environment where far-sighted economic planning was difficult and where polarizing ideologies could thrive at the expense of cooperation and compromise. The sad fate of European democracy in the 1930s is testimony to this point.

---

[1] This section builds on Eichengreen and Iversen (1999).

[2] The relevant points have been made by Maier (1987) and Toniolo (1996).

However disruptive the experimentation between the wars with solutions to the challenges for efficiency and legitimation posed by the new twentieth century industrial system, there is an important sense in which it nevertheless planted the seeds for success after World War II. The institutions of economic governance elaborated after 1945 were themselves outgrowths of these, for the most part, less-than-successful interwar experiments. The labor codes of the National Industrial Recovery Act in the United States, the labor policies of the Popular Front in France, and the Saltsjöbaden agreement in Sweden were all efforts to solve the problems of efficiency and legitimacy of the 1920s and the unemployment crisis of the 1930s. Such frameworks can be thought of, in part, as concessions to the labor movement by governments and elite interests seeking to head off more radical alternatives (Luebbert 1991). In part, they can be seen as cross-class alliances to advance the common interest in effective conflict-resolution mechanisms and macroeconomic recovery (Swenson 1991a). With the exception of Austria, this is particularly true in the small European countries where a divided right and hightened exposure to international competition intensified the search for common ground (Katzenstein 1985). Typically they involved negotiations with the political arm of the labor movement, which had acquired a parliamentary presence. PR electoral institutions guaranteed that they could not be ignored.

The structure of these settlements – one of industry-level negotiations conducted under broad guidelines set down by government – contrasted with the starkly centralized agreements reached by state unions and industry organs in Mussolini's Italy and Hitler's Germany, whose legacy nevertheless also persisted into the postwar era (in the German case, for example, in the form of a dozen and a half national unions). Neither were the postwar reliance on ministerial controls over wages and working conditions and formal and informal incomes policy in, inter alia, France, Italy and the United Kingdom unprecedented and radically new; these devices were direct outgrowths of experiments with state direction in the 1930s and the even greater state control made necessary by total war.

It is hard to exaggerate the role of World War II itself as a selection mechanism for which of the innovations of the 1930s and early 1940s persisted into the postwar golden age. The creation of more hierarchical arrangements designed to facilitate the efforts of governments to harness the market economy for war bequeathed a set of more centralized structures ready to be applied to peacetime use. Fascism, Nazism, and Bolshevism all worked to discredit the more radical solutions of left and right. And, of course, the fact that the United States was the only capitalist superpower left standing was conducive to the adoption of institutional solutions appealing to American foreign policy makers.

2.1.2. Labor Markets and Economic Growth

Reconstruction in Europe after World War II took place against a backdrop of capital scarcity and labor militancy. Productive capacity had been devastated in the war, and many of the conservative political parties and organizations that were the traditional counterweights to organized labor had been discredited by their acquiescence to or active participation in the Nazi war effort. This economic and social disarray was all the more alarming once the Soviet Union came to be seen as a threat to Western Europe. For the United States and its European allies, economic growth promised to solve all these problems in a stroke. It would give Western Europe the economic and military capacity to withstand the Soviet threat. It would give labor a stake in the market economy. And it would restore the respectability of the capitalist class and of conservative political organizations.

But in order to initiate and sustain economic growth, three interrelated problems that were highlighted by the polarized and turbulent interwar experience had to be solved.

1. *Short-termism and time inconsistency.* Given the destruction of plant, equipment, and infrastructure, investment was key to postwar recovery. And even after the recovery phase was complete, investment remained central to the process of transferring to Europe the technologies and mass production methods developed by American industry in the course of previous years. Given the disorganization of international financial markets, investment had to be financed at home. Faster growth and higher incomes in the future, thus, required sacrifices of consumption in the present. Wages had to be moderated to free up the profits to finance capacity modernization and expansion. Those profits had to be plowed back instead of being paid out to shareholders. A mechanism had to be created, in other words, to encourage labor and capital to trade current gratification for future gains, overcoming the problem of short-termism.

   In a closely related process, governments had to commit to policies that would encourage investments in the future, even while concern for reelection forced them to pay close attention to the present. In sofar as the government was itself an investor in capital and infrastructure, one issue was how to make such investments without advantaging future governments and hurting the government's own current electoral chances. Another issue was how to tax income without unions demanding compensation. As is argued later, the provision of wage protection through the welfare state was part of the solution, but such protection itself presented a problem. Even if voters understood that social insurance would be desirable from a long-term perspective, the inability of current and future voters to make binding agreements with each other created a time-inconsistency problem. This made underprovision of social protection a dominant strategy for short-term-oriented, vote-maximizing parties.

2. *Collective-action problems.* It is difficult to withhold the benefits of growth from those who refuse to support it. In the postwar setting, this meant that individual unions inevitably were tempted to raise their own wages even while benefiting from the favorable market conditions created by the restraint of other unions. The profits freed up by their restraint did not remain in the same sector; rather, they passed through the national capital market, boosting investment, productivity, and labor incomes economywide. Firms for their part were tempted to underinvest in research and development (R&D) and technical training in the belief that these investments benefited competing firms that did not help to defray the costs. Therefore, to sustain economic growth, collective-action problems had to be solved.

3. *Distributive conflict.* Like a messy divorce in which the family jewels are sold off to pay the lawyers' fees, a society riven by distributional conflict will be prone to dissipate the resources needed to sustain prosperity and growth. In particular, different groups of workers will only be willing to restrain their wages if they are confident that they reap a fair share of the benefits of that restraint: both a fair share vis-à-vis employers, who control the use of profits, and a fair share vis-à-vis other groups of employees, who may take advantage of their restraint sometime in the future. Additionally, an even distribution of the fruits of their labor today may be the only credible promise for an even distribution of those benefits tomorrow. Wage moderation, in other words, may presuppose wage solidarity and redistributive social policies.

Centralized and concertized bargaining of the form that emerged in northern Europe in the decades following World War II addressed these three problems simultaneously and became a central building block in a unique continental European welfare production regime. The coordination of bargaining across sectors encouraged individual unions to exercise wage restraint by convincing them that other unions would do likewise. Distributive conflicts could be solved through bargaining because the outcomes of such bargaining would have an immediate effect on relative wages and because future deviations from the compromise could be addressed through future bargaining. Finally, centralized bargaining allowed governments to assume a supporting role by providing unemployment, health, and retirement programs – central institutions of the welfare state – that reduced workers' uncertainty about their future welfare and, therefore, their temptation to engage in short-termism and industrial conflict (Korpi and Shalev 1979; Lange and Garrett 1985).

In turn, for workers who were less exposed to labor-market uncertainty, investing in their firm's success through wage restraint, acquisition of firm- and industry-specific skills, and shop floor cooperation became a more attractive strategy than militancy. If a worker lost her job, she could depend on a sizable income and a package of benefits (such as healthcare) from the state, and she would likely be hired back into a job with similar pay owing to standardized wage rates (what has previously been referred to as wage protection for the unemployed). At the macro-level, tax policies penalizing dividends, and conspicuous consumption reassured workers that wage restraint would translate into higher investment (Stephens 1979; Katzenstein 1985; Eichengreen 1997).

On the employer side, firms had to worry that the decision to invest would encourage their workers to raise their wage demands in order to appropriate the profits generated by that investment. But if wages were determined in economy-wide rather than enterprise-level negotiations, an individual firm's investment decision would no longer affect the wages it had to pay. In these circumstances, centralized wage negotiations led to a higher level of investment and, insofar as productivity was raised, to higher wages in equilibrium (Hoel 1990).

Interlocking directorships and cohesive employers associations operating under close government oversight avoided the underprovision of technical training and R&D. Firms that would have otherwise been reluctant to provide training to their workers for fear that they would be poached by competitors were restrained by the threat of sanctions by both government and industry associations. In addition, wage protection through the collective bargaining system, which ensures that similarly skilled workers are paid approximately equal wages, and income protection through the state enabled employers to place some of the cost of training on employees, thereby essentially creating an employee collateral in the company (in the case of firm-specific skills) and the industry (in the case of industry-specific skills). Institutionalizing union representation on corporate boards and in government agencies in charge of economic, social, and educational policy made it easier to monitor the parties' compliance with the terms of these agreements. It facilitated, to use a game-theoretic term, common knowledge about the cooperative equilibrium.

It is difficult to quantify the effects of cooperation on investment in human and physical capital, but the evidence that the period from the late 1940s to the late 1960s was characterized by an unprecedented growth in the capital stock and by a rapid expansion of both formal and vocational training is unambiguous. The particular forms that these investments took are discussed in Section 2.2.2.

Together, then, centralized bargaining, social protection, vocational training systems, and collective representation of interests combined to overcome the three key obstacles to growth. In turn, the capacity of countries to embrace this solution hinged on the presence of a set of historically specific structural conditions. First, cooperation was facilitated by the exceptional scope for rapid growth after the war. The European economy was functioning below capacity. The influx of labor from Eastern Europe and internal migration from low-productivity agriculture to high-productivity industry limited upward pressure on wages and supported the modern sector's growth. Above all, a backlog of unexploited technologies was left over from the years of war and depression, ready to be imported from the United States. For all these reasons, the return on investment was high. Wage restraint supporting that investment was generously rewarded, and institutional experimentation, even if it involved risks, carried high potential returns.

Second, centralization was facilitated by a relatively homogeneous labor force, which made it easier for workers to reach understandings about wage relativities and for employers to live with wage compression. The European adaptation of Fordist production methods, which relied on high-speed-throughput technologies and incremental innovation, an extensive division of labor, and semiskilled workers, was hindered very little by wage compression that pushed up the cost of unskilled labor and depressed the wages of the most highly skilled, because European industry did not made heavy use of workers in either tail of the feasible skill distribution. This skill structure was partly a result of a preindustrial craft tradition in many European countries, partly a result of widespread training facilities created during the war to boost the supply of skilled workers for the war economy, and partly a result of investments in a quality system of primary education by governments eager to modernize, but constrained by limited resources for basic education that would feed into the private training system. Almost every worker, therefore, received a good primary school education, supplemented by some period of vocational or on-the-job training. Additionally, a growing number of workers received long vocational training through apprenticeships, vocational schools, or some combination of the two. Unskilled workers gradually disappeared from the labor force or formed a small "flexible" segment that could more readily be dismissed during economic downturns.

Third, where unions were strong but politically unified and organized along industry lines, compromise between different segments of workers was easier to accomplish. Shifts in skill boundaries through reorganization and upskilling prompted less opposition than was the case in a craft-based union system like that in the United Kingdom, and this facilitated compromises with management over investment in new technology and training. It also appears to have been an important component to the continental European success story where unions and employers in the exposed manufacturing sector were the largest, best organized, and politically most influential actors. Because unions and employers in this sector had a strong incentive to reach wage settlements that would maintain international competitiveness, economy-wide wage moderation was easier to accomplish (Swenson 1989, 1991a).

A similar argument applies to the organization of employers. In many European countries, extensive cross-shareholding and strong representation on boards by large universal banks, interlocking directorships, and well-organized employer associations already existed prior to the end of the war and made it easier for employers to coordinate their behavior. This "coordinating capacity" (Soskice 1990) facilitated the creation of centralized bargaining institutions by making it possible for many employers to act jointly in the case of industrial conflict and by increasing the capacity for the implementation of agreements with unions. Peter Swenson (1991a) describes this capacity well in the case of Swedish employers using their lock-out capacity during the 1930s to force the union confederation (LO) to assume control over strike funds and cut off support to militant construction unions.

Finally, government policies supported cooperative bargaining by alleviating economic insecurity, addressing the distributive concerns of unions, and penalizing noncooperative behavior. Tax policies rewarded investment and punished consumption, as noted before. Subsidies and low-interest loans were channeled to sectors where unions displayed wage restraint and to firms willing to support apprenticeship training and finance R&D. Countercyclical monetary policies and fiscal stabilizers limited uncertainty about the future. Expansion of the welfare state encouraged workers to make additional investments in risky skills and addressed the problem of distributional conflict by supporting the maintenance of a "social wage" that satisfied egalitarian norms.

But how could the state be relied upon to perform these functions? This central question for political economy will be explored in detail in Chapter 4; however, some preliminary observations from a historical perspective can be made here. First, the mainstream parties that emerged from Europe's experience with left- and right-wing extremism before and during the war were more inclined to emphasize economic growth and social insurance than radical redistribution. The Cold War reinforced their pragmatism and moderation, and, with the notable exceptions of Britain, the antipodes, the United States, and (to a lesser extent) Japan, proportional-representation electoral systems gave party elites a strong incentive to seek compromise in order to form governing coalitions. Generally speaking, center parties allied with moderate left parties to pursue policies of labor peace and social insurance financed by moderately progressive tax and transfer policies. The center and left both benefited from redistribution, but only to the point where it did not seriously undermine investment incentives or jeopardize middle-class interests.[3]

Equally important, the phase of mass mobilization had gradually given way to a more or less "frozen" party system characterized by stable voting blocks. Some societies were highly segmented or "pillarized" by religious and other divisions, and no pillar could reasonably aspire to become hegemonic in a PR electoral system. This reduced the incentives of parties to try to buy off each others' constituencies through populist tax cuts and deficit spending.[4] In turn, elites' emphasis on growth, distributional justice, and

---

[3] These conditions will be made much more precise in Chapter 4.
[4] The notion of a frozen party system was put forth by Lipset and Rokkan (1967).

consensus building encouraged voters to judge government performance on precisely those dimensions. It also helped to build cooperative relations with unions on which the government depended for labor peace and the provision of other public goods such as constructive involvement in vocational training systems.

From the perspective of unions, proportional representation and center-left coalitions guaranteed that future governments would not move radically against their interests, thereby reducing future uncertainty. Insofar as parties owed their electoral success as much to the efforts of highly centralized organizations of capital and labor (the latter in particular) as to their own industriousness, governments also had an incentive to consult and involve labor organizations in the preparation of new legislation and to seek their consent in its implementation. This secured the consent of powerful unions but also limited policy flexibility. In effect, the existence of these disciplined mass organizations enabled the mainstream political parties to credibly commit to the consensus policies of postwar Social Democracy.[5]

In addition to these domestic institutional conditions, the international trade and monetary regime gave governments an important measure of fiscal and monetary policy autonomy by cushioning currencies against speculative attacks and by permitting governments to restrict and direct the international flow of capital. Likewise, the General Agreement on Trade and Tariffs (GATT) only brought down trade barriers slowly and allowed many exemptions to help European countries build their own industry (Ruggie 1983). Nontariff barriers were particularly dense in services where European governments argued that special considerations justified heavy state regulation and exclusion of foreign competition.

Public utilities were widely considered natural monopolies that required state ownership or tight regulatory control, and in areas such as telecommunication and postal services there was a national security interest in keeping foreign firms at bay. Regulation or nationalization of banking and insurance were considered necessary to protect markets against mass bankruptcy and to allow governments to steer the national economy in the event of a crisis. Protected service markets could also be used more directly as an employment buffer against business cycle swings, stabilizing the economy and facilitating the government's commitment to full employment. Finally, protection of services against competition was seen, rightly or wrongly, as a means to ensure universalism in service provision and as inherently

[5] Again, this insight will be developed further in Chapter 4.

inseparable from the goal of modernizing society by extending telephone, postal, transportation, and other services to rural and less-developed regions. Infrastructure, broadly speaking, was a precondition for industrial development, and the future depended on the spread of industry. By combining economic growth and full employment with some measure of social justice, regulating and sheltering services from international competition became part and parcel of the European growth strategy.

Table 2.1 summarizes the structural preconditions for the emergence of institutions and policies that overcame the problems of growth described previously. For the most part, the table refers to the situation that existed immediately after World War II. Each column provides a standardized measure of the variables discussed in this section. The first is based on countries' GDP per capita in 1950 and the ratio of this figure to per capita income in 1940. In both cases, lower numbers imply greater catch-up potential. The index numbers have been inverted so that higher numbers indicate greater catch-up potential. Unsurprisingly, the three big losers of the war – Germany, Italy, and Japan – score the highest on this measure.

Second, the strength and unity of the labor movement is a multiplicative index of unionization rates and the organizational unity of the union movement.[6] Here all northern European countries score high with the exception of Finland. The same pattern is evident for the capacity of business coordination, which is based on a simple division of countries into three groups according to the strength of business associations and cross-shareholding. The next indicator, concentration of educational attainment, is calculated from the distribution of the adult population across three categories of formal education in 1950. Not surprisingly, the United States and Canada come out at the bottom, while education in most European countries is concentrated in primary and secondary degrees. Finally, I have used Lijphart's measure of consensual democracy to capture the extent to which the political system encourages political compromise. The composite index of structural preconditions in the last column is the mean of all five indicators.

In countries where the structural preconditions were propitious, centralization of wage bargaining generally progressed the furthest, and social protection attained the highest levels. It is not easy to demonstrate this conjecture with any degree of statistical precision because there is a lack of systematic data for centralization and social protection that extends back to

---

[6] Both measures were standardized to vary between 1 and 2 before being multiplied.

Table 2.1. *Structural Preconditions for Economic Policies and Institutions, ca. 1950*

	Catch-Up Potential[a]	Strength and Unity of Labor[b]	Coordination Capacity of Business[c]	Concentration of Educational Distribution[d]	Consensual Democracy[e]	Index of Structural Preconditions
Canada	0.16	0.06	0.00	0.00	0.03	0.05
United States	0.04	0.00	0.00	0.00	0.22	0.05
United Kingdom	0.43	0.20	0.00	0.49	0.00	0.22
France	0.52	0.02	0.50	0.52	0.07	0.33
Italy	0.70	0.16	0.00	0.47	0.77	0.42
Switzerland	0.15	0.13	0.50	0.38	1.00	0.43
Japan	1.00	0.10	0.50	0.09	0.64	0.47
Belgium	0.54	0.18	0.50	0.37	0.77	0.47
Denmark	0.41	0.45	1.00	0.05	0.83	0.55
Netherlands	0.50	0.14	0.50	0.87	0.82	0.57
Germany, West	0.70	0.24	1.00	0.33	0.63	0.58
Austria	0.69	0.66	1.00	0.20	0.52	0.61
Finland	0.59	0.08	0.50	1.00	0.92	0.62
Sweden	0.29	1.00	1.00	0.22	0.68	0.64
Norway	0.50	0.46	1.00	0.56	0.62	0.63

[a] Average, after standardization, of two indicators: (i) GDP per capita in 1950 and (ii) GDP per capita in 1950 relative to GDP per capita in 1940. *Source:* Cusack (1991).

[b] Average, after 0–1 standardization, of three indicators: (i) unionization rates in 1950; (ii) political and organizational unity of labor movement (0 = several competing and divided confederations, 1 = a single dominant confederation; 0.5 = weak confederation or moderate division); and (iii) whether unions are organized by industry (= 1), craft (= 0) or a mixture of principle (= 0.5). *Sources:* Visser (1989) and Ferner and Hyman (1992).

[c] Standardized index with three values based on the extent of cross-shareholding and strength of employer associations.

[d] Standardized index based on the standard deviation of the share of adults with a primary, secondary, and postsecondary degree in 1950. *Source:* OECD's Education Database as compiled by Robert J. Barro, and Jong-Wha Lee (*www2.cid.harvard.edu/ciddata/barrolee*).

[e] Arend Lijphart's index of consensus democracy, based on the effective number of parliamentary parties, the percentage of minimal winning one-party governments, executive dominance, electoral proportionality, and corporatism. The index covers the period 1945–96, but there is little change over this period in any of the countries in the table. *Source:* Lijphart (1999, p. 312).

the war. In addition, as noted earlier, some of the institutions and policies that emerged after the war were an extension of institutions and policies that existed before the war. For these reasons, it is impossible to establish an unambiguous causality between preconditions and subsequent institutional developments. However, it is noteworthy that the index of structural preconditions is highly correlated with a centralization of a wage-bargaining index for the 1970s ($r = .9$),[7] as well as with an index of social protection that is explained later ($r = .8$). Since truly centralized bargaining systems – distinguished from the compulsory wage-setting measures that were instituted in some countries during the war – did not arise until the 1950s and 1960s, this is at least consistent with a story that emphasizes the importance of the structural-institutional preconditions highlighted here. Likewise, most of the cross-national differences in social protection that were evident in the 1970s and 1980s were the result of policies initiated in previous decades (discussed later).

After institutions and policies were in place, they reinforced one another through a set of interlocking complementarities (Hall and Soskice 2001). Governments supported centralized bargaining because it facilitated rapid growth that aided the electoral fortunes of the governing parties. Strong unions and employers' associations also helped maintain the political monopoly of mainstream parties by providing financial and organizational support. Politicians, in turn, nurtured the institutions of centralized bargaining by granting representational monopolies to the peak associations of capital and labor, rewarding unions for their restraint and attending to their distributional interests.

By and large, this ideal type description is best approximated in the Nordic countries, where centralized industrial relations and secure social democratic governments committed to full employment produced both wage compression and a rapid expansion of pensions and other social rights. Union cooperation was facilitated by drawing representatives of the main labor market organizations into the preparation and implementation of literally every new piece of social or economic legislation. As we move south and west from Scandinavia, one or more elements of the postwar model – centralized bargaining, government commitment to full employment, and egalitarian wage and social policies – are weakened, but in no case are all three completely missing.

Germany, Austria, Belgium, the Netherlands, and Switzerland all developed highly coordinated and ordered systems of industrial relations in the 1950s, although in none of these cases was bargaining centralized at the national level. While these countries differed from their Scandinavian counterparts in their level of public service provision and employment, they too passed generous entitlement legislation such as Adenauer's 1957 pension

---

[7] The centralization of wage bargaining index is from Iversen (1999, Chapter 3).

reform in Germany, which greatly increased social spending. The generosity of the Dutch social security system was second to none in Europe. Likewise, governments instituted extensive legal and regulatory protection for employment, and social insurance schemes introduced in the 1930s were bolstered by legislation and the creation of employee workplace representation.[8]

In the European context, France, Italy, and the United Kingdom deviate more sharply from the ideal type. All suffered coordination problems because of fragmented labor movements and weak employers' organizations. In France and Italy, unions were divided by ideological and confessional cleavages, and many had allied with politically marginalized communist parties. The latter saw the unions not just as vehicles for workers' material progress but also as an important organizational resource for the effort to mobilize and expand a mass base. Partly for this reason, governments in both countries were reluctant to pursue policies that might strengthen the communist unions. The French state, however, could rely to some extent on a strong independent bureaucracy to overcome coordination problems and pursue aggressive investment and industrial restructuring policies, and although Italy was one of the worst performers in terms of inflation and unemployment, cooperative solutions did emerge at the local and regional levels in areas where unions and the left were strong and entrenched.

By contrast, Britain never devised effective institutional solutions to any of the three obstacles to growth. After the war, a reform-minded Labour government nationalized several industries, but otherwise industrial policies were kept at arm's length, in part as a result of a market-based financial system that did not lend itself to French-style *dirigisme* (Zysman 1983). The financial system was also an important impediment to the pursuit of full employment. Because British banks were heavily oriented toward international banking, they opposed devaluation. Consequently, when the government tried to address internal imbalances through demand stimulation, it would often find itself reversing policies so as to not cause a politically unacceptable depreciation of the pound (Hall 1986, Chapter 4). The resulting "stop-go" pattern was clearly not conducive to farsighted investment and wage strategies. Finally, even though representatives of employers and unions were consulted on economic policy matters, legislation designed to difuse distributive conflict did little to induce wage restraint for the simple

---

[8] The laggard here is Denmark, partly because its industrial structure is so dominated by small firms.

reason that no individual union had much incentive to cooperate with the government's incomes policy given that membership was divided among a large number of mainly craft-based unions.

In several respects, the postwar British political economy can be seen as a problematic hybrid of northern European and U.S. capitalism. As in northern Europe, unionization rates were much higher in Britain than in the United States, but like the labor movement and business community in the United States, that in Britain was far more fragmented than that in northern Europe. Indeed, it can be argued that because of the concentration of American unions in the automobile industry and because unions in that industry were fairly well organized and engaging in pattern bargaining, U.S. wage setting was *more* coordinated than in Britain. Outside the much smaller unionized sector in the United States, wage pressures were kept in check by highly competitive labor markets.

The U.S. political economy is notable for the absence of any government employment guarantee or commitment to egalitarian wage and social policies. Although some aspects of the New Deal survived under Truman and Johnson, notably social security, there was neither the economic urgency nor the political support for interventionist policies, extensive social protection, or comprehensive incomes policies of the kind that emerged in Europe. American production capacity and infrastructure had not been destroyed in the war, and American firms enjoyed a significant productivity advantage vis-à-vis their European and Asian competitors after the war. Against this backdrop, the main issue was not how to accelerate domestic output but how to cultivate global demand for U.S. products. Aid to help rebuild Europe and stop any westward spread of communism, and a stable trading regime that kept foreign markets open to U.S. exports and investments were key ingredients in the U.S. global strategy. The Marshall Plan, Bretton Woods, and GATT became the main institutional vehicles for forwarding this strategy.[9]

Many of the key postwar U.S. welfare programs, such as food stamps, Medicaid, and public housing, were the result of mobilization by poor black constituencies and civil unrest, notably the Inner-city riots of the 1960s, and they had a distinctly redistributive impetus and effect. In a similar vein,

---

[9] This is not to say that postwar international institutions were unmediated expressions of U.S. hegemony. Rather, as argued by Ruggie, they were a compromise between the American desire for a liberal international economy and the social and political reality of Western European countries, which required some capacity of governments to shape policies to the needs of domestic social stability (Ruggie 1983).

affirmative action sprang from a racially based mobilization of the lower classes. With the major exception of Johnson's introduction of Medicare (and before that Social Security), most welfare programs were of little direct benefit to the white middle class; therefore, they were vulnerable to rollback when violence and protest subsided. Majoritarian electoral institutions eliminated the need for a compromise with the poor, and both major parties have always been to the right by European standards. The importance of electoral institutions for partisanship and redistribution is discussed further in Chapter 4.

In terms of protection against risks, the American middle class turned to education. Catering to centrist voters, the federal government and the states poured huge sums of money into the public university system, and individuals spent an ever-increasing share of their income to send their children to college. There was never an effective vocational alternative – partly because there was no deeply rooted craft tradition, and partly because business was inadequately organized to provide the necessary funding, training, and monitoring of such an alternative – consequently, a college degree was the only ticket to the American dream that could be bought with money and effort rather than luck.[10]

2.2. Comparison of Welfare Production Regimes[11]

2.2.1. Social Protection

The national differences in the social protection systems as they evolved during the first three decades after the war can be fairly well summarized by a comparison of employment and unemployment protection – two dimensions emphasized in the theoretical discussion in Chapter 1. Data for the first dimension are provided in Table 2.2. The first column is OECD's measure of legal and quasi-legal employment protection legislation (EPL) governing individual hiring and firing. The composite EPL index is based on provisions in the legal code as well as on collective bargaining agreements, hereunder what constitutes just cause for dismissals, required length of advance notice, mandated severance pay, compensation for unfair dismissals,

[10] A few large firms such as Boeing and IBM could promise life-time employment to workers who would go through many years of company training because of the position of these firms as technological and market leaders. Of course, as this position of leadership was eroded, so was the life-time employment system.

[11] This section builds on Estevez-Abe et al. (2001).

Table 2.2. *Employment Protection in Eighteen OECD Countries*

	(1) Employment Protection Legislation (EPL)[a]	(2) Collective Dismissals Protection[b]	(3) Company-Based Protection[c]	(4) Index of Employment Protection[d]
Sweden	2.8	4.5	3	0.94
Germany	2.8	3.1	3	0.86
Austria	2.6	3.3	3	0.84
Italy	2.8	4.1	2	0.81
Netherlands	3.1	2.8	2	0.80
Japan	2.7	1.5	3	0.76
Norway	2.4	2.8	2	0.66
Finland	2.4	2.4	2	0.64
France	2.3	2.1	2	0.61
Belgium	1.5	4.1	2	0.56
Denmark	1.6	3.1	2	0.53
Switzerland	1.2	3.9	2	0.49
Ireland	1.6	2.1	1	0.36
Canada	0.9	3.4	1	0.30
New Zealand	1.7	0.4	1	0.29
Australia	1.0	2.6	1	0.27
United Kingdom	0.8	2.9	1	0.25
United States	0.2	2.9	1	0.14

[a] Index of the "restrictiveness" of individual hiring and firing rules contained in legislation and collective agreements (the high numbers indicate the more restrictive regimes). *Source:* OECD (1999b). (Weight: 5/9).

[b] Index of the "restrictiveness" of collective dismissal rules contained in legislation and collective agreements (the high numbers indicate the more restrictive regimes). *Source:* OECD (1999b). (Weight: 2/9).

[c] Measure of company-level employment protection as explained in text. The French case has been assigned a score of 2 even though company-level protection is weak. The reason is that the Inspectorat du Travail can and does intervene to prevent redundancies, and this is not captured by OECD's legal measure of employment protection. See Berton, Podevin, and Verdier (1991) for a description of the French system. *Sources:* Income Data Services (1996); OECD (1998), pp. 142–52; David Soskice (1999). (Weight: 2/9).

[d] Weighted average of columns (1) and (2) after each indicator has been standardized to vary between 0 and 1.

the rights of employee representatives to be informed about dismissals and other employment matters, and the rights of workers to challenge dismissals in the courts.

The composite EPL index is constructed for both regular and temporary employment, but the skill argument is only relevant for the former because neither employers nor employees have much of an incentive to invest in firm-specific skills when employment is time-limited. The regular employment EPL index is calculated for two periods, the late 1980s and the late 1990s, but because it is nearly perfectly correlated between the two periods ($r = .99$), the figures are simple averages (shown first column of Table 2.2). The index is based on the regulation of individual contracts and does not incorporate measures for protection against collective dismissals. In OECD's latest update of the index (OECD 1999b), a separate index was created to reflect the regulation of collective dismissals, which is shown in the second column of Table 2.2.

Neither of the OECD measures fully take into account the employment protection that is built into the firm governance structure or into the workings of the industrial relations system. As the OECD acknowledges, "nonlegislated employment protection tends to be more difficult to measure and may therefore be under-weighted" (OECD 1999b, p. 51). Japan illustrates the problem because companies in Japan offer greater protection against dismissals for their skilled workers than the EPL index would suggest (See OECD 1994a, pp. 79–80). Indeed, dismissals and layoffs are extremely rare in Japan compared to other countries (OECD 1997, Table 5.12).[12] Instead, large Japanese firms engage in special work force loan practices with their suppliers, called "Shukko," which enable them to retain workers during recessions. In other countries, and to some extent also in Japan, firms must consult with works councils or other employee representative bodies before making decisions about layoffs, and industry unions are often in a strong position to oppose collective layoffs. This relationship is only partly reflected in the EPL index because it considers only the need for firms to *notify* works councils or unions about impending dismissals, not the power of unions or works councils to prevent or modify the implementation of decisions to dismiss.

These "private" employment protection arrangements are captured in column 3 of Table 2.2 by a simple index that measures the strength of

---

[12] These data are not fully comparable across countries, but the very low figures for Japan leaves little doubt that the numbers are much smaller in Japan than elsewhere.

institutions and practices at the firm level that increase the job security of especially skilled workers in a company. The measure is based on three criteria: (1) the presence of employee-elected bodies with a significant role in company manpower decisions; (2) the existence of strong external unions with some monitoring and sanctioning capacity (especially through arbitration); and (3) the systematic use of employee sharing practices between parent companies and subsidiaries or across companies. Where at least two of these conditions are met to a considerable degree, a score of 3 was assigned; where all three are largely absent, a score of 1 was assigned. Intermediary cases were assigned a score of 2. With the exception of Japan, the index of company-based protection is consistent with the rank-ordering implied by the composite index.

The final column combines the OECD and company-based measures in a composite index that captures both the legal and more informal aspects of employment protection. The index is a weighted average with the following weights: 5/9, 2/9, and 2/9. The first two weights are adopted unchanged from OECD's own weighing scheme (OECD 1999c, p. 118), and reflect the fact that collective dismissal rules tend to build on individual dismissal rules, which are already part of the EPL index. Because the influence of employee representative bodies over firm-level manpower decisions is also partly captured by the EPL index, I assigned the same (low) weight to the company protection indicator. Some would quibble with the assignment of these weights, but the relative numbers are not very sensitive to changes in these weights, and I think most agree that the resulting index of employment protection provides a reasonably good summary of the differences across countries.

Looking at the ranking of countries, it is not surprising to find the Anglo-Saxon countries at the low end and Japan and many of the continental European countries at the high end of protection. Belgium, Denmark, and Switzerland are in the lower half of the table, most likely because these countries have relatively large small-firm sectors, but in terms of actual numbers, the break in the employment protection index is between this group of countries and the Anglo-Saxon countries.

The measurement of unemployment protection is more straightforward, although there are some nontrivial issues concerning the *administration* of unemployment benefit systems. The most obvious and commonly used indicator is the unemployment replacement rates, the portion of a worker's previous wage that is replaced by unemployment benefits (see column 1 of Table 2.3). I here consider a "typical" worker, defined as a 40-year-old

Table 2.3. *Unemployment Protection in Eighteen OECD Countries*

	(1) Net Unemployment Replacement Rates[a]	(2) Generosity of Benefits[b]	(3) Definition of Suitable Job[c]	(4) Index of Unemployment Protection[d]
Denmark	60	76	3	0.91
Netherlands	58	74	3	0.89
Switzerland	(40)	94	2	0.86
Belgium	57	99	2	0.82
Austria	43	78	3	0.81
Germany	43	66	3	0.77
Norway	40	40	3	0.64
Sweden	30	52	3	0.63
France	48	44	2	0.54
Finland	45	20	2	0.43
Ireland	(38)	59	1	0.37
Japan	10	48	2	0.33
Canada	32	49	2	0.30
New Zealand	31	44	1	0.27
Australia	32	30	1	0.22
Italy	5	18	2	0.18
United Kingdom	23	15	1	0.11
United States	14	26	1	0.10

[a] Net unemployment replacement rates for a 40-year-old representative worker. *Source:* Restricted OECD data reported in Esping-Andersen (1999a, Table 2.2, p. 22). Net figures for Ireland and Switzerland are missing and have instead been estimated by taking gross replacement rates for these countries as proportions of average gross replacement rates and then multiplying these proportions by average net replacement rates. *Source:* OECD, *Database on Unemployment Benefit Entitlements and Replacement Rates* (undated).

[b] The share of GDP paid in unemployment benefits as a percent of the share of unemployed in the total population. Average for the period 1973–89. *Sources:* Huber, Ragin, and Stephens (1997); OECD, *Economic Outlook* (various years), OECD, *Labour Force Statistics* (various years).

[c] Index that measures the restrictiveness of the definition of a suitable job in the administration of benefits to unemployed. 1, Any job qualifies as a suitable job; 2, skilled unemployed are given some discretion in rejecting jobs they deem unsuitable to their skills, but choice is restricted in time and/or to certain job categories, 3, skilled unemployed exercise wide discretion in accepting or rejecting jobs on the grounds of the suitability of the job to their skills. *Sources:* OECD (1991, pp. 199–231); *European Commission, Employment in Europe* (various years); and national sources.

[d] Average of columns (1)–(3) after each indicator has been standardized to vary between 0 and 1.

industrial production worker, "averaged" across several different family types (single, married to working spouse, and married to nonworking spouse). Additionally, I focus on *net* replacement rates after adjusting for cross-national differences in tax systems and non-income subsidies for the unemployed (such as rent support). Given that taxation of unemployment benefits varies considerably across countries, gross replacement rates (for which much more detailed data exist) can be misleading.

As in the case of employment protection, the Anglo-Saxon countries again score at the bottom. But note that the three continental European countries falling in the lower half of the employment protection index – Belgium, Denmark, and Switzerland – now figure at or near the top of the table. On the other hand, two countries – Italy and Japan – have very low replacement rates compared to their position on the employment protection indicators. The pattern is broadly similar, though not identical, when looking instead at the actual amount of money the government spends on unemployment benefits (as a share of GDP), compared to the number of unemployed people (as a share of the population). As before, the three countries in northern Europe with relatively low employment protection are among the five countries with the most generous unemployment benefit systems.

Table 2.3 also includes a more qualitative measure of the administration of unemployment benefits: the restrictiveness of the definition of a suitable job. All national unemployment systems stipulate that in order to receive benefits a person cannot refuse a suitable job, but what constitutes a suitable job varies significantly from one system to another. In principle, such variation is important for our purposes. For example, if a skilled worker is required to take any available job, regardless of whether it is commensurable with the worker's skills, high unemployment benefits are of limited value from the perspective of reducing the riskiness of specific skills investments. In practice, it is difficult to get any precise comparable figures for this variable. Consequently, I am using only a very simple three-tiered classification based on a variety of national and international sources. Though basically reinforcing the pattern revealed by the other two indicators, it does affect the rank-order position of some countries slightly.

As in the case of employment protection, I combined the various indicators into an index of unemployment protection (see column 4). With the possible exception of Italy, this index gives a good sense of cross-national differences in the extent of unemployment protection. The number for Italy probably underestimates the extent of protection because of quasi-public insurance schemes that do not show up in the official statistics. Thus, about a third of (mainly large companies) covered by Casa Integrazione have replacement rates between 70 and 80 percent, and there are normally good unemployment benefit schemes for artisans (i.e., craftsmen) administered at the regional level by associations representing small firms, in cooperation with regional governments.[13]

In addition to employment and unemployment protection, Chapter 1 distinguished a form of insurance called *income protection*. Income protection is secured both through the collective wage bargaining system in the form of negotiated standard wage rates and through the public tax and transfer system.[14] Income protection helps reduce the variability of after-tax and transfer income and, hence, helps to manage the risks associated with investing in skills that cannot easily be transferred from one job or occupation to another. Table 2.4 seeks to capture income protection with three different measures. The first is an index of total taxes and transfers (both weighed equally) as a proxy for publicly mediated income protection. The second is d9/d1 earnings ratios used as a proxy for (the inverse of) protection of wages through the private wage-setting system. The third is after-tax and transfer Gini coefficients, which are a function of both wage and public income protection. In principle, Gini coefficients are the key data for our purposes, but because they are only available at the level of households, they do not directly measure individual income protection. Even if individual income is highly protected, after-tax and transfer household income can be quite dispersed owing to differences in the labor force participation rates of household members. As in Tables 2.2 and 2.3, the final column is an index of protection based on all three indicators (after standardization).

As can be seen from the correlation matrix at the bottom of Table 2.4, the different indicators are all fairly highly correlated with one another, and the income protection index produces an ordering of countries that is quite similar to that for the unemployment protection index. Japan, Ireland, and the Anglo-Saxon countries are at the bottom of the scale, while the Low Countries and Scandinavia are at the top. Italy has moved up compared to the unemployment index and is probably more accurately located, but Switzerland is now an outlier. Without Switzerland, the correlation between the income and unemployment indexes rises to .75. In Chapter 4,

---

[13] Michele Salvati provided this information.

[14] More precisely, this was called *income protection for the unemployed* in Chapter 1.

Table 2.4. *Income Protection in Eighteen OECD Countries, 1973–1995*

	(1) Taxes and Transfers[a]	(2) D9/D1 Earnings Ratios[b]	(3) After-Tax and Transfer Gini Coefficients[c]	(4) Index of Income Protection[d]
Sweden	0.77	2.07	19.40	0.94
Belgium	0.78	2.34	21.67	0.85
Denmark	0.61	2.18	21.50	0.81
Norway	0.50	2.00	21.50	0.80
Finland	0.41	2.08	20.00	0.79
Netherlands	0.89	2.56	26.00	0.74
Germany	0.42	2.80	26.16	0.52
Austria	0.57	3.54	–	0.46
France	0.67	3.25	29.40	0.46
Italy	0.37	2.33	31.33	0.44
Switzerland	0.16	2.72	30.50	0.32
Australia	0.03	2.81	28.50	0.31
Japan	0.01	3.07	–	0.26
United States	0.10	3.21	30.00	0.24
Ireland	0.33	4.06	–	0.21
Canada	0.20	4.19	27.80	0.18
United Kingdom	0.22	4.06	32.00	0.10

Correlation matrix:

(1) Transfers as percentage of GDP	1			
(2) d9/d1 earnings ratios	−.66	1		
(3) After-tax/transfer Ginis	−.59	.68	1	
(4) Income protection	.79	.85	.85	
Unemployment protection	.68	−.60	−.53	.65

[a] Taxes and transfers is the mean of total taxes as a percentage of GDP and total transfers as a percentage of GDP, after both measures have been standardized. The transfer data are from the OECD, *National Accounts, Part II: Detailed Tables* (various years), and the tax data are from the OECD (2002).

[b] d1/d9 earnings ratios are the gross earnings (including all employer contributions for pensions, Social Security, etc.) of a worker at the top decile of the earnings distribution relative to the worker at the bottom decile (OECD, *Electronic Data Base on Wage Dispersion*, undated);

[c] Ginis are calculated on the basis of LIS data on posttax and transfer income for households with working-age adults.

[d] Average of columns (1)–(3) after each indicator has been standardized to vary between 0 and 1.

Table 2.5. *Percentage of Population over 25 with a Postsecondary Education*

	1950	1960	1970	1980	1990	2000
North America	**13.6**	**18.3**	**20.9**	**33.6**	**44.0**	**51.6**
United States	13.6	16.5	21.3	29.8	45.2	50.1
Canada	n.a.	20.0	20.4	37.4	42.7	53.0
Europe[a]	**1.9**	**4.5**	**6.3**	**10.0**	**13.9**	**19.6**
France	1.8[b]	2.1	3.0	8.5	11.4	18.4
Germany	n.a.	1.8	3.1	6.9	10.4	17.5
Italy	1.5	2.1	2.6	4.1	9.0	14.7
Sweden	n.a.	7.5	8.3	15.4	18.3	23.1
Difference	**11.7**	**13.7**	**14.5**	**23.6**	**30.0**	**32.0**

[a] Average for the following thirteen countries: Austria, Belgium, Denmark, Finland, France, Germany, Ireland, Italy, Netherlands, Norway, Sweden, Switzerland, United Kingdom;
[b] 1955.

Source: OECD's Education Database as compiled by Robert J. Barro and Jong-Wha Lee (*www2.cid.harvard.edu/ciddata/barrolee/Appendix.xls*).

it is argued that Switzerland is an outlier when it comes to redistributive policies because the Swiss government has a collective executive that gives right-wing parties veto power over redistributive policies. As noted in Chapter 1, the pattern in other PR systems has been coalition governments that *exclude* the right.

2.2.2. Skills and Training Systems

The differences between the American and European educational systems were clearly visible already in the immediate postwar period. Thus, in 1950, 14 percent of the American population over 25 years of age had a postsecondary degree compared to less than 3 percent in most European countries. By 1970, the figure had risen to more than 21 percent, compared to 6 percent in Europe (see Table 2.5). The pattern is very similar for Canada, and the gap between North America and Europe has been growing over time (contrary to a simple catch-up hypothesis). In Europe, the university was the providence of the privileged few during the 1950s and 1960s, and whereas most postsecondary education in the United States leads to general degrees, in Europe more of this education is taking place through professional schools using more targeted occupational curricula.

The figures for upper-secondary education also hide more subtle differences in the *content* of education. In the Anglo-Saxon countries, university education tends to be very general, and even engineering and

Table 2.6. *Skill Systems in Eighteen OECD Countries*

	(1) Vocational Training Share[a]	(2) Median Length of Tenure[b]	(3) Vocational Training System[c]
Austria	22	6.9	Dual apprenticeship
Germany	34	10.7	Dual apprenticeship
Sweden	36	7.8	Vocational colleges
Norway	37	(6.5)	Vocational colleges
Belgium	53	8.4	Mixed
Japan	16	8.3	Company-based
Finland	32	7.8	Vocational colleges
Italy	35	8.9	Company-based
France	28	7.7	Mixed
Ireland	6	5.3	Weak
Netherlands	43	5.5	Mixed
Switzerland	23	6.0	Dual apprenticeship
Denmark	31	4.4	Mixed
Canada	5	5.9	Weak
Australia	9	3.4	Weak
New Zealand	7	n.a.	Weak
United Kingdom	11	5.0	Weak apprenticeship
United States	3	4.2	Weak

[a] The share of an age cohort in either secondary or postsecondary (ISCED5) vocational training. *Source:* UNESCO (1999).
[b] The median length of enterprise tenure in years, 1995 (Norwegian figure refers to 1991). *Sources:* OECD *Employment Outlook*, 1997b, Table 5.5. For Norway: *OECD* (1993, Table 4.1).
[c] The character of the vocational training system according to whether most of the training occurs at the company level (as in Japan), through a dual apprenticeship system (as in Germany), through vocational colleges (as in Sweden), or through some mixture of the latter two (as in the Netherlands). Where vocational training is weak, I have not distinguished between the type of system. *Sources:* Streeck (1992); Finegold and Soskice (1988); Soskice (1999); Crouch, Finegold, and Sako (1999).

business schools provide very broad training that is not linked to particular industries or trades. By contrast, in Japan and most continental European countries, many university degrees are more specialized and there tends to be close linkages from engineering and trade schools to private industry.

But the part of the educational system that most clearly distinguish continental Europe (and Japan) from the Anglo-Saxon countries (and Ireland) is vocational training (see Table 2.6). The share of an age cohort that goes through a vocational training in the latter (column 1) varies between 3 and

11 percent (counting short-term postsecondary degrees), and there is little involvement of companies in the training system. In the former countries, the percentage of an age cohort going through vocational training is generally between a quarter and one half of an age cohort. At 16 percent, the figure for Japan is somewhere in the middle, but much training in this country goes on in large financially secure companies and is not recorded in the data.

As noted in Chapter 1, vocational training is closely related to how well adults perform on Statistics Canada and OECD's international literacy tests. In particular, those who leave the formal educational system early are much more likely to do well on these tests in countries with extensive vocational training programs than in countries emphasizing formal education. This fact would appear to be a result of the additional training afforded by the presence of good vocational training opportunities and the incentives to work hard in school that such opportunities create for young people at the lower end of the academic ability distribution.

The main difference among the countries with strong vocational training systems is in the emphasis on company as opposed to industry-level training. Whereas in Japan, and to a lesser extent in France and Italy, the emphasis is on company training, the remaining countries have some combination of on-the-job training and school-based training, with heavy involvement of employer organizations and unions. Formally, the systems can be divided into the apprenticeship systems of the German type, the vocational school systems of the Swedish type, or mixtures between the two, but they all combine theoretical, industry-specific, and direct workplace training (column 2). The relative importance of the three is difficult to gauge, but Belgium, The Netherlands and the Scandinavian countries tend to place more emphasis on school-based training (i.e., provision of non-firm-specific skills) than do Austria or Germany.

The difference in skill systems can also be gauged by median enterprise tenure rates – the median number of years workers have been with their current employer (based on national labor force surveys). These numbers contain relevant information about the firm-specificity of skills because firms and individuals investing heavily in such skills become increasingly dependent upon one another for their future welfare. The greater the investment, the higher the opportunity costs of severing the relationship and the lower the incentive for either party to do so. Indeed, short tenure rates may be not only an indicator of the *absence* of firm-specific skills but also a positive measure of *presence* of general skills. The reason is that general skills are developed in part by accumulating job experience from many different firms.

The drawback of using tenure rates to measure firm-specific skills is that they may also in part reflect the costs of dismissing workers as a result of employment protection. However, if higher tenure rates were unrelated to the extent of firm-specific skills, then the association between employment protection and tenure rates would be weak at best because most job switching is known to be voluntary. But, in fact, the cross-national association between the two variables is rather high ($r = 0.75$). Where data are available, tenure rates are strongly negatively related to quit rates. From this relationship, it seems clear that at least part of the effect of employment protection on tenure rates must go through the effect of the former on the stock of firm-specific skills. This interpretation is supported by considerable evidence showing tenure rates across industries *within* countries to be closely associated with the skill intensity of these industries (OECD 1993, 141–5).

Used as a measure of firm-specific skills (column 2 in Table 2.6), tenure rates suggest that the stock of such skills is low in the Anglo-Saxon countries compared to Japan and most of the continental European countries. The exceptions are Denmark, The Netherlands, and Switzerland, where firm tenure rates also tend to be quite short. In these countries, firms tend to be small with lower organizational capacity to adapt to the business cycle and limited R&D capacity. Although these countries have developed vocational training systems, firms typically depend more on industry technologies and skills, as well as employment and income protection at the industry level. Generous unemployment benefits, for example, allow small firms to "park" skilled workers in the unemployment benefit system during downturns without undermining the incentives of workers to invest in relevant skills.

The general pattern emerging in Table 2.6 is supported by a recent detailed comparative study of training systems in France, Germany, Italy, Japan, Sweden, the United Kingdom, and the United States (Crouch et al. 1999). In this comparison, the United Kingdom and especially the United States stand out as general skills countries, coupled with a weak, but vanishing, apprenticeship system in the case of the United Kingdom. Large American machine-tool firms with good apprenticeships abandoned these in the 1970s as weak employers associations and fragmented wage bargaining could not prevent rampant poaching behavior (Finegold et al. 1994). In this comparison, France and especially Sweden stand out as having good school-based vocational training systems (but with more emphasis on in-firm training and internal labor markets in France), while the German system is highlighted for its capacity to cultivate deep vocational skills through a combination of school and on-the-job training. Japan has little school-based vocational training but combines a good basic education with extensive training inside large corporations. Italy, finally, ranks low in terms of formal training institutions, but it provides good firm-based training in regions with well-organized unions and employer associations.

2.2.3. Product Market Strategies and the International Division of Labor

Figure 2.1 plots the eighteen OECD countries on the employment and unemployment protection indexes. Because income protection is so closely related to unemployment protection, the picture does not change radically if the former is used in place of the latter. Note that countries are distributed along a primary axis, corresponding to the southwest-northeast diagonal

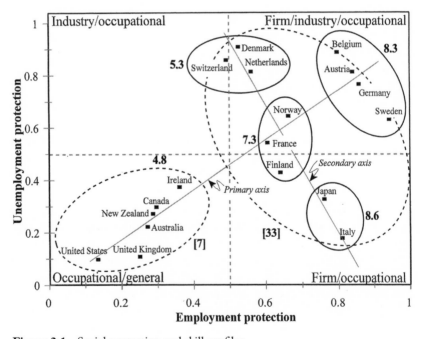

Figure 2.1 Social protection and skill profiles.
Notes: Bolded numbers are mean tenure rates for the cluster of countries circled; bracketed numbers are the percentage of an age cohort going through a vocational training.
Sources: See Tables 2.2, 2.3, and 2.4.

in Figure 2.1, with some countries further divided along a secondary axis, corresponding to the northwest-southeast diagonal in Figure 2.1. The main axis separates countries into two distinct welfare-production regimes: one combining weak employment and unemployment protection with a general skills profile, represented by the Anglo-Saxon countries and Ireland, and one combining high protection on at least one of the two social protection dimensions with firm- and/or industry-specific skills, represented by the continental European countries and Japan. The secondary axis divides the latter group into one with greater emphasis on employment protection and the creation of firm-specific skills, exemplified primarily by Japan and Italy,[15] and one with greater emphasis on unemployment protection and the production of industry-specific skills, exemplified by Denmark, The Netherlands, and Switzerland.

The data on skills presented in Table 2.6 have been summarized in the form of averages for each cluster of countries (only tenure rates are relevant for the division along the secondary axis). The high protection countries are also those with the best developed vocational training systems, and tenure rates decline with employment protection. Clearly, the empirical patterns we observe are quite consistent with the notion that skill formation is closely linked to social protection.

The coupling of social protection and skill systems helps us understand the product market strategies of companies and the creation of comparative advantages in the global economy. Thus, where there is a large pool of workers with advanced and highly portable skills and where social protection is low, companies enjoy considerable flexibility in attracting new workers, laying off old ones, or starting new production lines. This flexibility allows for hightened responsiveness to new business opportunities and facilitates the use of rapid product innovation strategies. In economies with a combination of firm- and industry-specific skills, such strategies are hampered by the difficulty of quickly adapting skills to new types of production and by restrictions in the ability of firms to hire and fire workers. On the other hand, these welfare-production regimes advantage companies that seek to develop deep competencies within established technologies and to upgrade and diversify existing product lines continuously.

Although this book is not intended as a comprehensive test of these propositions, they are broadly consistent with accounts in the comparative

---

[15] Although the position of Italy is probably exaggerated by the failure to account for semipublic unemployment insurance arrangements, as noted earlier.

literature of the international division of labor that had evolved during the 1950s and 1960s as a result of institutional and policy differences. Porter (1990), Streeck (1991), Soskice (1999), and Hollingsworth and Boyer (1997) all describe a pattern where firms in continental European countries, especially in northern Europe, were producing for established product markets but continuously upgrading and diversifying their product lines to take advantage of the most lucrative market niches. Porter, using data from the early to mids 1980s, shows that countries such as Germany, Switzerland, and Sweden had competitive advantages in a broad range of machinery industries and that the number of industries with an advantage was an order of magnitude greater than in the United States or the United Kingdom. The reverse pattern was apparent in industries using rapidly changing new technologies, as well as in internationally traded service industries where there is a premium on being able to hire highly mobile and well-educated employees from the external market (Porter 1990).

These findings are echoed by quantitative evidence developed by Thomas Cusack using U.S. Patent Office data. Broken into thirty technology classes, Cusack counted the number of references to scientific articles for patents in each technology class and country and then divided this number by the world number of scientific citations per technology class.[16] The idea is that the number of scientific citations, as opposed to citations to previous patents and nonscientific sources, is a good proxy for the extent to which national firms are engaged in radical innovation strategies. The results are shown in the first column of Table 2.7, with countries ranked by the average ratio of scientific citations for patents secured by national firms. As it turns out, the Anglo-Saxon countries and Ireland all have ratios that are significantly higher than in the specific skills countries of continental Europe and Japan. This is precisely as expected, although much work is clearly needed to establish a conclusive linkage between institutions and innovation strategies – a task outside the scope of this book.

At the low-tech end of product markets, it is necessary to rely on a different type of data to detect cross-national differences. Column 2 of Table 2.7

---

[16] The data are coded into references to previous patents and "others," where many of the latter are references to scientific articles. To get a good estimate of the number of scientific articles in the other category, the proportion of scientific references to other references was calculated for a random sample (6,000) for each country and technology class. These factors were then used to correct the overall data set so as to get a better measure of scientific citations.

Table 2.7. *Scientific Citation Rates and Low-Wage Service Employment in Eighteen OECD Countries*

	(1) Scientific Citation Ratio[a]	(2) Private Service Employment[b]
Ireland	1.514	–
United States	1.310	23
New Zealand	1.267	–
Canada	1.032	20
United Kingdom	0.837	16
Australia	0.804	26
Sweden	0.757	14
Netherlands	0.754	14
Norway	0.690	17
Switzerland	0.639	–
France	0.601	11
Belgium	0.598	13
Germany	0.592	14
Japan	0.586	–
Austria	0.575	–
Finland	0.552	11
Denmark	0.536	11
Italy	0.491	9

[a] The average number of scientific citations per patent by national firms in each of thirty technology classes as a proportion of the average number of citations in each class for the entire world, 1985–95. *Source:* U.S. Patent Office data.

[b] The number of people employed in wholesale, retail trade, restaurants and hotels, and community, social and personal services, 1982–91 as a percentage of the working age population. *Source:* OECD, *International Sectoral Data Base* (1996).

uses the proportion of the working age population employed in private social and personal services as a proxy. As I will show later, firms that rely heavily on low-skilled and low-paid labor for profitability tend to be concentrated in these industries. Although there is only data for a subset of countries, the numbers display a rather clear cross-national pattern. Producers of standardized and low-productivity services thrive in general skills countries such as Australia and United States because they can hire from a large pool of unskilled workers who are afforded little job protection and whose wages are held down by low unemployment protection. By contrast, firms trying to compete in this space in specific skills countries such as

Germany and Sweden are inhibited by higher labor costs and lower flexibility in hiring and firing. These differences were magnified during the 1980s and 1990s, and Britain is now closer to the mean for the general skills countries.

One of the catalysts for greater diversification in industrial structures and the supporting social and labor market institutions was the economic crisis of the 1970s. Starting with the "hot" summer of 1968, wage moderation collapsed in some countries, and inflation exploded. The increases won by strikers in 1968–9 were about twice those of the preceding three years (Allsopp 1983, Table 3.4). One of the sources of inflationary wage pressure was the rising demand for labor, which caused unemployment to reach unprecedented low levels across the continent. With the share of employment in agriculture having declined to less than 15 percent, elastic supplies of underemployed labor from the agricultural sector no longer capped industrial wage demands. Johansen's (1987, pp. 148–9) description of the situation in Denmark is representative: "In the mid-1960s," he writes, "the registered unemployed were either workers who were in the process of changing from one job to another and had a few idle days in between, or older people staying in isolated municipalities in Northern Jutland or the smaller islands from where they did not want to move." Under such conditions, the threat of unemployment no longer disciplined wages. Memories of high unemployment faded as the postwar generation of workers aged and retired. The Soviet threat was perceived as less immediate, removing one incentive for labor and capital to pull together. With the weakening of the Bretton Woods System and its breakdown in the early 1970s, inflationary expectations lost their anchor.

The result was a great downward pressure on industrial employment that was exacerbated by the beginning shift in consumer demand away from manufactures and toward services. Governments responded to the consequent unemployment by increasing their spending to sustain demand. They responded to the breakdown of wage moderation by encouraging further centralization of negotiations and more formal incomes policy arrangements (Scharpf 1991). Unions were promised increased health and unemployment payments and larger social security stipends as the quid pro quo for restraint. Public spending as a share of gross domestic product rose from 24 percent in 1967–9 to 30 percent in 1974–6.[17] While the growth in spending as a percentage of GDP had been rapid in the 1960s, its

---

[17] This is an unweighted average for thirteen European countries.

expansion was even faster in the 1970s. It was particularly dramatic in The Netherlands, Denmark, and Sweden, where public spending was tied to the expansion of transfer payments and social programs.

This strategy worked best where the institutions of corporatism and centralized wage bargaining were most advanced.[18] Fiscal expansion and accommodating monetary policy stimulated employment rather than inflation, given agreements by the unions to restrain their wage demands. Where private-sector employment growth lagged, governments supplemented it with increases in public employment or early retirement schemes. Contrary to popular notions, the pressures of the international crisis, especially rising unemployment, did not force or induce generous welfare states to cut back. This is most evident with respect to unemployment protection, as illustrated in Figure 2.2. The figure splits countries into high- and a low-protection categories, based on the unemployment protection index introduced earlier, and then shows the evolution of average unemployment replacement rates in each category during the period from 1971 to 1995. Note that whereas high-protection countries significantly raised replacement rates, low-protection countries kept them low.[19]

Although the administration and long-run generosity of unemployment benefits have everywhere been tightened, which is not apparent in the figure, the cross-country pattern is consistent with the argument in this book since support for generous unemployment protection among unions, employers, and individual workers should be a function of their exposure to risk. Because risk is linked to skills, and because specific skill countries tend to have relatively generous protection, when exogenous shocks raise the level of risk, it is not surprising that the effect is greater in the specific skills countries with already high generous protection. The one exception is Japan where unemployment benefits were relatively low and remained low. In this case, as argued in Chapter 1, because skills are almost entirely firm-specific, high-employment, not unemployment, protection is the key to insurance against risk.

Of course, in all the specific skills countries, there was a greater premium on retaining employment, partly to reduce the exposure to risk but also to lighten the fiscal burden of generous benefits. In many countries, the corporatist solutions to the economic crisis, described earlier, worked quite

[18] Typically, in the smaller European democracies. See Katzenstein (1984, 1985).
[19] There are exceptions to this pattern. In Ireland, replacement rates were raised during the 1970s only to be cut back again in the 1990s. In Germany, there is little change over time.

well. In Austria and Sweden, for example, unemployment was kept remarkably low at 1.9 percent of the labor force in 1973–83 (see Table 2.8). In Germany, where the unions similarly restrained wages but macroeconomic stimulus was subdued as a result of the strong antiinflationary predisposition of the Bundesbank and deficit reductions by capital-market-constrained state and local governments, unemployment still averaged less than 5 percent during this turbulent period. By comparison, in countries like Britain, Italy, Canada, and the United States where corporatist institutions were missing or less well developed, demand stimulus aggravated inflation instead of reducing unemployment. In the United States, this was exacerbated by the Vietnam War and the accommodating stance of the central bank.

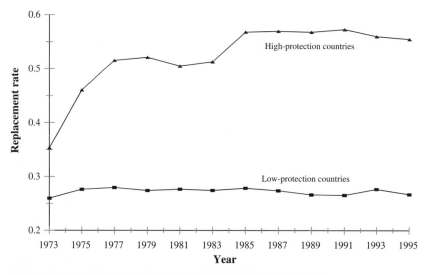

Figure 2.2 Unemployment replacement rates, 1973–1995.
Notes: This division of countries into the high- and low-protection groups is based on the unemployment protection index introduced in Chapter 1. High-protection countries: Austria, Belgium, Finland, France, Germany, Netherlands, Norway, Sweden, and Switzerland; low-protection countries: Australia, Canada, Ireland, Italy, Japan, New Zealand, United Kingdom, and United States. Because time-series data for this index do not exist, the figures in this graph are based on gross replacement rates for the first year of unemployment for a representative 40-year-old worker (averaged over different family situations). These rates do not necessarily correspond to the protection index across countries, but it is assumed that change over time in underlying protection levels is correlated with changes in gross replacement rates.
Source: OECD, *Database on Unemployment Benefit Entitlements and Replacement Rates* (undated).

Table 2.8. *Unemployment in Selected Countries, 1950–1996*

	1950–59	1960–72	1973–83	1984–96
Switzerland[a]	0.8	0.1	0.4	1.7
Sweden	2.2	1.5	1.9	4.2
Austria	3.9	1.8	1.9	3.6
Norway	1.5	1.2	2.0	4.3
Japan	1.3	1.1	2.0	2.6
Finland	1.3	2.0	4.5	9.4
Germany	6.1	1.0	4.7	8.0
France	0.6	0.9	5.4	10.5
Netherlands	2.0	1.3	6.5	8.4
United Kingdom	1.6	2.3	6.5	9.1
Denmark[a]	9.5	3.5	7.1	7.9
United States	4.4	4.9	7.2	6.3
Italy	9.3	5.3	7.4	11.2
Canada	4.2	5.4	7.9	9.7
Belgium	9.1	3.4	8.2	10.2
Ireland	–	5.2	8.5	15.6

[a] Figures for Denmark and Switzerland are not directly comparable to the rest because of different definitions of unemployment.

Source: OECD Employment Outlook, various years.

In addition to differences in the capacity of governments to respond to macroeconomic pressures, new technology and diverging product market strategies started to create a more fundamental divide between the social market economies of continental Europe, the corporate welfare model of Japan, and the more liberal Anglo-Saxon countries. As the postwar wave of Fordist mass production methods gave way to more skill-intensive, science-based technologies and flexible specialization, firms that were in long-term cooperative relations with their employees and had access to workers with good vocational training thrived. Firms in countries with adversarial labor-management relations suffered not only because they had more difficulty containing wage pressures, but also because they had no effective way to provide their employees with the kind of deep firm- and industry-specific skills that were required to compete effectively in the new high-quality, and hence high-value-added, product markets.[20]

---

[20] These differences are evident in a wave of industrial relations reforms in high-protection countries during the 1970s. Although varying in depth and breadth, these reforms all improved employee representation at the plant level and in some cases in corporate board rooms. By and large, the reforms were consistent with the production model that emerged

The loss of competitive edge for American firms was a major concern in several in-depth studies. Thus, the research team led by Michael Porter found relative decline in such industries as automobiles, machinery, machine tools, consumer electronics, and office products, and they detected a beginning deterioration in many others (Porter 1990, p. 519). A team of MIT researchers came to similar conclusions, emphasizing that U.S. products were often lacking in quality, timeliness of service, flexibility, and other business aspects where Japanese and European firms excelled (Dertouzos et al. 1989, p. 33). In both studies, the institutional sources of weakness were precisely those that gave coordinated market economies an edge during this period: a weak vocational training system, hierarchical corporate governance structures, arms-length relationship between buyers and suppliers, and short-termism in the equity-based financial system.

Based on the competitive advantage in diversified quality markets, and despite the slowdown resulting from the global recession, firms in both Europe and Japan were well positioned to take advantage of new export opportunities, and they kept unemployment below the level in most other countries. In Japan, growth was actually accelerating, and equity markets took off in the early 1980s. By contrast, growth fell sharply in Britain and the United States, and unemployment rose more rapidly than elsewhere. International trade, the one area of the world economy experiencing rapid growth, became increasingly dominated by Japan and continental Europe, and both Britain and the United States experienced a slowdown in exports in the latter half of the 1970s (in Britain, export growth actually fell below the domestic rate of growth). Commensurate with poor economic performance, British and American equity markets went through protracted bear markets, and commentators started to sound alarmist about the future of Anglo-Saxon capitalism (e.g., Zysman and Cohen 1987; Barlett and Steele 1992; Madrick 1995).[21]

It is against this backdrop that one must understand the radical deregulation of the British and U.S. economies during the 1980s and 1990s. Instead

in these countries and were broadly consistent with the interests of high-quality producers and skilled workers (Windolf 1989).

[21] James Cramer, a highly successful hedge fund manager, recalls the defensive mood among U.S. investors in the early 1980s: "my clients were scared to death that the Japanese were going to destroy us in the '80s as they took over every one of our industries. My pitch was always the same: 'One thing that is never going to happen is that you won't ever see a bottle of Mitsubishi ketchup on the table. It will always be good old Heinz.'" Commentary, December 5, 1999, TheStreet.com (*www.thestreet.com*).

of trying to emulate the welfare production regimes of northern Europe and Japan, and despite political rhetoric to that effect during the late 1970s and early 1980s,[22] these countries embarked on reforms that would strengthen their comparative institutional advantage: low-cost mass-produced services and high-tech radically new products. For the continental European countries and Japan, despite the manufacturing successes of the 1970s, new tensions associated with the rise of services threatened the long-term viability of the high-protection strategy during the 1980s and 1990s. As I discuss in the next section, a strategy of wage compression, high job protection, and high taxes was not conducive to the growth of labor and low-pay intensive services, *even though* it was entirely compatible with manufacturing competitiveness.

To summarize, by the early 1970s, advanced economies had divided into two broad categories: one with generous social protection, specific skills, and competitive advantages in established product markets, and one with low social protection, general skills, and comparative advantages in new product markets. There is no simple causal story behind this bifurcation. It resulted from a complex interaction between economic conditions, inherited organizational capacities of employers and unions, initial differences in skill systems, and differences in political structures. Where institutional capacities were high, where there existed a craft tradition, where there were consensual rather than majoritarian institutions, and where the potential for economic growth was high, cooperative solutions of institutionalized wage restraint and an expansion of the welfare state emerged. In turn, these solutions reinforced comparative advantages in product markets requiring specific skills investments and long-term cooperative relationships between firms and their employees. Where institutional capacities were low, on the other hand, high social protection tended to exacerbate collective action problems and pushed governments toward deregulation and welfare state cutbacks, while encouraging individuals to seek self-insurance, primarily through heavy investments in general skills.

2.3. A Change of Fortunes: The Rise of the Service Economy

The high-protection countries with relatively egalitarian distributions of income performed remarkably well during the 1950s and 1960s on most economic measures. The insecurity and inequality of capitalist markets

---

[22] See especially Reich (1983).

had been tempered by high levels of social protection and wage equality while simultaneously giving European firms a comparative advantage in relatively established but high-quality segments of international product markets. It was not simply that European firms learned to live with a generous social protection system, but that they depended on this system to overcome worker disincentives to invest in specific skills and to secure union cooperation in wages and work organization. Centralized wage bargaining, in particular, appears to have played a key role in adjusting to the international economic crisis of the 1970s, as argued by many students of corporatism.

Yet, somewhere in the mid- to late 1970s, the fortunes of different welfare production regimes started to change. In some countries, this was probably tied to the extension of egalitarian norms to the point where it became counterproductive for skill formation and interfered with the introduction of new technology (Hibbs and Locking 2000). Relatively stable wages between skill categories provide a protection of skill investments, but in some countries solidaristic wage policies significantly reduced wage differentials across skill groups. I have discussed these problems at length elsewhere (Iversen 1996). On the whole, however, these problems probably only made a small dent into the international market shares of European companies, and they were dealt with by reorganizing collective bargaining institutions and macro-economic policy regimes without significantly reducing the overall level of social protection for full-time skilled employees.

But while industrial relations reforms may have helped restore any lost competitiveness by European firms, high-protection countries experienced a growing employment problem that did not go away with the success of European exporters. The problem is illustrated in Figure 2.3, which shows the gap in unemployment and private sector employment performance in manufacturing and services between the United States and eleven high-protection countries in Europe starting in 1950.[23] A positive number for unemployment means that European rates exceed those in the United States, while a positive number for employment means that private sector employment as a percentage of the working age population is higher in Europe than in the United States. Note that Europe outperformed the United States on unemployment until the mid-1980s, and that private sector employment in manufacturing and private services almost caught up to

---

[23] The eleven countries are Austria, Belgium, Denmark, Finland, France, Germany, Italy, Netherlands, Norway, Sweden, and Switzerland.

U.S. levels in the early 1960s where it remained until the 1970s. Thereafter a gap in the United States' favor quickly opens up.

Figure 2.4 provides a breakdown of the employment numbers by sector. One trend is unsurprising: because Europe began the period with about two to three times more employment in agriculture than in the United States (19 percent of the working age population in Europe versus 8 percent in the United States), agricultural employment was bound to decline faster in Europe relative to that in the United States. By 1995, agricultural employment converged to the low U.S. figure of about 2 percent. Expansion of employment in European manufacturing by and large made up for losses until 1963, when manufacturing employment likewise began a process of convergence to U.S. levels. By 1995, average manufacturing employment in Europe was 18.1 percent of the working age population compared to 17.4 percent in the United States. This is essentially complete convergence.

In a very similar fashion, although with "opposite sign," the period up until the late 1960s was characterized by a gradual convergence of European

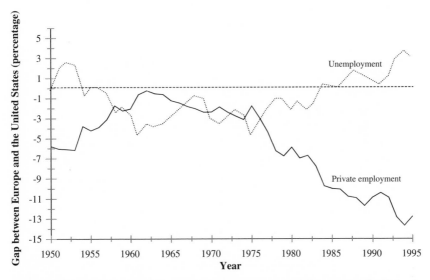

Figure 2.3 The (un)employment gap between continental Europe and the United States. The gap is defined as average European (un)employment minus U.S. (un)employment. Above the zero line, absolute (un)employment is higher in Europe. Employment is measured as a percentage of the working age population in private sector employment. Unemployment is measured as standardized unemployment rates. Continental Europe refers the following countries: Austria, Belgium, Denmark, Finland, France, Germany, Italy, Netherlands, Norway, and Sweden.

service employment to U.S. figures. Had this trend toward convergence continued, Europe and the United States would essentially have had an identical sectoral employment structure by the mid-1990s (as indicated by the dotted line). But starting around 1970, the process of convergence in services ended, and Europe and the United States grew increasingly apart. In 1968, employment in private services was about 26 percent in the United States and about 21 percent in Europe. Twenty-seven years later, the figures were 42 percent for the United States and 28 percent for Europe. Measured as a share of the adult population, almost 50 percent *more* people were employed in private services in the United States than in Europe. If we are to understand the shift in private employment performance captured by Figure 2.3, it is therefore critical to understand the causes of divergence in private service employment performance.

The explanation advanced in this book is simple and follows directly from the welfare production regime argument. Even though the egalitarian social welfare regimes of northern Europe created comparative advantages in high-value added manufactures, they created disadvantages in precisely

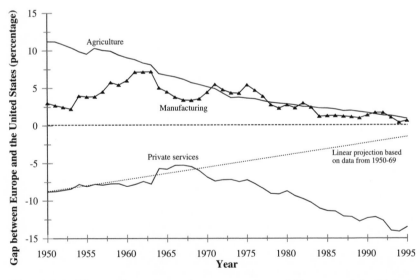

Figure 2.4 The employment gap between continental Europe and the United States, by sector. The gap is defined as European employment minus U.S. employment. Above the zero line, absolute employment in a sector is higher in Europe than in the United States. Employment is measured as a percentage of the working age population.

Table 2.9. *Average Annual Rates of Growth in Total Factor Productivity for Fourteen OECD Countries, 1970–1994*

	1970– 1974	1975– 1978	1979– 1982	1983– 1986	1987– 1990	1991– 1994	1970– 1994
AGRICULTURE [a]	*4.6*	*1.2*	*3.6*	*2.5*	*2.7*	*n.a.* [c]	*3.7*
INDUSTRY	*2.0*	*1.5*	*−0.1*	*1.5*	*1.4*	*1.8*	*1.6*
Manufacturing	*2.8*	*1.8*	*0.1*	*1.6*	*1.3*	*2.7*	*2.1*
Textiles	3.2	0.8	0.3	1.3	0.2	2.2	1.7
Chemicals	3.8	3.7	0.6	0.7	1.4	4.1	2.6
Machinery and equipment	3.6	0.7	0.5	1.7	1.6	3.4	2.6
Electricity, gas, and water	*3.0*	*1.5*	*−1.3*	*1.0*	*0.6*	*0.5*	*1.8*
Transport, storage, and communication	*2.2*	*1.7*	*0.3*	*2.1*	*3.2*	*2.0*	*2.7*
Construction	−1.2	0.0	−0.4	0.7	0.3	−0.4	−0.4
SERVICES	*0.2*	*0.2*	*−0.5*	*0.4*	*−0.4*	*−0.5*	*−0.2*
Private services	*0.8*	*0.2*	*−0.6*	*0.7*	*−0.4*	*−0.5*	*0.4*
Wholesale, retail, restaurants, and hotels	1.8	0.5	−0.9	1.1	0.1	−0.5	0.9
Finance, insurance, and real estate	0.4	0.2	−0.4	0.9	−0.4	−0.2	0.0
Community, social, and personal services	0.4	0.1	−0.4	0.3	−0.7	−0.6	−0.2
Productivity gap [b]	*1.8*	*1.3*	*0.4*	*1.1*	*1.8*	*2.3*	*1.8*

[a] Based on estimated *labor* productivity.
[b] Difference between industry and private services.
[c] n.a.: data not available.
Source: OECD, *International Sectoral Data Base* (1996).

the type of service production that was generating the most jobs during the 1980s and 1990s. As we shall see in Chapter 6, most of the differential in service sector employment performance was the result of relatively low-skilled industries that were hurt by wage compression at the bottom end of the wage scale as well as by inflexible labor contracts and high costs of social protection for low-skilled workers.[24] In addition, because productivity growth in most services seriously lagged behind that in manufacturing (see Table 2.9), a tightly coupled wage-setting system raised the relative prices

---

[24] Although the problem could potentially have been addressed by specializing in high-value-added services for exports, this option was unavailable at the time because of the very limited trade in most services. I return to the issue of liberalization of services trade in Chapter 6.

71

on these services and reduced demand.[25] How important this "Baumol cost disease" (Baumol 1967) is for employment depends on the price elasticity of demand, but in a range of services where the product is not essential to the consumer, the effect is substantial.

This argument is related to problems of unemployment in the following way. Although the government can cope with sluggish private sector employment growth by limiting the entry of new workers into the labor market, by encouraging the exit of older workers, or by increasing public sector employment, the incentives and opportunities for unemployed workers with specific skills to find work outside the industry or sector where their skills are appropriate are very small. Therefore, when unemployment is rising not as a result of temporary swings in the business cycle or shifts in the relative performance of companies within a sector but because of a secular decline in an entire industry, unemployment is likely to change from a transitional to a structural problem as workers with specific skills become longterm unemployed. Combined with high unemployment protection, unemployed workers have neither good opportunities nor strong incentives to look for employment outside their sector.

Finally, the confluence of workers with high industry- and sector-specific skills, rapidly declining employment in manufacturing, and sluggish growth in new employment opportunities in services help explain the rapid growth of the welfare state. Essentially, the new labor market insecurities could not be dealt with inside the "private" protection system of wage coordination and employment security. Deindustrialization threatened to force workers out of the industries for which their skills had been developed. This had two effects. First, if the incentives underpinning the specific skills equilibrium were to be retained, income protection through the public insurance system had to rise to compensate for a lower effective rate of "private" wage protection. Second, the higher the probability of transitioning between jobs with different skill requirements, the higher the preferred level of protection at any given level of skill specificity and income. This implication of the

---

[25] Productivity in services is notoriously difficult to measure. However, a large empirical literature supports the productivity gap evident in the OECD data. See especially Gordon (1987) and Van Ark (1996). Gordon, widely considered the leading authority on productivity, finds that services productivity lagged manufacturing productivity in Europe and the United States by a factor of about 2 to 4 from the early 1970s to the mid-1980s. There is also evidence for a productivity gap between services and manufacturing in the sizable economic literature on real exchange rates. I discuss this literature in Chapter 6.

theory of social policy preferences is developed in Chapter 3. The broader political, institutional, and economic consequences of deindustrialization are considered in Part III.

2.4. Conclusion

This chapter has outlined the historical origins of the different welfare production regimes that came to define the postwar political economies of Europe, North America, and Japan. The emphasis has been on tracing the processes leading to divergent institutional developments that are roughly approximated by two ideal types or institutional equilibria. Each is characterized by distinct couplings of social protection, skill systems, and political institutions, and a key objective of this study is to provide an understanding of the political underpinnings of these couplings.

Following Hall and Soskice (2001), a central theme is why social, political, and economic institutions tend to coevolve in a manner that reinforces rather than undermines one another. The welfare state is not "politics against markets," as commonly assumed, but politics *with* markets. Although it is popular to think that markets, especially global ones, interfere with the welfare state, and vice versa, this notion is simply inconsistent with the postwar record of actual welfare state development. The United States, which has a comparatively small welfare state and flexible labor markets, has performed well in terms of jobs and growth during the past two decades; however, before then the countries with the largest welfare states and the most heavily regulated labor markets exceeded those in the United States on almost any gauge of economic competitiveness and performance.

Despite the change in economic fortunes, the relationship between social protection and product market strategies continues to hold. Northern Europe and Japan still dominate high-quality markets for machine tools and consumer durables, whereas the United States dominates software, biotech, and other high-tech industries. There is every reason that firms and governments will try to preserve the institutions that give rise to these comparative advantages, and here the social protection system (broadly construed to include job security and protection through the industrial relations system) plays a key role. The reason is that social insurance shapes the incentives workers and firms have for investing in particular types of skills, and skills are critical for competitive advantage in human-capital-intensive economies. Firms do not develop competitive advantages *in spite of* systems of social protection but *because of* it.

Continuing this line of argument, the changing economic fortunes of different welfare production regimes probably has very little to do with growing competitive pressure from the international economy. To the contrary, it will be argued in Chapter 6 that the main problem for Europe is the growing reliance on services that have traditionally been closed to trade. In particular, labor-intensive, low-productivity jobs do not thrive in the context of high social protection and intensive labor-market regulation, and without international trade, countries cannot specialize in high value-added services. Lack of international trade and competition, therefore, *not* the growth of these, is the cause of current employment problems in high-protection countries.

The rest of this study seeks to spell out both the political foundations of the persistence of institutions and the political responses to the economic forces that challenge them. Part II considers the comparative politics of social protection and focuses on electoral politics. Specifically, Chapter 3 develops a human capital model of popular preferences for social protection, while Chapter 4 explores the institutional conditions that facilitate or retard the translation of these preferences into policy outcomes. Finally, Part III focuses on the challenges to existing welfare production regimes caused by deindustrialization and other forces of structural change. First, Chapter 5 relates deindustrialization to the expansion of the welfare state, and how it has been conditioned by skill systems and political institutions. Second, Chapter 6 discusses the economic tradeoffs engendered by deindustrialization and how governments have responded to these.

PART II

Political Foundations of Social Policy

3

---

*Explaining Individual Social Policy Preferences**

As noted in Chapter 1, human capital rivals physical capital as a source of personal and national wealth, and it is the single most important determinant of personal income in advanced industrialized countries. Viewing human capital as an *investment* or asset, this chapter asks how the character of that investment affects workers' preferences for social protection. The fundamental idea is that investment in skills that are specific to a particular firm, industry, or occupation exposes their owners to risks for which they will seek nonmarket protection, whereas skills that are portable, by contrast, do not require extensive nonmarket protection.

The asset theory of preferences does not necessarily contradict a long tradition in the study of the welfare state that emphasizes redistribution as a key political motive behind the welfare state (e.g., Korpi 1983; Esping-Andersen 1990). Indeed, Meltzer and Richard's (1981) influential median voter result for government spending, which focuses on the redistributive aspect of social protection, emerges as a special case in the model. Given a particular composition of skills, workers with higher incomes are likely to demand less social protection than workers with lower incomes. The asset model parts ways with the Meltzer-Richard model, however, because it explicitly recognizes that social protection also has an insurance aspect (Sinn 1995; Moene and Wallerstein 2001) and that demand for insurance varies between workers according to their degree of exposure to labor market risks (Baldwin 1990).

---

* This chapter is an expanded version of a co-authored paper with David Soskice published in the *American Political Science Review* under the title of "An Asset Theory of Social Policy Preferences" (Iversen and Soskice 2001).

The model is tested on public opinion data from eleven advanced democracies. Income and skill specificity, which is measured in a variety of ways, turn out to be the overriding determinants of preferences for a range of different social polices that broadly correspond to the various types of protection identified in Chapter 1. Gender is also important for explaining policy preferences, and the effect is precisely what we would predict from the discussion of gender and social protection in Chapter 1. Unlike the impression one often gets from a largely nontheoretical comparative public opinion literature, there is, thus, a great deal of structure to peoples' social policy preferences.

The chapter is organized into three sections. In the first, the model and its main empirical implications are presented. The second tests these implications on public opinion data from the International Social Survey Program. The concluding section discusses the broader implications of the model for explaining differences in social protection across countries.

3.1. The Model

3.1.1. Assumptions

Workers derive their incomes from skills that can be either general or specific. Specific skills are skills that are valuable only to a single firm or to a group of firms (whether an industry or a sector), whereas general skills are portable across all firms. Three different employment situations, or states of the world, are distinguished, each associated with distinct levels of income. In State I, a worker is employed in a firm that utilizes both his or her specific and general skills; in State II the worker is employed in a firm that only utilizes his or her general skills; and in State III the worker is unemployed (i.e., none of his skills are being utilized).

In State II, g defines the market value of a worker's general skills when his or her specific skills are not being used. In State I (when the specific skills are being used as well), the worker is paid sg, the value of his or her combined specific and general skills. A worker that has no specific skills ($s = 1$) is always employed at the market value of his or her general skills. The key assumption is that general skills are marketable in all sectors of the economy, whereas specific skills are marketable only in one sector (the size of which is defined by the specificity of skills).

In addition to market income, which includes both wage and non-wage compensation, workers receive transfer income from the government, hereunder unemployment benefits, healthcare benefits, pensions, and other forms of nonwage compensation. Although some of these benefits are received by people who are outside the labor market, what matters to the argument is that they are viewed by workers as part of their compensation (what in the neocorporatist literature is sometimes referred to as the "social wage"). Those who are most fearful of losing the labor market power of their skills, and, hence, their ability to secure good health and pension plans through their employer, will also be most concerned about guaranteeing a high level of benefits, even if the benefits are "deferred" to the future.

Transfers are assumed to come in the form of a flat-rate payment, R, which incorporates the idea in the Meltzer-Richard model that there is a redistributive aspect to social protection.[1] Following the terminology in Chapter 1, one can distinguish between transfers that go to support the income of employed workers, *wage protection*, and transfers that go to the unemployed, *unemployment protection*. As the model is developed, we will discuss what happens if R only goes to unemployment protection. But in the main model, we will assume that all workers receive the same flat-rate subsidy, which may simply be referred to as *income protection*. *Employment protection* could be modeled as a probability of keeping a job where a worker's skills are fully utilized, and it will be considered separately in the empirical analysis along with the other types of protection.

Transfers are paid out of a flat-rate tax (t) on all wages. Total per capita receipts are T, and all receipts are spent on transfers (i.e., budgets are assumed to be balanced). As in the Meltzer-Richard model, taxation is assumed to create work disincentives, captured here by the following simple labor supply function:

$$l(t) = 1/(1 + t) \tag{3.1}$$

where $l(t)$ is the number of hours worked or the intensity of effort (the particular form of this function is chosen for mathematical convenience). Define w as average hourly pretax earnings. Then tax income per capita is

$$T = t \cdot w \cdot l(t) = \frac{t \cdot w}{1 + t} = R \tag{3.2}$$

---

[1] This is also a realistic assumption with after-tax income distributed significantly more equally than pre-tax income (see Gottschalk and Smeeding 2000; Huber and Stephens 2001; Bradley et al. 2003).

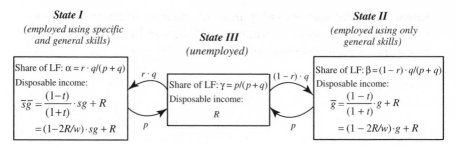

Figure 3.1   The three states of an individual in the labor market.

Figure 3.1 illustrates the three states of labor market and shows the disposable (after tax) income associated with each state: I, $\overline{sg}$; III, R; and II, $\overline{g}$.

For a given period of time, there is a probability, p, of losing one's job and another probability, q, of reemployment. In equilibrium $p \cdot e = q \cdot \gamma$, where e is the share of employed workers and γ is the share of the work force that is unemployed ($e = 1 - \gamma$). This implies that in equilibrium $e = q/(p + q)$. Furthermore, if r is the probability that an employed worker is reemployed into State I (i.e., into a job where both general and specific skills are utilized), then the equilibrium share of the labor force employed in State I is

$$\alpha = r \cdot e = r \cdot q/(p + q) \tag{3.3}$$

Likewise, the share of the labor force employed in State II is

$$\beta = (1 - r) \cdot e = (1 - r) \cdot q/(p + q) \tag{3.4}$$

while the share of the labor force in State III (unemployment) is

$$\gamma = p/(p + q) \tag{3.5}$$

For any individual worker with both specific and general skills, the proportions α, β, and γ can be interpreted as probabilities in a lottery with three possible outcomes. An employed sg-worker will therefore seek to maximize the expected utility of income across all three states. Ignoring the discounting of future income (which makes no substantive difference to the results), this is captured by the following utility function:

$$V = \alpha \cdot u(\overline{s}\,\overline{g}) + \beta \cdot u(\overline{g}) + \gamma \cdot u(R) \tag{3.6}$$

80

where $u(\cdot)$ is the worker's utility from net income, which for simplicity is assumed to be spent on consumption. Using standard assumptions, the following constraints are imposed on u:

$$u_c > 0,$$
$$u_{cc} < 0, \tag{3.7}$$

and

$$\lim_{c \to 0} u'(c) = \infty$$

A number of the following results hold for this general form of utility function (notably the Meltzer-Richard results). However, because the insurance function of the social wage will play an important role and because we then need specific conditions on risk aversion, the standard assumption of a constant Arrow-Pratt relative risk aversion (RRA) utility function is used. Specifically,

$$u(c) = \frac{c^{1-a}}{1-a} \quad \forall \quad a > 0, \quad \neq 1 \tag{3.7a}$$
$$= \log c \quad \text{for} \quad a = 1$$

With these assumptions in mind, it is not possible to determine workers' utility-maximizing preferences for social protection.

3.1.2. Optimizing Social Preferences

The logic of the presentation in this section is as follows. First, we consider a simple base-line model with no insurance effects, no tax disincentives, only general skills, and no unemployment (Model I). Then tax disincentives are introduced to get the Meltzer-Richard result (Model II), followed by insurance effects (and unemployment) to explore the effects of risk-aversion (Model III). Finally, we see what happens to the demand for social protection when the composition of skills is allowed to vary (Model IV). To keep the presentation simple, all proofs are put in the appendix at the end of this chapter.

Model I. No insurance effects, no disincentive effects: the $t = 1$ model. In solving the workers' maximization problem, begin by assuming a labor force with only general skills ($s = 1$) and no unemployment ($e = 1$). The simplest case is where there are no tax disincentive effects on the number of hours supplied [so that $l(t) = 1$ rather than $l(t) = 1/(1 + t)$ as subsequently will be assumed].

When $s = 1$, $e = 1$, and $l(t) = 1$, Equation (3.6) reduces to

$$V = u((1 - t)g + tw) = u(g(1 - R/w) + R) \qquad (3.8)$$
$$= \frac{1}{1 - a} \cdot (g(1 - R/w) + R)^{1-a}$$

We want to choose R to maximize V, where R is bounded between $R = 0$, corresponding to $t = 0$, and $R = w$, corresponding to $t = 1$. Because

$$V_R = (g(1 - R/w) + R)^{-a} \cdot (1 - g/w)$$

and, because $0 \le R \le w$, $g > w$ implies that V_R is uniformly negative for all values of R and hence t: Maximization of V, therefore, requires $t = 0$. Thus, voters with above average income will choose a zero tax rate. An analogous argument for $g < w$ implies that voters with below average income will choose the maximum tax rate of 100 percent. This is the standard result: In the absence of insurance functions and tax disincentives, voters will want the maximum R (i.e., $t = 1$) if $g < w$ and a zero R ($t = 0$) if $g > w$. Thus, if the median voter, M, has an income less than the average income of w, the median voter will always vote for a maximum tax rate. The result is illustrated in Figure 3.2a.

Model II. Disincentive effects, no insurance effects: the Meltzer-Richard model. If we now include the tax disincentive effect that $l(t) = 1/(1 + t)$, we have

$$V = u\left(\frac{1 - t}{1 + t}g + \frac{tw}{1 + t}\right) = u\left(g\left(1 - \frac{2R}{w}\right) + R\right) \qquad (3.9)$$
$$= \frac{1}{1 - a} \cdot \left(g\left(1 - \frac{2R}{w}\right) + R\right)^{1-a}$$

This implies

$$V_R = (g(1 - 2R/w) + R)^{-a} \cdot (1 - 2g/w) \qquad (3.10)$$

so that in the Meltzer-Richard model, only voters with a g level below that of half the average hourly wage ($g = w/2$) will vote for a maximum tax rate. As illustrated in Figure 3.2b, if the median voter has a g level above $w/2$ he or she will, therefore, not vote for the maximum tax rate. Because of the simplicity of the tax disincentive function, voters with g levels below $w/2$

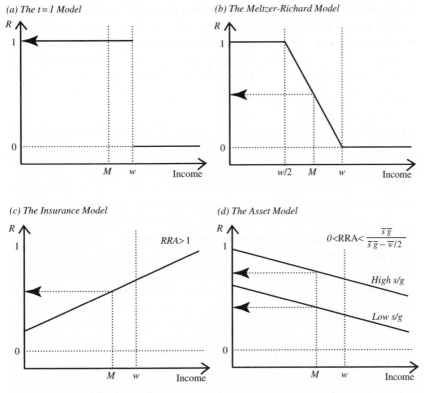

Figure 3.2 Four models of social policy preferences. Arrows indicate preferred level of social protection by the median voter.

will vote for $t = 1$, and voters with g levels above $w/2$ will vote for $t = 0$.[2] With the more complex tax disincentive function used by Meltzer-Richard, workers with income in the range $[w/2, w]$ will prefer taxation up to the point where the benefits to them from redistribution are exactly outweighed by the efficiency costs of tax disincentives. If the median voter is in this range, as the Meltzer-Richard model assumes, then he or she may vote for a positive tax rate less than 1 (as illustrated in Figure 3.2).

One of the implications of the Meltzer-Richard model is that voter turnout will be positively related to the level of government transfers because nonvoting tends to be concentrated among low-income people

---

[2] Meltzer-Richard have a more general tax disincentive function than that used here. Consequently, the tax rate that maximizes tax revenue can be less than one.

(Lijphart 1997). There is some cross-national evidence for this proposition (see Franzese 1998). On the other hand, there is little empirical support for another key implication of the model, developed by Alesina and Rodrik (1994), namely that relatively inegalitarian societies will exhibit greater pressures for redistributive spending than relatively egalitarian ones (see Perotti 1996 for a review of the evidence). Among advanced countries, the relationship is actually the reverse (Bénabou 1996).

Model III. Disincentive effects, insurance effects: the insurance model. Moene and Wallerstein (2001) offer one possible explanation for this puzzle by introducing insurance effects (see also Sinn 1995). For insurance effects to matter, we need at least two states of the world. By contrast to the Moene-Wallerstein model (where there are two categories of employees, high and low wage, in addition to the unemployed), it is assumed that workers can either be employed at a gross wage equal to their "tax-incentivised" skill level $g/(1 + t)$ or be unemployed. There are no specific skills ($s = 1$), so Equation (3.6) becomes

$$V = \beta \cdot u(\overline{g}) + \gamma \cdot u(R) \tag{3.11}$$

In this model, if relative risk aversion is constant and greater than unity, workers will choose a higher tax rate as they become wealthier; in other words, their aversion to risk outweighs the increased cost to them of insurance as their income increases. Thus, the relationship between income and preferred level of spending is positive (see Figure 3.2c).[3]

To get this result, it is assumed that $\overline{g} = g \cdot (1 - 2R/w)$ so that R is only paid to those who are unemployed. It can then be shown (as is done in Appendix 3.A) that

$$dR/dg < 0 \quad \text{iff} \quad RRA < 1 \tag{3.12}$$

and

$$dR/dg > 0 \quad \text{iff} \quad RRA > 1 \tag{3.13}$$

---

[3] This differs from the Moene-Wallerstein model because workers with high incomes in that model are assumed not to be exposed to labor market risks and, hence, prefer zero spending and taxation. Because no distinctions are made in the risk exposure of different income groups, model III is referred to as the insurance model rather than as the Moene-Wallerstein model. In the empirical section the insurance model, not the Moene-Wallerstein model, is tested.

A key implication of the result for RRA > 1 is that, contrary to the Meltzer-Richard model, a means-preserving increase in inequality will *reduce* the median voter's preferred level of social protection (provided that the income distribution is skewed to the right). The reason is that such a rise in inequality lowers the income of the median voter, and because the insurance motive dominates the redistribution motive (RRA > 1), demand for social protection will decline. In the Meltzer-Richard model, there is no insurance motive, so a fall in the income of the median voter always leads to a rise in the demand for social protection. Risk aversion, thus, poses one potential solution to the empirical puzzle of why income equality is linked to redistributive spending.

Yet, despite the neatness of this result, the econometric estimations clearly reject its implication that people prefer less redistribution at lower levels of income. This leaves the negative relationship between redistribution and inequality as an important unsolved puzzle for comparative political economy. In the conclusion to this chapter, how the distinction between specific and general skills permits an alternative and more plausible interpretation is discussed.

Model IV. Disincentive effects, insurance effects, specific and general skills: the asset model. This is the most general model and requires us to consider all three states in Figure 3.1. We therefore return to the present value of utility given by Equation (3.6):

$$V = \alpha \cdot u(\bar{s}\,\bar{g}) + \beta \cdot u(\bar{g}) + \gamma \cdot u(R) \tag{3.6}$$

where

$$\bar{s}\,\bar{g} = s \cdot g \cdot (1 - 2R/w) + R$$
$$\bar{g} = g \cdot (1 - 2R/w) + R$$

In addition, an important new variable is introduced, expected hourly income before taxes and transfers, y. It is simply defined as

$$y \equiv \alpha \cdot sg + \beta \cdot g$$

Now we can ask, first, up to what value of y is the chosen R maximal (i.e., $t = 1$); second, under what RRA conditions does R fall or rise as y rises above this value; and, third, what happens to the choice of R as the balance of general and specific skills changes, holding y constant?

In the first result, a worker will only choose the maximum tax rate if $y \leq w/2$. It is stated formally (the proof is in Appendix 3.A) in Result I.

Result I. *Given the assumptions of Model IV,* $t = 1$ *iff* $y \leq w/2$.

With this property established, we now consider what happens to R when y increases. As shown in Appendix 3.A, this yields Result II.

Result II. *Given the assumptions of Model IV, holding s constant and with* $y > w/2$,

$$\text{sgn} \frac{\partial R}{\partial y} = \text{sgn} \left[\text{RRA}(\bar{s}\,\bar{g}) - \frac{\bar{s}\,\bar{g}}{\bar{s}\,\bar{g} - \bar{w}/2} \right]$$

What this equality says is that the direction of the relationship between R and income (the sign, sgn, of $\partial R/\partial y$) depends on the level of risk aversion, just as in the simple insurance model. However, for income to be positively related to support for spending, the RRA requirement is more stringent ($\text{RRA} > \bar{s}\,\bar{g}/(\bar{s}\,\bar{g} - \bar{w}/2)$) than before ($\text{RRA} > 1$). The reason is that R now goes to the employed as well as to the unemployed, and because employed workers in the insurance model only have an insurance incentive in relationship to unemployment, RRA must be higher for the insurance motive to dominate the redistribution motive. This implication is also demonstrated by Moene and Wallerstein.

Now we come to the critical result, which differentiates the proposed approach from previous ones. Central to the argument in this chapter is the proposition that an increase in specific skills relative to general skills, holding constant the level of expected income, implies an increase in preferred R; put broadly, workers with specific skills will prefer higher taxes and social protection than workers with general skills. The following result is also proved in Appendix 3.A.

Result III. *Assuming a constant relative risk aversion utility function and* $RRA > 0$, $\partial R/\partial s > 0$ *holding y constant.* In other words, as s rises, the preferred level of R also rises. The intuition behind this key result is that workers with specific skills have more to fear if they lose their job than workers with general skills. This is because specific skill workers who are laid off face the risk of being reemployed in a sector where their skills are not needed. If this happens, they will lose some of their previous income, including employer-provided insurance against illness and old age. General skill workers do not face this problem because they are always compensated at the value of their general skills. Hence, the more income derived from specific as opposed to general skills (i.e., the higher the ratio s/g), the greater the demand for income protection, R. The logic is illustrated in

Figure 3.2d and implies that the median voter's support for social protection depends on the composition of his or her skills.

The results in this section can be summarized as follows: With the simplest set of assumptions – only one state of the world (employment), only general skills, and no tax disincentives – the politics of social spending is all about redistribution (class politics if you will); those with a wage below the mean will want a maximum rate of taxation ($t = 1$) whereas those above the mean will want zero taxation. If we add tax disincentives, however, the cost of redistribution may deter those low-income workers closest to the mean from demanding confiscatory taxation, and the median voter is likely to be among those workers. This is the Meltzer-Richard model.

When an unemployment state is added to the model, an entirely new motive enters into workers' calculations of their interests: insurance against loss of income. If workers are sufficiently risk-averse and if all transfers go to the unemployed, rising income may in fact be associated with *higher* demand for protection because high-income workers have more to lose than low-income workers. This is the simple insurance model. If some transfers go to the employed, however, the threshold of risk-aversion for which this relationship holds goes up because transfers to the employed only serve redistributive purposes.

Finally, when differences in the specificity of skills, which require at least two employment states (States I and II in the model), are introduced, the insurance motive plays a crucial role *even* when workers are only moderately risk-averse ($0 < \text{RRA} < 1$) and *even* when transfers are distributed to both employed and unemployed workers. The reason is that employed workers risk losing the income from their specific skills, regardless of their exposure to unemployment. This coupling between skills and demand for insurance thus transforms the relationship between income and social policy preferences.

3.1.3. The Role of Gender

The asset model has implications for understanding gender differences in social policy preferences. The possibility of a gender gap emerges when marriage contracting is incomplete and termination of the contract is an ever-present possibility. In this case, spouses will have conflicting preferences over who receives family benefits, and they will differ over any policies that affect their outside options should the marriage break up. This is not simply because spouses could one day be forced to take the outside option but also because outside options affect the current bargaining power inside the family (Iversen and Rosenbluth 2003).

As soon as outside options matter for family bargaining power, men and women will differ over the policies that affect these options. The most obvious matter of disagreement between husbands and wives is over publicly subsidized daycare. Because women are much more likely to end up as the primary care givers, their welfare is disproportionately affected by the availability of high-quality, low-cost daycare. Men may prefer to spare the public purse, and hence their tax bill, if their wives are default child-care givers. This logic also applies to public care for the elderly and the sick because it helps women escape some of their traditional duties and thereby permits more time to be spent in paid employment. In addition, as has been stressed throughout, the welfare state is an important source of employment for women precisely because so many of the jobs replace caring functions that are otherwise provided "for free" in the family.

Men and women are also likely to disagree about a range of social transfer programs. First, as pointed out in Chapter 1, research based on the Luxembourg Income Study has shown that transfers always result in a reduction of inequality (Bradley et al. 2003), and because women are on average paid less than men, they tend to have a stronger interest in redistributive spending (assuming again that they care about their outside options).[4] Social transfers are also important insofar as they allow women temporary career interruptions without significant loss of income. As argued by Estevez-Abe (1999), social protection for women involves two factors that are not equally relevant for men: (i) protection against dismissal during and after pregnancy, such as maternity, parental, and family leave policies; and (ii) income maintenance during leaves and guarantees of reinstatement to the same job at the same wage level upon return to work.

The asset argument enters into the story because women will find it harder to get jobs in occupations that require extensive specific skills. For a woman to invest in specific skills, she needs to be assured that potential career interruptions, if temporary, will not lead to dismissal or reduce her

---

[4] The gap in income between men and women may be the result of "statistical discrimination" where employers pay women less than men because women are on average more likely than men to leave the labor market for purposes of child birth and rearing, and because women are more likely than men to trade off working time for time on domestic duties, including care for sick family members (see Daly 1994; Rubery, Fagan, and Maier 1996). There is a vicious circle here because as women are paid less their bargaining position in the family becomes weaker and they will spend more time on household duties to the detriment of their attractiveness to employers.

wage level in the long run. A high probability of dismissal reduces the incentives to acquire firm-specific skills. Likewise, a high probability of reduction in wages after becoming a mother reduces the incentives to invest in either firm-specific or industry-specific skills (Estevez-Abe 2002).

One key implication of the asset model is that women, provided that outside options *do* matter, at any given level of income and skill specificity will prefer higher social protection than men. This gender gap is magnified by an indirect effect through income because women earn less than men. On the other hand, the effect is reduced to the extent that women invest more in general than in specific skills. An interesting corollary of this argument is that women should be more supportive than men of public investment in general education. The reason is that inexpensive access to good formal education presumably benefits women disproportionately because they have a comparative advantage in general skills.

Using the logic developed in this section, we can revisit some broader claims that are sometimes made about the gender and political preferences. Orloff (1999) and O'Connor, Orloff, and Shaver (1999), for example, strongly suggest that women are most disadvantaged in countries such as those in southern Europe and eastern, Asia, where female labor force participation rates are low, stratification on the labor market is high, and the distribution of domestic work is very unequal. If access to paid work and the ability to form autonomous households are the fundamental interests of women, as Orloff and others argue, one would expect gender conflicts to be most intense in these countries. Yet, these are the countries in which the policy preferences of men and women appear the most *similar*, and where there does not appear to be a strong gender gap in electoral politics (Iversen and Rosenbluth 2003). One plausible explanation is that the family as an institution is heavily protected, legally and normatively, in these countries. The likelihood of a first marriage ending in divorce in Italy is less than one in ten – even lower than the rate of divorce in the United States in the 1950s. Following Becker, if divorce is a highly unlikely prospect, men and women are much less likely to adopt conflicting policy preferences.

Another recent controversy surrounds the role of the public-private sector division in Scandinavia. According to some, this division, which concerns issues of public sector size, relative pay, and public sector job protection, has emerged as a salient cleavage in electoral politics. The high gender segregation in the public sector also helps explain a widening gender gap. Paul Pierson points out (Pierson 2000) that because men in the private sector tend to be married to women in the public sector, there is no compelling reason that spouses should quibble over issues of relative pay. At the end of the day, the income of both spouses simply adds to family income. But this logic only applies when husband and wife have few reasons to concern themselves with outside options. Because pay in the public sector is financed by taxing the private sector, policies affecting relative pay are a perfect example of an area where gender conflict is likely to be intense.

3.2. Testing the Model

3.2.1. Statistical Model

In Section 3.1.3, it was demonstrated in Model IV that the relationship between the "preferred" level of R and the two exogenous variables y (expected income) and s (skill specificity) is given by the implicit equations:

$$V_R(R, s, g) = 0$$
$$y = \alpha \cdot s \cdot g + \beta \cdot g \tag{3.14}$$

And from (3.14) was derived Result II that

$$\frac{\partial R}{\partial y} < 0 \quad \text{if} \quad 0 < \text{RRA} < \frac{\bar{s}\,\bar{g}}{\bar{s}\,\bar{g} - \bar{w}/2}$$

and Result III

$$\frac{\partial R}{\partial s} > 0 \quad \text{if} \quad 0 < \text{RRA}$$

It is shown in Appendix 3.B that

$$R = K + \frac{\partial R}{\partial y} \cdot y + \frac{\partial R}{\partial s} \cdot s$$

is the first-order Taylor expansion of (3.14). Thus, the regressions take the form

$$R = k + b \cdot y + c \cdot s \tag{3.15}$$

By implication, if the estimate of b is significantly different from zero and negative, we can infer that $0 < \text{RRA} < \bar{s}\,\bar{g}/(\bar{s}\,\bar{g} - \bar{w}/2)$. If c is significantly different from zero and positive, $0 < \text{RRA}$, so that skill specificity increases the demand for social protection. This is the main argument and hypothesis.[5]

---

[5] The model also implies that the coefficients of y and s are independent of cyclical variations in the unemployment rate. This implication can be tested through multilevel modeling as discussed in the next section and Appendix 3E.

More generally, Model IV encompasses Models I, II, and III. Hence, we can test for these models as well. Model I (Meltzer-Richard without tax disincentives) implies that $b = c = 0$. Model II (Meltzer-Richard with tax disincentives) implies that $b < 0$ and $c = 0$. And Model III (the insurance model with RRA $> \bar{s}\,\bar{g}/(\bar{s}\,\bar{g} - \bar{w}/2)$) implies that $b > 0$ and $c = 0$.[6]

3.2.2. The Data

The empirical analysis is based on individual-level data from eleven advanced democracies obtained from two sets of national mass surveys conducted under the auspices of the International Social Survey Program, one in 1996 and the other in 1997 (ISSP 1999; 2000).[7] These surveys offer by far the best individual-level data on skills and preferences for social protection. These individual-level variables are supplemented with economy-wide unemployment data. The following two sections describe the operationalization of the dependent and independent variables.

Dependent Variables The 1996 survey contains four spending questions that are closely related to the three protection variables introduced in Chapter 1. Three of the four are used in a cluster of questions that asks whether the respondent would like to see more or less government spending on (a) unemployment benefits, (b) healthcare, and (c) pensions (see Appendix 3.C for details). Reflecting an assumption in the model, each respondent was warned that more spending may require higher taxes. The fourth variable is based on a question that asks whether the respondent favors government spending on declining industries for the purpose of protecting jobs (see Appendix 3.C for details). Although the respondent was not explicitly told about the potential costs of government subsidies, such subsidies are widely acknowledged to be problematic for economic efficiency.

The four variables are closely related to the conceptual framework presented in Chapter 1. The first item is obviously a measure of unemployment

---

[6] Any general insurance model is, of course, consistent with the present model. The hypothesis about the insurance model being tested is the particular version (Model III) together with the assumption of RRA $> \bar{s}\,\bar{g}/(\bar{s}\,\bar{g} - \bar{w}/2)$. This solves the inequality-spending puzzle by implying a positive relationship between income and support for redistributive spending.

[7] The eleven countries are Australia, Britain, Canada, France, Germany, Ireland, Italy, Netherlands, Norway, Sweden, and the United States. Japan, used in both ISSP surveys, could not be included because of missing data on a key occupational variable (explained later).

protection, while healthcare insurance and pensions are the two main sources of publicly provided wage protection. Together, healthcare and public pensions make up the bulk of total transfers, and from Chapter 1 we know that transfers reduce pretax and transfer income inequality. Hence, these types of spending smooth out income for workers moving between different employment states and, therefore, constitute a form of wage protection. Finally, the question about job protection is a reasonable proxy for the concept of employment protection, and we would expect specific skills workers to be more concerned than general skills workers with keeping their present jobs.

The survey also asked people whether they favored more or less spending on "culture and the arts" and "the environment." These policy areas are clearly unrelated to social protection, but they are nevertheless relevant to the argument because general education is often argued to *increase* support for spending on "postmaterialist" activities, whereas the theory says that it reduces support for spending in the social policy area (cf. Kitschelt 1994).[8] Because one might object that the findings for skills reflect general ideological opposition to government spending among those with long formal educations, it is useful to be able to show that the relationship between skills and support for spending varies by policy area.

For presentational purposes I used confirmatory factor analysis (CFA) to create two spending indexes: one for social spending and one for postmaterialist spending (both constructed to have a standard deviation of one). The adjusted goodness of fit index of the CFA model applied to all eleven countries is 0.94 and varies little by country (the range is 0.90–0.98).[9] The social spending index is closely related to the concept of income protection (R) in the theoretical model, and it makes for a parsimonious presentation of results. I subsequently show the findings for each of the four component

---

[8] Duch and Taylor (1993) make a similar argument concerning postmaterialist attitudes (though they do not directly discuss spending).

[9] LISREL Version 8.5 was used to conduct the confirmative factor analysis, using the resulting factor loadings to construct the two indexes from the individual spending variables. The model was estimated from the covariance matrix for the six spending variables, assuming that the variables are indicators of two latent spending variables: social and postmaterialist spending. The factor loadings for each latent variable are as follows: (i) *social spending*: .52 (subsidies to protect jobs), .48 (health insurance), .58 (pensions), and .55 (unemployment insurance); (ii) *postmaterialist spending*: .58 (environment) and .51 (culture and the arts). Alternatively the indexes can be constructed from the results of fitting confirmatory factor models to the covariance matrixes for individual countries, but the regression results are only marginally affected.

items in the overall protection index, which allows for a discussion of each of the three protection areas discussed in Chapter 1.

Independent Variables Two different approaches to the measurement of skill specificity are employed, each reflecting different aspects of the theoretical model. The first is to classify workers' skills, or the skills required to perform certain jobs, according to their degree of specialization or specificity. This approach is an attempt to gauge s directly. The second starts from the model assumption that the difficulty of finding a job where one's skills are needed is proportional to their specificity. This approach is an attempt to gauge s indirectly through rq: the probability of reemployment into State I.

The first approach is based on the ILO's detailed classification of people's occupations: the International Standard Classification of Occupations (ISCO-88). ISCO-88 classifies workers in "occupations" based on two criteria: the *level* of skills required for an occupation and the *degree of specialization* of those skills. ISCO-88 distinguishes between four broad skill levels, which are a function of "the range and complexity of the tasks involved" and are explicitly dependent on informal as well as formal training (ILO 1999, p. 6). Skill level, thus, corresponds to $(s + g)$ in the model. All other distinctions between occupations are based on the specialization of skills required to carry out particular jobs, reflecting "the type of knowledge applied, tools and equipment used, materials worked on, or with, and the nature of the goods and services produced" (ILO 1999, p. 6). Guided by this logic, the subdivision of skills proceeds through four levels of aggregation until a high degree of skill homogeneity is reached within each group.[10] At the most disaggregated level, called the unit level, there are 390 occupational categories with highly specific job descriptions.[11]

Because the occupation of every respondent in the ISSP surveys was classified according to ISCO-88 at either the most detailed or second most detailed level (for exceptions, see Appendix 3.C), one can exploit the skill-based hierarchical structure of ISCO-88 to capture the specialization of

[10] There is no claim that homogeneity is equivalent in every unit group. Yet, skills that are clearly distinct from one another are unlikely to be in the same group at the most disaggregated level, and major groups with a highly diverse skill structure therefore will tend to have more minor and unit groups.

[11] Unit group 3144, for example, represents "air traffic controllers," a member of the minor group "ship and aircraft controllers and technicians," which is itself one of five categories in the major group called "technicians and associate professionals."

workers' skills. This is accomplished by comparing the share of unit groups in any higher-level class to the share of the workforce in that class. The logic is that the number of unit groups in any higher-level class will be a function of the size of the labor market segment captured by that class *and* of the degree of skill specialization of occupations found in that particular labor market segment. For example, 8 percent of the workforce across all countries are classified as "plant and machine operators and assemblers" (major group 8), whereas this group accounts for 70 out of the 390 unit groups, or 18 percent of all unit groups. If occupations at the unit group level are, on average, equally homogeneous in terms of skills, the dispropor-tionate share of unit groups in major group 8 will reflect a greater degree of specialization of skills found within that major group. By dividing the share of unit groups (.18) by the share of the labor force (.8), one can, therefore, generate a measure of the average skill specialization within that particular major group (3.1). This calculation can also be done at the lower submajor level, and the mean of these calculations has been used to get proxy for s.[12] The resulting variable has 27 values ranging from 0.4 to 4.7.

Because the theoretical concept of skill specificity is a *relative* variable, the final step is to divide the absolute skill specialization measure, s, by the ISCO measure of the *level* of skills.[13] This gives us a proxy for $s/(s + g)$ that we will refer to as s_1. Alternatively, we can divide s by a proxy for peoples' general skills, g, which gives us a measure for s/g. This alternative mea-sure is called s_2. The proxy used for g is the respondent's highest academic degree as recorded by the respondent (see Appendix 3.C for details).

The second approach to measuring skill specificity is based on the obser-vation that the probability of moving from any particular job into one that makes use of a worker's skills (State I) is rq for specific skills workers and q for general skills workers, where $r < 1$. If we conceive of rq as an element in the continuum $[0, q]$, r would then be a measure of the asset specificity of a worker's skills. At the heart of the concept of job specificity is the idea

---

[12] The sensitivity of s to small differences in the number of unit groups assigned to each higher-level group is greater at lower levels of aggregation, and these differences may not accurately reflect differences in skill specificity. This source of error is minimized at the highest level of aggregation. However, the greater variance of the measure at lower levels of aggregation helps reduce the standard error on the estimated parameter for the skill variable.

[13] Using an absolute measure of s generates results that are downward biased. At the limit, if the (unknown) correlation between s and g is 1, s will have no effect on preferences. It is, therefore, important to develop relative measures.

that outside options are more limited for workers with specific skills than for workers with general skills.

The 1997 ISSP survey contains a question that precisely taps workers' assessments of their outside options (ISSP 2000). The question reads as follows:

If you were looking actively, how easy or difficult do you think it would be for you to find an acceptable job?

The respondent could answer "very easy," "fairly easy," "neither easy nor difficult," "fairly difficult," and "very difficult." The key here is that the difficulty of finding an acceptable job is likely to be related to how portable a person's skills are. High skill specificity means that there are fewer jobs where these skills are used, and the number of job openings is also likely to be smaller because asset-specific investments by employers and employees tend to lengthen tenure and limit turnover. In addition, the probability of finding an appropriate job close to a person's current residence, which is also a likely component of what an individual considers "acceptable," falls with the number of job openings in a given geographical area.[14] Asking people about the probability of finding an acceptable job is, therefore, likely to generate answers that are systematically related to a person's skills. In the absence of extensive information about individual work histories, and employment conditions in particular labor market niches, the question is, therefore, about as good a measure of rq as one could hope for. It is referred to as s_3.

There is, however, an ambiguity in the relationship of s_3 to the theoretical concept of s. The reason is that we cannot know for sure if peoples' responses reflect their *absolute* level of specific skills or the *relative* share of their skills that is specific. To make sure that the skill measure is a relative measure, as required by the theoretical model, we can divide s_3 by g. This alternative measure is called s_4. If s_3 is already a relative measure, we simply get another relative measure that should also be positively related to preferences for social spending.

The different skill measures, and their intercorrelations, are listed in Table 3.1. Not surprisingly, the correlations are higher between measures

[14] In a path-breaking analysis, Scheve and Slaughter (2001) argue and show empirically that home ownership can be treated as a relatively immovable asset that affects people's preferences for trade protection. It would be interesting to include an interaction term for home ownership and the question about the difficulty of finding an acceptable job. But residential status is unfortunately not recorded by ISSP.

Table 3.1. *Summary of Independent Skill Variables*

Variable Name	Definition	Intercorrelations				Comment
		s_1	s_2	s_3	s_4	
s_1	(Share of ISCO-88 level 4 groups)/(Share of labor force) ÷ ISCO level of skills[a]	1				
s_2	(Share of ISCO-88 level 4 groups)/(Share of labor force) ÷ (Level of general education)[a]	0.8	1			
s_3[b]	Response to question about difficulty of finding an acceptable job	0.4	0.5	1		Not clear whether this is a measure of absolute or relative skills
s_4[b]	s_3 ÷ (Level of general education)	0.7	0.6	0.6	1	Assumes that s_3 measures absolute skills (though s_4 will always be a relative measure)

[a] Shares are calculated at both the first and second ISCO-88 level and then averaged.
[b] The number of categories on s_3 and s_4 have been reduced to the same number as on s_1 and s_2 before calculating the intercorrelations.

using either the survey question *or* the ISCO classification. The lowest correlations are between s_3 and s_1 or s_2. To some extent, this may reflect that s_3 is an absolute rather than a relative measure, but the main reason is simply that s_3 is influenced by a number of factors (such as how much people like their current co-workers) that are unrelated to either skills or social policy preferences. These factors will wash out in the regression, but they reduce the correlation with the other measures. To facilitate comparison of the effects of the different variables in the subsequent regression analysis, all proxies for s have been divided by their standard deviations.

One final methodological issue needs to be addressed. Because the question used as the basis for s_3 and s_4 was asked only in the 1997 survey, whereas all the questions about spending were asked only in the 1996 survey, it was necessary to "translate" the 1997 information on s_3 so it could be used in the 1996 survey (s_4 can be always be calculated from s_3). For this purpose, averages for s_3 were calculated at the three-digit ISCO-88 level in the 1997 survey and then assigned to individuals in the 1996 survey based on their three-digit ISCO classification in that survey.[15] Because the classification of occupations is motivated by the skills required in these occupations, it is reasonable to expect that original information about s is preserved to a considerable extent in this translation. Moreover, because the 1996 and 1997 samples are drawn from the same populations,[16] it is shown in Appendix 3.D that s_3, averaged by ISCO level 3 groups, is an unbiased estimator for the original variable.

In addition to the skill variables (s_1-s_4), self-reported pretax and transfer income was used as a proxy for y (converted into dollars at 1996 exchange rates). Gender also enters as a key variable in the regression for the reasons outlined previously. In addition, the regression includes the following set of controls:

Age. Older workers are likely to be more concerned with job security and income than younger workers because their time to retirement is shorter and their ability to find new employment is likely to be more limited.

Union membership. Because one of the main functions of unions is to insure their members against labor market risks, it is reasonable to expect that union members are particularly concerned with social protection (see, for example, Korpi 1989).

Part-time employment. Part-time employees are often in vulnerable labor market positions, which may cause particular concern for job security and income protection. On the other hand, part-time employees depend more on flexible labor markets to generate nonstandard jobs, which suggests a countervailing effect.

Nonemployed. Esping-Andersen (1999) has argued that some outsider groups may share an interest in social and economic policies that maximize their ability to enter employment. But this is an extremely heterogeneous group that may not have common policy preferences. We need to include the variable to control for the possibility that the nonemployed have very different attitudes than the employed.

Unemployed. The expectation is obviously that the unemployed, relying as they do on transfers, will support high levels of income protection.

---

[15] There are 116 unique groups at the three-digit level. The more fine-grained four-digit level is not available for some countries and contains a large number of empty categories where it is.

[16] With the minor qualification that those who turned 18 between the 1996 and 1997 surveys were not part of the population in the former survey.

Self-employment. The self-employed are expected to favor free markets and low levels of social protection because they depend on flexible labor markets and often on relatively low-paid workers.

Information. It is conceivable that better information about the economy yields particular views on the desirability of social spending. There was an intense public debate about the proper role of the state in the 1990s, and it could be argued that better informed people may reflect the predominant view in this debate, which tended to see cut-backs as necessary on efficiency grounds (corresponding to a higher cost of distortionary taxation in the model). Information is measured by respondents' subjective understanding of politics (see Appendix 3.C for details).

Left–right position. Attitudes to social protection may in part be a reflection of people's ideological predispositions, or perhaps the socializing effects of political parties.[17] This possibility is controlled for by including positions on a left–right scale based on the respondent's declared support for parties that are ranked from far left to far right (see Appendix 3.C for details).

National unemployment. Although the theory implies that individuals discount cyclical unemployment, it has been suggested that such unemployment could have an impact on individual-level social preferences. Testing this assumption requires a multilevel modeling procedure, with countries as level 1 and individuals as level 2. Collapsing both levels into a single equation (as shown in Appendix 3.E) implies the inclusion of the product variables $U_j \cdot y_{ij}$ and $U_j \cdot s_{ij}$ in the regression model, where U_j is the rate of unemployment in country j (see Appendix 3.C for details on measurement).

3.2.3. Findings

The regression model in Equation (3.15) was estimated on all countries simultaneously (technically speaking as a single-stage multilevel procedure to incorporate the possible impact of national macroeconomic conditions).[18] To cope with problems of missing observations, a multiple imputation technique developed by Gary King and his associates was used (see Honaker

---

[17] Note that party support may in part be endogenous to skills. If so, the effect of skills will be underestimated by the parameter for s.

[18] All data analysis was done using Stata 6.0 for Windows.

et al. 1999). This strategy is superior to the traditional approach of "list-wise deletion," which is both inefficient and potentially biased (King et al. 2001).[19] The following presentation is divided into a section with the key results and a section that tests the robustness of these results and discusses potential objections to the way the results are being interpreted.

The Basic Results To give a sense of the central tendency of the estimates, Table 3.2 shows the results from a pooled analysis, including a full set of country dummies. Because the Italian survey was conducted in 1990 and lacks information on several of the control variables, it was not included in the calculation of these pooled results. In the next section, the results for Italy are shown to be consistent with those presented in Table 3.2.

The model in column (1) uses the average of the four measures of skills, called $s_{composite}$, as a summary variable for skill composition. The next four columns show the results for each of the component measures (s_1-s_4). Model (6) is identical to (1) except that the regression now includes union membership as an independent variable. Because union membership was not recorded in Australia, the estimation of model (6) excludes this country.

In interpreting the results, first note that the parameters for income, y, and the four measures of skill, s_1-s_4, are in the predicted direction and highly statistically significant. The negative effect of income implies that people's risk-aversion is not sufficiently high to make their demand for transfers rise with income. Technically speaking, $RRA < \overline{s}\,\overline{g}/(\overline{s}\,\overline{g} - \overline{w}/2)$, which means that the Meltzer-Richard redistribution logic dominates the insurance logic. As expected, the relationship is little affected by differences in national unemployment rates, despite considerable variation in unemployment in the survey year. Thus, a one standard deviation increase in unemployment would only change the parameter on y from .0033 to .0038.

Yet, for my purposes, the key finding is the positive effect of specific skills on preferences for spending (which implies that $RRA > 0$). Each of the four (standardized) skill variables is associated with significantly higher support for spending, and three of the four measures exhibit similar magnitudes of effects. Again, these relationships hold for all levels of unemployment as can be seen from the negligible parameters for $U_j \cdot s_{ij}$.[20] The parameter for s_3 is

---

[19] In practice, however, the results are very similar to those obtained by using listwise deletion. The effects of the theoretical variables tend to be slightly stronger when listwise deletion is used, but the standard errors are also larger.

[20] For example, a one standard deviation increase in U_j only reduces the effect of $s_{composite}$ from .23 to .22.

Table 3.2. *Support for Social Spending among the Publics of Ten OECD Countries, 1996 (standard errors in parentheses)*

	Dependent Variable: Support for Social Spending[a]					
	(1)	(2)	(3)	(4)[b]	(5)[b]	(6)[c]
Income	−0.0033**	−0.0036**	−0.0038**	−0.0044**	−0.0035**	−0.0036**
	(0.0002)	(0.0002)	(0.0002)	(0.0002)	(0.0002)	(0.0002)
$s_{composite}$	0.233**	−	−	−	−	0.219**
	(0.014)					(0.013)
s_1	−	0.148**	−	−	−	−
		(0.010)				
s_2	−	−	0.150**	−	−	−
			(0.010)			
s_3	−	−	−	0.105**	−	−
				(0.013)		
s_4	−	−	−	−	0.218**	−
					(0.014)	
Age	0.0029**	0.0043**	0.0034**	0.0042**	0.0018**	0.0027**
	(0.0006)	(0.0006)	(0.0005)	(0.0006)	(0.0006)	(0.0006)
Gender (female)	0.215**	0.208**	0.205**	0.124**	0.148**	0.198**
	(0.018)	(0.018)	(0.018)	(0.019)	(0.019)	(0.019)
Union membership	−	−	−	−	−	0.185**
						(0.023)
Part-time employment	−0.029	−0.041	−0.033	−0.076*	−0.058	−0.031
	(0.028)	(0.028)	(0.028)	(0.031)	(0.031)	(0.029)
Unemployed	0.293**	0.313**	0.311**	0.320**	0.309**	0.325**
	(0.041)	(0.041)	(0.042)	(0.047)	(0.046)	(0.043)
Nonemployed	−0.079**	−0.081**	−0.086**	−0.080**	−0.074**	−0.038
	(0.025)	(0.025)	(0.025)	(0.026)	(0.026)	(0.026)
Self-employed	−0.232**	−0.235**	−0.250**	−0.222**	−0.221**	−0.184**
	(0.029)	(0.028)	(0.028)	(0.028)	(0.029)	(0.027)
Informed	−0.041**	−0.045**	−0.047**	−0.069**	−0.050**	−0.043**
	(0.008)	(0.008)	(0.008)	(0.010)	(0.010)	(0.009)
L–R party support	−0.050**	−0.051**	−0.050**	−0.047**	−0.047**	−0.041**
	(0.004)	(0.004)	(0.004)	(0.005)	(0.005)	(0.005)
$U_j \cdot y_{ij}$	−0.0002**	−0.0002**	−0.0002**	−0.0003**	−0.0004**	−0.0003**
	(0.0001)	(0.0001)	(0.0001)	(0.0001)	(0.0001)	(0.0001)
$U_j \cdot s_{ij}$	−0.008	−0.004	−0.002	−0.008	−0.012*	−0.012*
	(0.005)	(0.004)	(0.004)	(0.005)	(0.005)	(0.004)
Adjusted R-squared	0.21	0.20	0.20	0.18	0.20	0.22
N	14,101	14,101	14,101	10,956	10,956	11,950

* Significant at the .05 level; **significant at the .01 level.

[a] All regressions included a full set of country dummies (not shown).

[b] Excludes Australia, Ireland, and Italy for which data are not available.

[c] Excludes Australia for which union membership data are not available.

lower than for the other measures, but this is not entirely unexpected given that this variable may capture absolute rather than relative endowments of specific skills (or a combination of absolute and relative endowments). For all correlations between s and g that are greater than -1, absolute measures of s will yield lower parameter estimates than relative measures.[21]

Considering the very different approaches to measuring skills, it is reassuring that the results are consistent across definitions. Yet, statistically significant effects do not necessarily imply large substantive effects. Table 3.3, therefore, shows the estimated portion of the explained variance accounted for by each of the independent variables, as well as the impact on preferences of a one standard deviation change in each of the independent variables. The estimates are based on the results of model (6) in Table 3.2, which includes all the relevant variables.

Although it is not possible to attribute precisely the proportion of explained variance to each of the independent variables, it is possible to calculate likely ranges. The *upper* bounds of these ranges are found by recording the increase in explained variance (measured as a percentage of the total explained variance) when a variable is included as the *first* predictor (apart from the country dummies). This number encompasses every direct, indirect, and spurious effect of the variable. The *lower* bounds are calculated as the increase in explained variance (as a percent of the total explained variance) when a variable is entered as the *last* predictor. This procedure eliminates all hypothesized individual-level spurious effects of the variable but also discounts all possible indirect effects. The true explanatory power of any variable is likely to be somewhere between these bounds.

Using this method, Table 3.3 shows that income and skills are unambiguously the most important variables in explaining social policy preferences among the ones included in this analysis. Thus, income accounts for between 11 and 51 percent of the total explained variance, whereas skills account for between 26 and 38 percent. Jointly, income and skills capture between 38 and 73 percent of the explained variance, with the rest accounted for by the controls.

The key role of income and skills in explaining social policy preferences is confirmed when we consider the impact of a one-standard deviation change in these variables (column 3). A standard deviation change in either variable is associated with about 20 percent of a standard deviation change

---

[21] In fact, the correlation between s_3 and a measure of g based on general education is close to 0 in the data, which implies that an estimated effect of s_3 is half the "true" effect of skills.

Table 3.3. *Estimates of the Magnitude of the Effects of Independent Variables*

	Proportion of Explained Variance[a]		Impact of a 1 Standard Deviation Change[d]
	Lower Bound[b]	Upper Bound[c]	95% Confidence Interval
Income	11	51	−0.22 −0.19
$s_{composite}$	26	38	0.19 0.22
Age	1	2	0.03 0.05
Gender (female)	6	17	0.09 0.11
Union membership	1	4	0.07 0.09
Part-time employment	0	0	−0.02 −0.00
Unemployed	3	9	0.06 0.08
Nonemployed	0	8	−0.03 −0.01
Self-employed	2	8	−0.07 −0.05
Informed	1	8	−0.05 0.04
L–R party support	5	5	−0.09 −0.07
$U_j \cdot y_{ij}$	1	13	
$U_j \cdot s_{ij}$	0	8	
Income and $s_{composite}$	38	73	0.38 0.44
All controls combined	27	52	0.36 0.47

[a] Increase in explained variance by each variable as proportion of the total explained variance of all (nondummy) variables (based on model (6) in Table 3.2).

[b] Increase in explained variance (compared to model with only country dummies) when each variable is included as the last variable.

[c] Increase in explained variance when a variable is included as the first variable.

[d] The change in support for social spending (measured in standard deviations) as a result of a one standard deviation increase in each of the independent variables (in the cases of income and $s_{composite}$, unemployment is kept at its mean). The last two rows assume changes in the independent variables that raise support for spending (and take into account that some combinations of the employment variables are impossible).

in preferences (since the dependent variable is standardized, the recorded effects can be interpreted directly in terms of standard deviations). Together, the impact of income and skills is as great as the joint effect of a standard deviation change in all controls simultaneously. Note also that the effects of both variables are estimated very precisely, varying in a narrow range between (−)0.19 and (−)0.22 (95-percent confidence interval).

The results for the controls also generally confirm the expectations. Individuals who are particularly exposed to labor market risks – the unemployed, women, and older workers – are more favorably disposed to increasing social spending than others. The same is the case for union members, whereas the self-employed are more likely to oppose social spending. Those who consider themselves well informed about politics are also more likely to oppose spending, perhaps reflecting a political reality at the time that was hostile to the welfare state. Supporters of right parties, not surprisingly, also express less support for social spending than supporters of left parties. Finally, note that the attitudes of part-time employees and those outside the labor market are indistinct from the attitudes of others. These groups are evidently too heterogenerous to share any common interest in social policies.

Table 3.4 shows the results for each spending area separately.[22] They are quite similar across issue areas for the theoretical variables, although the effects are somewhat stronger for employment protection.[23] From the perspective of the insurance model, as defined previously, it is notable that the negative effect of income is just as strong for unemployment protection where transfers go only to those out of employment. This result holds even when we exclude high-income earners, casting some doubt on the Moene-Wallerstein argument that egalitarian societies, all else being equal, spend more on social insurance than inegalitarian ones because the median voter's income is higher (Moene and Wallerstein 2001). Higher income appears to be always linked to preferences for lower spending.

The most notable differences across spending areas are, for the most part, easy to explain. Thus, it is no surprise that unemployed are far more concerned with unemployment protection than any other policy area. Likewise, it is pretty obvious why older people are particularly keen to raise pensions (see the effect of age on the pension variable), and it is perhaps also understandable that nonemployed are less enthusiastic about doing this given that pensions are, for the most part, linked to employment. It is perhaps more puzzling that those who consider themselves well informed are particularly opposed to employment protection. However, recall that the survey question referred to protection of jobs *in declining industries*, which might be perceived by the well informed as particularly damaging to overall economic efficiency. A more intriguing result is that the effect of skills on support for employment protection is weaker in countries with high unemployment. Yet, this is the only policy area where the unemployment rate has this effect, and because there are so many potentially confounding variables at the national level, we should perhaps not attach too much weight to this

---

[22] Each variable ranges between 1 and 5, and all are defined so that higher values means greater support for protection.

[23] This is partly, though not fully, explained by more variation in the answers to the job protection question. The standard deviation for this item is 1.15, whereas for the others it is .94 (unemployment protection), .83 (health insurance), and .81 (pensions).

Table 3.4. *Support for Spending in Four Areas of Social Protection (standard errors in parentheses)*

	Dependent Variable[a]			
			Wage Protection	
	Employment Protection	Unemployment Protection	Health Insurance	Pensions
Income	−0.0033**	−0.0019**	−0.0017**	−0.0018**
	(0.0003)	(0.0002)	(0.0002)	(0.0002)
$S_{composite}$	0.248**	0.144**	0.079**	0.138**
	(0.015)	(0.016)	(0.012)	(0.012)
Age	−0.0013*	0.0027**	0.0011*	0.0051**
	(0.0007)	(0.0005)	(0.0005)	(0.0005)
Gender	0.269**	0.072**	0.134**	0.088**
(female)	(0.021)	(0.018)	(0.016)	(0.015)
Part-time	−0.028	0.027	−0.027	−0.047*
employed	(0.033)	(0.027)	(0.024)	(0.023)
Unemployed	0.120*	0.536**	0.043	0.066
	(0.048)	(0.040)	(0.037)	(0.036)
Nonemployed	−0.063*	−0.014	−0.070**	−0.061**
	(0.029)	(0.022)	(0.021)	(0.021)
Self-employed	−0.191**	−0.273**	−0.060*	−0.084**
	(0.029)	(0.024)	(0.027)	(0.025)
Informed	−0.068**	−0.004	−0.016**	−0.020**
	(0.010)	(0.008)	(0.007)	(0.007)
L–R party support	−0.043**	−0.040**	−0.029**	−0.019**
	(0.005)	(0.004)	(0.004)	(0.004)
$U_j \cdot y_{ij}$	−0.0003**	−0.0001	−0.0002**	−0.0001
	(0.0001)	(0.0001)	(0.0001)	(0.0001)
$U_j \cdot s_{ij}$	−0.016**	−0.005	0.004	−0.002
	(0.006)	(0.005)	(0.004)	(0.004)
Adjusted R-squared	.15	.16	.13	.14
N	14,101	14,101	14,101	14,101

* Significant at the .05 level; **significant at the .01 level.
[a] All regressions included a full set of country dummies (not shown).

result. Overall, the findings by area are intuitive and consistent with the overall argument.

Gender Differences Gender stands out among the control variables. It accounts for between 8 and 17 percent of the total explained variance, and it has the greatest impact after income and skills. As argued earlier, the likely reason is that women require more protection than men in comparable jobs because they need to be able to leave the labor market for the purpose of child rearing and then *return* to it. This suggests that the gap in gender preferences depends on the extent to which women participate in the labor market. Because the welfare of nonworking women relies more on the income of men than does the welfare of working women, nonworking women have a stronger incentive to support policies that raise the take-home pay of males. Nonworking women will still care about their outside options, but policies that reduce the relative wage of men also reduce the income of families where the woman does not work.

To explore this possibility, the first column in Table 3.5 adds labor force participation and a term for the interaction between gender and labor force participation. Labor force participation is coded 1 for those who are full-time employed, 0.5 for part-time employed, and 0 for those who are less than part-time employed or outside the labor market. As a consequence, two of the employment variables (part-time and nonemployment) from Table 3.4 had to be dropped.

Adding the interaction term creates some problems of collinearity, with 68 percent of the variance in this variable explained by its constituent terms. Still, the results are statistically significant and make sense in terms of the theoretical argument. Thus, when a woman is *not* working (the value on the labor force participation variable is zero), her predicted support for more social protection is .16 higher than men's, whereas it is .24 higher than men's when she is working full-time. In other words, women are more likely to share policy preferences with men when they are not working. This pattern is the same across categories of protection.

Columns 2 and 4 of Table 3.5 look at two predicted *indirect* effects of gender. Column 2 uses income as the dependent variable and shows that women, not surprisingly, earn less than men. On average, they make about $400 less than men (in 1996), and this figure roughly doubles if we also take into account that women participate less in the labor market. Because lower income translates into greater support for social spending, the effect of gender on preferences is obviously magnified by income.[24]

---

[24] The regression uses education, instead of skill specificity, to capture the effects of past skill investment on income. In principle, we should be using total skills, but the variable that can be derived from the ISCO classifications is very crude. At any rate, it does not matter much for the effect of gender.

Table 3.5. *Gender Effects on Preferences, Income, and Skills (standard errors in parentheses)*

	Dependent Variable[a]		
	Support for Social Protection	Income	Skill Specificity
Income	−0.003***	−	−
	(0.000)		
$S_{composite}$	0.243***	−	−
	(0.012)		
Gender (female)	0.179***	−20.00***	−0.266***
	(0.026)	(0.73)	(0.015)
Labor force participation	0.044	57.83***	−0.219***
	(0.028)	(0.96)	(0.017)
Gender × labor force participation	0.071**	−	−
	(0.034)		
Education	−	11.304***	−
		(0.301)	
Age	0.003***	0.764***	0.005***
	(0.001)	(0.025)	(0.000)
Unemployed	0.309***	−52.20***	0.410***
	(0.039)	(1.71)	(0.037)
Self-employed	−0.224***	−1.85	−0.059**
	(0.023)	(1.28)	(0.022)
Informed	0.039***	−	−
	(0.008)		
L–R party support	−0.050***	−	−
	(0.004)		
$U_j \cdot y_{ij}$	−0.0002***	−	−
	(0.0001)		
$U_j \cdot s_{ij}$	−0.009**	−	−
	(0.004)		
Adjusted R-squared	.15	.16	.13
N	14,101	14,101	14,101

***Significant at the .05 level; ** significant at the .01 level.
[a] All regressions included a full set of country dummies (not shown).

On the other hand, about half of this effect is canceled out by another indirect effect: the lower propensity of women to invest in specific skills (column 2). The skill specificity variable is 0.27 standard deviations lower for women than it is for men. Because women know that they are likely to leave their jobs before they can reap the full returns on specific skill investments, they are dissuaded from making such investments in the first place. Put differently, because women have a comparative advantage of investing in general skills, they will tend to specialize in these. This provides micro-level support to the interpretation of the macro-level data on occupational segregation presented in Chapter 1, and it explains why almost half the effect of gender on preferences disappears if the skill variable is removed from the regression.

Robustness Tests   In this section, the robustness of the results are tested and some potential objections to the interpretation of the results are addressed. It can first be noted that the findings for y and s stand up to any combination of the controls included previously, and they are robust to the inclusion of any other variable used in the survey, hereunder region, public sector employment, urbanization, and supervisory position – in any combination.[25] Even though income and skills are powerful explanatory variables in the pooled analysis, pooling can disguise considerable cross-national variation in the strength of the results, and sometimes estimated parameters can even reverse in particular cases. In addition, pooling usually yields exaggerated t-scores compared to those found for individual countries.[26] The regressions for each of the eleven countries were, therefore, run individually. The results for the theoretical variables are shown in Table 3.6.

Note that every regression yields results that are consistent with the pooled analysis, with each of the sixty parameters recording the correct sign and most being significant at the .01 level or better. The composite skill variable is always significant at a .01 level or better, and for nine of the eleven countries the parameter estimates for s vary in a fairly narrow range between 0.16 and 0.29 (the parameter in the pooled analysis is .23). Only Ireland and Italy fall slightly out of the pattern with parameters just below .12. Yet, the effects for these countries are still statistically highly significant, and it should be noted that $s_{composite}$ in both cases are based on only two proxies for s. In the case of Italy, these proxies also use a crude

---

[25] None of these variables were used in every survey, so instead of cluttering the presentation with several additional columns, these variables are out of the main analysis.

[26] The reason is that the standard error has the form (Standard error of equation error)/(Standard error of variable). Because the denominator is the square root of the sum of squares of the explanatory variable divided by N, this normally increases with N since a squared term is added on the top and 1 is added to the bottom (though it does not have to be so).

Table 3.6. *Income, Skills, and Support for Social Spending in Eleven OECD Countries (t-scores in parentheses)[a]*

	Income[b]	$s_{composite}$	s_1	s_2	s_3	s_4	N
Australia	−0.0030**	0.156**	0.129**	0.127**	n.a[c]	n.a	2151
	(−0.0004)	(0.027)	(0.023)	(0.026)			
Britain	−0.0029**	0.219**	0.105**	0.121**	0.135**	0.181**	989
	(−0.0006)	(0.042)	(0.026)	(0.027)	(0.039)	(0.046)	
Canada	−0.0054**	0.219**	0.102*	0.140**	0.087*	0.220**	1182
	(−0.0008)	(0.053)	(0.042)	(0.045)	(0.041)	(0.047)	
France	−0.0055**	0.235**	0.158**	0.147**	0.097**	0.111**	1312
	(−0.0007)	(0.038)	(0.035)	(0.028)	(0.037)	(0.026)	
Germany	−0.0027**	0.255**	0.182**	0.155**	0.115**	0.212**	2361
	(−0.0007)	(0.030)	(0.028)	(0.023)	(0.035)	(0.028)	
Ireland	−0.0030**	0.116**	0.092**	0.122**	n.a	n.a	994
	(−0.0008)	(0.028)	(0.029)	(0.027)			
Italy	−0.0021	0.105**	0.104*	0.095**	n.a	n.a	983
	(−0.0016)	(0.037)	(0.040)	(0.034)			
Norway	−0.0026**	0.257**	0.139**	0.165**	0.076**	0.250**	1344
	(−0.0006)	(0.033)	(0.024)	(0.027)	(0.027)	(0.030)	
New Zealand	−0.0049**	0.176**	0.125**	0.094**	0.134**	0.131**	1198
	(−0.0007)	(0.038)	(0.030)	(0.030)	(0.041)	(0.034)	
Sweden	−0.0055**	0.282**	0.130**	0.140**	0.156**	0.278**	1238
	(−0.0010)	(0.039)	(0.030)	(0.028)	(0.033)	(0.030)	
United States	−0.0024*	0.294**	0.192**	0.189**	0.042	0.272**	1332
	(−0.0010)	(0.052)	(0.030)	(0.037)	(0.036)	(0.058)	

* Significant at the .05 level; ** significant at the .01 level.
[a] All regressions included the same set of controls as in Table 3.2, column (1).
[b] The effect of income is only shown for $s_{composite}$ but varies little across the four measures of s.
[c] n.a.: Data not available to estimate this parameter.

occupational variable that maps rather poorly onto ISCO-88, potentially diluting the skill distinctions between categories.

As in the case of the pooled analysis, it should be noted that the results for s_3 are somewhat weaker across all cases than for the other skill measures, but only in one instance (the United States) is the result statistically insignificant. Given the variety of countries and the differences in measurements, the combination of results provides clear support for the theory.

Another objection that can be raised to the findings for skills is that they may in part be capturing an ideological aversion to government spending among those with higher education. Two of the measures of s have formal education in the denominator, and the other two implicitly assume that such skills are part of the denominator. In quantitative terms, general education accounts for roughly one third of the variance in $s_{composite}$. It is, therefore, conceivable that the proxies for skills may in part capture an ideological effect of higher education. For example, much of the economic theory taught to university students during the 1990s emphasized the efficiency of free markets over state intervention.[27]

To some extent, I have already controlled for this possibility by including variables for people's assessment of their own level of information, as well as their support for parties on the left–right scale. If the highly educated consider themselves better informed about the costs of generous social spending, this is likely to show up in the variable measuring information. Likewise, those ideologically committed to a small welfare state are presumably more likely to support right parties. The fact that a large effect of skills persists after control for these variables suggests that the conception of skills as assets is correct.

But there may still be unmeasured aspects of formal education that somehow confound the effects of the skill variable. One way to address this issue is simply to include general education as a separate variable. In that way, the effect of $s_{composite}$ will only pick up the effects of specific skills. In this setup, one should expect formal education to have the opposite effect of the specific skills variable, and the separating out of general skills will necessarily weaken the effect of the original variable if general education is indeed a measure of general skills. However, we can be certain that whatever effect remains of s, it cannot be attributed to general education.

The first column of Table 3.7 shows the results of reestimating model (1) in Table 3.2, using formal education as a separate independent variable. Formal education has a strong *negative* effect on support for social protection. This is consistent with the skill asset argument. But more importantly, the parameter on the specific skills variable remains positive and statistically significant. Not surprisingly, the effect of s falls from 0.23 to 0.14, but this is still a very considerable impact. Even if one were to discount the effect of general education as a measure of general skills completely, the results lend unambiguous support to the argument.

---

[27] In terms of the formal model this can be captured by different assessments of the distortionary effects of taxation.

Table 3.7. *Formal Education and Support for Two Types of Spending in Ten OECD Countries, 1996 (t-scores in parentheses)*

	Support for Social Spending	Support for Postmaterialist Spending	
Formal education	−0.105**	0.130**	−
	(0.008)	(0.007)	
$s_{composite}$	0.143**	−	−0.097**
	(0.015)		(0.014)
Income	−0.0027**	−0.0004	0.0004
	(0.0002)	(0.0002)	(0.0002)
Age	0.0015*	−0.0064**	−0.009**
	(0.0006)	(0.0006)	(0.001)
Gender (female)	0.203**	0.092**	0.087**
	(0.018)	(0.018)	(0.019)
Part-time employment	−0.025	0.104**	0.112**
	(0.028)	(0.029)	(0.030)
Unemployed	0.303**	0.085*	0.089*
	(0.040)	(0.043)	(0.044)
Nonemployed	−0.067**	0.077**	0.093**
	(0.025)	(0.024)	(0.025)
Self-employed	−0.243**	0.021	0.011
	(0.028)	(0.025)	(0.026)
Informed	−0.031**	0.069**	−0.083**
	(0.008)	(0.009)	(0.009)
L–R party support	−0.049**	−0.060**	−0.059**
	(0.004)	(0.005)	(0.005)
$U_j \cdot y_{ij}$	−0.0002	0.0000	0.0001
	(0.0001)	(0.0001)	(0.0001)
$U_j \cdot s_{ij}$	−0.006	0.008	0.007
	(0.005)	(0.005)	(0.006)
Adjusted R-squared	0.22	0.09	0.07
N	14,101	14,101	14,101

* Significant at the .05 level; ** significant at the .01 level.
Note: Regressions included a full set of country dummies.

Yet, results for the postmaterialist spending index explained earlier suggest that it would be a mistake to treat general education as a proxy for unmeasured ideological effects. Surely, if highly educated individuals believe in the efficiency of free markets and the waste of government spending, they should also oppose public spending on the environment, culture, and the arts.[28] But the exact opposite is true as shown in column (2) of Table 3.7. People with high general education are much *more* likely to support government spending on these areas than others. Conversely, if we use the composite measure of specific skills (column 3), the effect of skills is reversed: Specific skill workers want less postmaterialist spending, even though they support more social spending. Evidently people prefer government spending in areas that are particularly conducive to their personal welfare. General skills workers demand little social protection but are enthusiastic consumers of a clean environment and state-subsidized culture. Specific skill workers are deeply concerned with social protection but are not enthusiastic about state subsidization of environmental causes and the arts. There is no blanket support for, or opposition to, government spending among any particular group of workers.

3.3. Conclusions

Because a substantial portion of both national and personal income can be attributed to human capital, broadly conceived, it is not surprising that the asset specificity of this capital matters a great deal for the amount of social insurance demanded by individual workers. Like physical capital, human capital can be more or less mobile, and workers who have made heavy investments in asset-specific skills stand a greater risk of losing a substantial portion of their income than workers who have invested in portable skills. For this reason, specific skill workers have a greater incentive to support policies and institutions that protect their jobs and income.

Because social protection tends to benefit low-income people more than high-income people, position in the income distribution also divides public opinion. However, at any given level of income, workers with specific skills are more inclined to support high levels of protection than workers with general skills. This may help us understand cross-national variance in social protection because, as explained in Chapter 1, the profile of skills varies depending on the structure of the educational system. If these differences are

---

[28] It is true that "the environment" may be conceived as a collective good improving overall welfare (it is a little harder to argue this with respect to subsidies to the fine arts), but by the same token social protection may be conceived as welfare-improving insurance. The point is not that the highly educated are more informed about what is "good" and "bad" spending, that is already controlled for, but that they may have internalized a general aversion to government spending through their educational experience.

reflected in the political preferences of electorates, and if political parties adopt policies to attract the support of voters, it suggests a new explanation of the welfare state based on differences in national skill profiles. As explained in Chapter 4, however, the translation of policy preferences into policies is not direct. Even if the median voter is pivotal in electoral competition, the long-term social preferences of the median will not necessarily be reflected in policies. Nevertheless, having a theory of preferences, such as the one presented in this chapter, is the first step toward explaining cross-national variance in social policy.

The model also suggests a solution to the long-standing puzzle that income equality is linked to higher social spending when comparing across countries. As we know from Chapter 1, vocational training activity is strongly positively related to pretax income equality (the correlation coefficient is .73 using d9/d1 earnings ratios), and if a specific skill structure is simultaneously linked to more spending, as suggested by the model and evidence presented in this chapter, it follows that income equality and social spending will go hand in hand. In the pure Meltzer-Richard model, this is ruled out because the pressure for redistribution is always greatest in countries with the most skewed distribution of income.

Appendix 3.A. Mathematical Proofs

Derivation of Results (3.12) and (3.13) in Model III

The choice of the optimal R requires that

$$V_R \geq 0 \Leftrightarrow \beta \cdot u'(\bar{g}) \cdot 2g/w = \gamma \cdot u'(R)$$

Totally differentiating both sides we get

$$\frac{dR}{dg} = \frac{\dfrac{2\beta}{w} \cdot [\bar{g} \cdot u''(\bar{g}) + u'(\bar{g})]}{\beta \cdot \left(\dfrac{2g}{w}\right)^2 \cdot u''(\bar{g}) + \gamma \cdot u''(R)}$$

Because the denominator is negative,

$$\frac{dR}{dg} > 0 \qquad \text{iff} \qquad [\bar{g}u''(\bar{g}) + u'(\bar{g})] < 0$$

which implies

$$\mathrm{RRA}(\overline{g}) \equiv -\frac{\overline{g}u''(\overline{g})}{u'(\overline{g})} > 1$$

where $\mathrm{RRA}(x)$ is the Arrow-Pratt definition of relative risk aversion defined at $c = x$. The inequality conditions specified in (3.12) and (3.13) follow directly.

Proof for Result I in Model IV

1. Note first that $t = 1$ maximizes $t/(1 + t)$ when $0 \le t \le 1$. Also, if $t = 1$, $R = w/2$.
2. From (3.6) the necessary condition for optimal R is

$$\alpha \cdot u'(\overline{s}\overline{g}) \cdot \left(1 - \frac{2sg}{w}\right) + \beta \cdot u'(\overline{g}) \cdot \left(1 - \frac{2g}{w}\right) + \gamma \cdot u'(R) \ge 0$$

$$(A3.1)$$

If $R = w/2$, $\overline{s}\,\overline{g} = \overline{g} = R$; hence, the maximum combination of sg and g at which $R = w/2$, assuming it exists, requires that this condition holds with equality and that $u'(\overline{s}\,\overline{g}) = u'(\overline{g}) = u'(R)$. These conditions imply directly that

$$\alpha \cdot sg + \beta \cdot g = (\alpha + \beta + \gamma) \cdot \frac{w}{2} = y = \frac{w}{2}$$

Proof for Results II and III of Model IV

The necessary condition for optimal choice of R is $V_R(R, s, g) = 0$. This is given by (A3.1).

Totally differentiating V_R gives

$$\alpha \cdot \left[u''(\overline{s}\,\overline{g}) \cdot \left(\frac{2sg}{w} - 1\right) \cdot \left(1 - \frac{2R}{w}\right) \cdot g + u'(\overline{s}\,\overline{g}) \cdot g \cdot \frac{2}{w}\right] \cdot ds$$

$$+ \alpha \cdot \left[u''(\overline{s}\,\overline{g}) \cdot \left(\frac{2sg}{w} - 1\right) \cdot \left(1 - \frac{2R}{w}\right) \cdot s + u'(\overline{s}\,\overline{g}) \cdot s \cdot \frac{2}{w}\right] \cdot dg$$

$$+ \beta \cdot \left[u''(\overline{g}) \cdot \left(\frac{2g}{w} - 1\right) \cdot \left(1 - \frac{2R}{w}\right) + u'(\overline{g}) \cdot \frac{2}{w}\right] \cdot dg$$

$$= \left\{\alpha \cdot u''(\overline{s}\,\overline{g}) \cdot \left(\frac{2sg}{w} - 1\right)^2 + \beta \cdot u''(\overline{g}) \cdot \left(\frac{2g}{w} - 1\right)^2 + \gamma \cdot u''(R)\right\} \cdot dR$$

$$(A3.2)$$

Note: (1) The term in curly brackets on the right-hand side, which will be called B, is negative. (2) We can write $(\overline{s}\,\overline{g} - \overline{w}/2) \cdot (1 - 2R/w) = \overline{s}\,\overline{g} - \overline{w}/2$. And (3)

$$[u''(\overline{s}\,\overline{g}) \cdot (\overline{s}\,\overline{g} - \overline{w}/2) + u'(\overline{s}\,\overline{g})]$$

$$= u'(\overline{s}\,\overline{g}) \cdot \left[1 - \text{RRA} \cdot \frac{\overline{s}\,\overline{g} - \overline{w}/2}{\overline{s}\,\overline{g}}\right] \equiv u'(\overline{s}\,\overline{g}) \cdot L(\overline{s}\,\overline{g}) \qquad \text{(A3.3)}$$

So (A3.2) can be written as

$$u'(\overline{s}\,\overline{g}) \cdot L(\overline{s}\,\overline{g}) \cdot \alpha \cdot g \cdot ds + u'(\overline{s}\,\overline{g}) \cdot L(\overline{s}\,\overline{g}) \cdot \alpha \cdot s \cdot dg + u'(\overline{g}) \cdot L(\overline{g}) \cdot \beta dg$$
$$= (w/2) \cdot B \cdot dR \qquad \text{(A3.4)}$$

Since $dy = \alpha \cdot g \cdot ds + \alpha \cdot s \cdot dg + \beta \cdot dg$, we can further rewrite (A3.4) as

$$dR = \frac{2\alpha \cdot \beta \cdot g}{wB} \cdot \left[\frac{u'(\overline{s}\,\overline{g}) \cdot L(\overline{s}\,\overline{g}) - u'(\overline{g}) \cdot L(\overline{g})}{\alpha s + \beta}\right] \cdot ds$$

$$+ \frac{2}{wB} \cdot \left[\frac{u'(\overline{s}\,\overline{g}) \cdot L(\overline{s}\,\overline{g}) \cdot \alpha s + u'(\overline{g}) \cdot L(\overline{g}) \cdot \beta}{\alpha s + \beta}\right] \cdot dy \qquad \text{(A3.5)}$$

To prove Results III and IV, note that in terms of (A3.5) $\partial R/\partial y = dR/dy$ and $\partial R/\partial s = dR/ds$. First, it is shown that $L(\overline{s}\,\overline{g}) < L(\overline{g})$. From the definition in (A3.3), this follows if $s > 1$ – as is the case apart from purely general skills – and if RRA > 0. Result III is that sgn $\partial R/\partial y < 0$ *if* RRA $< \overline{s}\,\overline{g}/(\overline{s}\,\overline{g} - \overline{w}/2)$. Since $B < 0$, $L(\overline{s}\,\overline{g}) < L(\overline{g})$ and $u'(x) > 0$, this follows from (A3.5) if $L(\overline{s}\,\overline{g}) > 0$. This requires that RRA $< \overline{s}\,\overline{g}/(\overline{s}\,\overline{g} - \overline{w}/2)$. This is a sufficient condition: A necessary and sufficient condition is that the numerator of the second term in square brackets on the right-hand side of (A3.5) is positive.

Result IV is that sgn $\partial R/\partial s > 0$. Since $B < 0$, this requires that the numerator in the first square bracket on the right-hand side of (A3.5) is negative. Since $u'(\overline{s}\,\overline{g}) < u'(\overline{g})$ from diminishing marginal utility, a sufficient condition is that $L(\overline{s}\,\overline{g}) < L(\overline{g})$, which is true so long as RRA > 0 and $s > 1$. So Result IV follows from the existence of risk aversion and specific skills.

Appendix 3.B. Deriving the Estimating Equation

In this appendix, it is demonstrated that the estimating equation used in the analysis

$$R = k + b \cdot y + c \cdot s \tag{A3.6}$$

is equal to

$$R = k + \frac{\partial R}{\partial y} \cdot y + \frac{\partial R}{\partial s} \cdot s \tag{A3.7}$$

where (A3.7) is a first-order Taylor expansion of $V_R(R, s, g) = 0$ and $y = \alpha \cdot s \cdot g + \beta \cdot g$ evaluated around $(R, s, g) = (\widetilde{R}, \widetilde{s}, \widetilde{g}) \equiv \widetilde{x}$.

Proof. The first-order Taylor expansion of V_R is given by

$$R = K + \frac{V_{R,s}}{V_{R,R}} s + \frac{V_{R,g}}{V_{R,R}} g \tag{A3.8}$$

In terms of (3.5A),

$$\frac{V_{R,s}(\widetilde{x})}{V_{R,R}(\widetilde{x})} = \frac{u'(\widetilde{s}\,\widetilde{g}) \cdot L(\widetilde{s}\,\widetilde{g}) \cdot \alpha \cdot \widetilde{g}}{(w/2) \cdot B} \tag{A3.9.1}$$

and

$$\frac{V_{R,g}(\widetilde{x})}{V_{R,R}(\widetilde{x})} = \frac{u'(\widetilde{s}\,\widetilde{g}) \cdot L(\widetilde{s}\,\widetilde{g}) \cdot \alpha \cdot \widetilde{s} + u'(\widetilde{g}) \cdot L(\widetilde{g}) \cdot \beta}{\dfrac{w}{2} \cdot B} \tag{A3.9.2}$$

The first-order Taylor expansion of y is

$$y = k(\widetilde{x}) + [\alpha \cdot \widetilde{s} + \beta] \cdot g + [\alpha \cdot \widetilde{g}] \cdot s \tag{A3.10}$$

Rewrite (A3.10) as

$$g = \frac{y - k(\widetilde{x}) - \alpha\widetilde{g}}{\alpha\widetilde{s} + \beta}$$

and substitute into (A3.8), using (A3.9.1) and (A3.9.2). This yields (A3.7).

Appendix 3.C. Detailed Information about Variables

Dependent Variables

The spending variable, R, is based on four issue items in the ISSP surveys. The first three are based on the following question:

> Listed below are various areas of government spending. Please show whether you would like to see more or less government spending in each area. Remember that if you say 'much more', it might require a tax increase to pay for it. The respondent is then presented with the different spending areas (unemployment, health, retirement) and the following range of possible responses: 1. Spend much more; 2. Spend more; 3. Spend the same as now; 4. Spend less; 5. Spend much less; 8. Can't choose, don't know.

The fourth variable is based on the following question:

> Here are some things the government might do for the economy. Please show which actions you are in favor of and which you are against. Please tick one box in each line. One of the actions is: Support for declining industries to protect jobs: 1. Strongly in favor of; 2. In favor of; 3. Neither in favor of nor against; 4. Against; 5. Strongly against; 8. Can't choose, don't know; 9. NA, refused.

Independent Variables

s_1 **and** s_2 In some countries individuals were classified using an earlier version of ISCO (ISCO-68). However, these classifications can be translated into ISCO-88 with considerable consistency using a coding scheme developed by Harry Ganzeboom at Utrecht University (see Ganzeboom and Treiman 1996 and *www.fss.uu.nl/soc/hg/ismf* for details). The Swedish occupational classification is based on an amended version of an older edition of ISCO. *Statistiska Centralbyràn* (Statistics Sweden) provided us with a conversion table to translate these codes into ISCO-88 in a reasonably consistent manner. Britain uses its own national classification system, but it is closely related to ISCO-88 and likewise uses skills as the basis for the classification. The British translation codes were received from *U.K. National Statistics*. The only problematic case is Italy, where the few broad categories used in the 1996 ISSP survey are completely unrelated to the ISCO-88 categories. Instead, I went back to an earlier 1990 ISSP study (ISSP 1993), which contains a somewhat more detailed occupational variable for Italy. Using this variable in conjunction with information on educational levels enabled us to map the Italian codes to the one-digit ISCO-88 level in a fairly consistent manner. Yet, because of the lack of direct correspondence, the results for Italy must be viewed with caution.

General Skills (used in the denominator of s_2 and s_4)   The variable is used as a proxy for g and has five levels: 1, still at school; 2, incomplete primary; 3, completed primary degree or lower; 4, incomplete secondary; 5, completed secondary; 6, incomplete and completed semi-higher degree, or incomplete university degree; and 7, completed university degree. Alternatively, one could have used years of formal schooling as a measure of g, but the results are very similar.

Information   Gauged by a question that asked people to declare their degree of agreement with the following statement: "I feel that I have a pretty good understanding of the important political issues facing our country." Respondents could indicate five levels of agreement: 1, strongly agree; 2, agree; 3, neither agree nor disagree; 4, disagree; 5, strongly disagree. The variable was reversed so that higher values measure more information.

Left–Right Position   This variable is based on the classification of parties from left to right developed by the International Social Survey Program to facilitate comparison of party support across countries. Individual parties are classified as follows (data on party support are not available for Italy).

National unemployment   The standardized rate of unemployment at the time of the national surveys (1996 unless noted otherwise below) minus the OECD rate of unemployment at that time (the subtraction eliminates problems of multicollinearity while leaving the substantive results unaltered).

	Far left (1)	Left, Center Left (2)	Center, Liberal (3)	Right, Conservative (4)	Far Right (5)
Australia	Greens	Labour	Democrats	Liberal Party	
Britain		Labour	Liberal Democrats	Conservatives	
Canada	Communists	NDP, Bloc Quebecois, Greens	PC, Liberal Party	Reform Party	

	Far left (1)	Left, Center Left (2)	Center, Liberal (3)	Right, Conservative (4)	Far Right (5)
France	Communists, Far Left	Socialist Party	UDF	RPR	National Front
Germany	PDS	SPD, Greens	FDP	CDU/CSU	Republicans
Ireland		Worker's Party, Sinn Fein, Democratic Left	Fianna Fail, Fine Gael, Labour, Greens	Progressive Party	
Norway	Red Alliance	Labor, Socialist Left	Christian Democrats, Center Party, Liberal Party	Conservatives, Progress Party	
New Zealand	Alliance	Labour	New Zealand First	National Party	
Sweden		Labor, Socialists	Center Party, Liberals, Christians Democrats, Greens	Conservatives	
United States		Democrats	Independent	Republicans	

Source: OECD (2000). Unemployment rates were: Australia, 8.5; Britain, 8.2; Canada, 9.6; France (1997), 12.3; Germany, 8.9; Ireland, 11.6; Italy, 11.7; Norway, 4.9; New Zealand (1997), 6.7; Sweden, 9.6; United States, 5.4.

Appendix 3.D. Statistical Appendix

A problem arises in the use of s_3 and s_4 as explanatory variables. (Because it is the same in both cases, it will simply be referred to as s.) Because the question used as the basis for s was asked only in the 1997 survey, whereas all the questions about spending were asked only in the 1996 survey, it was necessary to "translate" the 1997 information on s so that it could be used in the 1996 survey. For this purpose, averages for s were calculated at the three-digit ISCO-88 level in the 1997, and then these values were assigned to individuals in the 1996 survey based on their three-digit ISCO classification in that survey. It is shown here that the estimated coefficient of b is consistent but has an approximate small sample bias that biases down the estimated coefficient toward zero if $b > 0$, and biases it upward toward zero if $b < 0$.

The structural model is

$$R_{i,j}^{96} = k + b \cdot y_{i,j}^{96} + c \cdot s_{i,j}^{96} + \varepsilon_{i,j}^{96} \tag{A3.11}$$

where each observation is drawn from the 1996 survey and where i indexes the ith individual in the jth ISCO three-digit level occupation group. There are no data on $s_{i,j}^{96}$. Assume $s_{i,j}^{96}$ is generated by the process

$$s_{i,j}^{96} = s_j + \eta_{i,j}^{96} \tag{A3.12}$$

where s_j is exogenous. s_j itself is unobservable, but data are available from the 1997 survey generated by the same process:

$$\begin{aligned} s_{i,j}^{97} &= s_j + \eta_{i,j}^{97} \\ E\eta_{i,j}^{9x} &= 0 \qquad \forall i, j, x \\ E\eta_{i,j}^{96} \cdot \eta_{r,j}^{97} &= 0 = E\eta\varepsilon \qquad \forall i, r, j \\ E\eta^2 &= \sigma_\eta^2; \qquad E\varepsilon^2 = \sigma_\varepsilon^2 \end{aligned} \tag{A3.13}$$

that is, η_{ij}^{96} and η_{ij}^{97} can be thought of as random drawings from the same distribution. We now run the regression

$$R_{i,j}^{96} = k + b y_{i,j}^{96} + c \bar{s}_j + \varepsilon_{i,j}^{96} + v_{i,j}^{96}$$

$$\text{where} \qquad \bar{s}_j \equiv \frac{\sum s_{i,j}^{97}}{N_j} \qquad \text{and} \qquad v_{i,j}^{96} \equiv c\left[s_{i,j}^{96} - \bar{s}_j\right] \tag{A3.14}$$

where N_j is the number of individuals in ISCO category j in the 1997 survey. From (A3.12) and (A3.13)

$$v_{i,j}^{96} = \eta_{i,j}^{96} - \frac{\sum \eta_{i,j}^{97}}{N_j} \tag{A3.15}$$

The exposition can be simplified considerably by assuming that there is no correlation between $\bar{s}$ and y. This implies

$$E\hat{b} = a$$

$$E\hat{c} = c \left(1 - E \frac{\sum_j \bar{s}_j \cdot \bar{\eta}_j}{\sum_j \bar{s}_j^2} \right) \tag{A3.16}$$

By making the appropriate probability limit assumptions, it is not difficult to show that $\hat{c}$ is a consistent estimator of c. We can get a better insight from the expectation of the exact first-order Taylor expansion of $\sum \bar{s} . \eta / \sum \bar{s}^2$ around the expected values of numerator and denominator:

$$
E \frac{\sum \bar{s}\eta}{\sum \bar{s}^2} \approx E \left[\frac{E \sum \bar{s}\eta}{E \sum \bar{s}^2} + \frac{1}{E \sum \bar{s}^2} \cdot \left(\sum \bar{s}\eta - E \sum \bar{s}\eta \right) \right.
$$
$$
\left. - \frac{E \sum \bar{s}\eta}{\left(E \sum \bar{s}^2 \right)^2} \cdot \left(\sum \bar{s}^2 - E \sum \bar{s}^2 \right) \right]
$$
$$
= \frac{E \sum \bar{s}\eta}{E \sum \bar{s}^2}
$$

Let there be $\mathcal{J}$ ISCO categories and assume for convenience that $N_j = N \forall j$. Then this approximation produces

$$
E\hat{c} = c \left(1 - \frac{\sigma_\eta^2}{\sigma_\eta^2 + N \cdot \dfrac{\sum s_j^2}{\mathcal{J}}} \right) \tag{A3.17}
$$

Since $\mathcal{J}$ is constant, (A3.17) tells us first that as N increases the approximate bias goes to zero. Second and more importantly, it implies that for a small sample

$$
c < E\hat{c} < 0 \; if \; c < 0
$$
$$
c > E\hat{c} > 0 \; if \; c > 0 \tag{A3.18}
$$

Finally, it implies that

$$
If \, c = 0 \; \Rightarrow \; E\hat{c} = 0 \tag{A3.19}
$$

and the standard significance tests hold.

Appendix 3.E. Multilevel Model

Write the level 2 observation on individual i in economy j as

$$R_{ij} = \gamma + \eta y_{ij} + \mu s_{ij} + \mathbf{X}'_{ij}\delta + \varepsilon_{ij}$$

where $\mathbf{X}_{ij}$ is the vector of controls, and define level 1 by the fixed effects model $\eta = \bar{\eta} + \eta_1 U_j$ and $\mu = \bar{\mu} + \mu_1 U_j$. The single-stage regression model is derived by substituting the level 1 model into level 2:

$$R_{ij} = \gamma + \bar{\eta} y_{ij} + \eta_1 y_{ij} U_j + \bar{\mu} s_{ij} + \mu_1 s_{ij} U_j + \mathbf{X}'_{ij}\delta + \varepsilon_{ij}$$

Making the assumption that U_j s are exogenous and that this is a nonrandom effects model implies that the single-stage multilevel equation conforms to the standard ordinary least squares conditions.

4

Credible Commitment, Political Institutions, and Social Protection*

In Chapter 3, peoples' preferences for social protection were explained as a function of the level and composition of human capital assets (i.e., as a function of income and skill specificity). Any theory that seeks to understand collective choice in democratic societies must begin with an account of individual preferences. But we know from the seminal works of Arrow, Olson, North, Shepsle, and Weingast that the aggregation of preferences into public policy is anything but straightforward. Indeed, preferences may never get translated into policies, even when a single (median) voter is decisive in electoral competition.

One fundamental problem in the provision of social protection arises because current pivotal voters choose policies that yield benefits to them only at some future point in time when these same voters are no longer pivotal. This poses a problem because current voters can only commit the government for one term at a time and because there is no way to bind future voters to the policy preferences of current voters (for a similar logic, see Franzese 2002, Ch. 2). This dilemma is referred to in this chapter as *the time-inconsistency problem in social policy provision*, and it is shown that it can lead to serious underprovision of social protection compared to the long-term preferences of voters. This is particularly true in specific skill systems because the underlying demand for protection is higher.

The time-inconsistency problem is closely related to another incomplete contracting problem in democratic politics. Political parties present policy platforms in order to win elections, but they are simultaneously representing party-internal constituents who may not share the policy preferences

* This chapter builds on two unpublished papers with David Soskice (Iversen and Soskice 2002, 2004).

of the voters who are being courted in the election. This *problem of representation* is particularly severe in majoritarian systems where the support of the median voter is critical to win the election, but it is also severe where parties' core constituents can be expected to have preferences that are clearly distinct from the median voter's. Because the electoral platform is not an enforceable contract, the median voter must worry about the actions that a party may take after it wins the election. As we will see later in this chapter, this affects the voting behavior of strategic voters and leads to outcomes that are systematically different from the preferences of the median voter.

Two arguments are advanced in this chapter to show how these contracting problems may be (partially) solved. The first is that political parties with detailed policy programs and highly developed party organizations, especially links to unions, limit the ability of leaders to give in to short-term electoral incentives and constrain the choice set of voters to alternatives that are optimal in the long run (see also Franzese 2002, Ch. 2). These mechanisms of commitments can work even when parties have the option of adopting flexible organizations and even when third parties are allowed to enter into the electoral competition with any platform or organization they desire. However, in majoritarian systems, this solution magnifies the problem of representation because parties will deviate from the policy preferences of the median voter. The result is that parties in majoritarian systems have a strong incentive to adopt parties with strong leaders at the expense of the ability to commit to long-term investment in social protection. This incentive is weaker under PR where it is not critical for parties to win the support of the median voter.

In addition to nurturing programmatic and responsible parties, PR electoral systems also give centrist parties an incentive to ally with left parties for purposes of redistribution. The reason is that the poor and the middle class have a common interest in taxing the rich and distributing the revenues among themselves. As I have argued already, such redistribution in turn serves insurance functions because those who are experiencing a complete or partial unemployment of their assets as a result of adverse labor market conditions will also benefit. Like wage protection through the collective wage bargaining system, redistributive social spending serves as a protection of income.

Majoritarian electoral systems are different because governments are not (typically) chosen through coalition bargaining but directly by the electorate. Whichever party gets a plurality wins, which, as we know well, places the median voter in a very strong position. This is where the incomplete contracting problem in representation matters. If parties have a nonzero probability of deviating from their electoral platforms after they are in power, the median voter has an incentive to vote for the center-right party because the median voter shares with the rich a common interest in limiting redistribution to the poor. Hence, although both parties have an incentive to cater to the median voter during elections, their incentive to deviate from the platform after the election will make the center-right party more attractive to the median voter. This undermines spending for both redistributive and insurance purposes.

This chapter is organized into three sections. The first section provides a precise definition of the time-inconsistency problem in the context of social policies. A model of parties and voters that is then presented, which shows the conditions under which the problem can be overcome. The next section develops the electoral system argument, while the third explores both arguments using micro-level electoral data as well as macro-level data on institutions, government partisanship, and redistribution. In equilibrium, electoral and party systems with high institutional capacity for commitment (PR with programmatic parties) are always found in political economies where specific skills are important, whereas the opposite (majoritarian systems with leadership-dominated parties) are always found in general skills systems.

The broader ambition of this chapter is to tie economic institutions and behavior to democratic institutions. Even though the varieties of capitalism literature have explored the complementarities that link economic institutions together, little theoretical or empirical energy has gone into exploring the linkages between economic and political institutions. Here I focus on the key institutions shaping democratic politics – political parties and electoral systems – and show how they are linked to the production system.

4.1. The Time-Inconsistency Problem

Assume that all individuals have identical preferences and face the same risk of a wide range of adverse events occurring, including ill health, unemployment, loss of employment that uses workers' specific skills, and so on. Against some of these events, individuals can insure privately; against others, market failure (such as moral hazard) rules private insurance out. Under what circumstances will a democratically elected government implement the will of the majority to provide appropriate public income protection?

Elections take place at regular intervals with government terms lasting T years. To simplify the argument, consider the following set of assumptions, which expose the bare bones of the problem. At the start of each term, individuals have a probability p of some adverse event happening to them during the T-year period. It is simple to think of this as a spell of unemployment, although it can refer to any event that adversely affects the earnings capacity of a worker, such as a skill becoming obsolete. In terms of the model in Chapter 3, it refers to unemployment of any asset that the individual possesses. After the election, it is revealed which individuals will be unemployed during the electoral term. Finally, voters vote in a first-past-the-post-election for one of two parties; each party's platform is a tax t on those who find themselves employed to finance an unemployment benefit $R = (1 - p) \cdot t/p$ (given to those who have found themselves unemployed). The goal of the parties is to win power, and the winning party is committed to carrying out its platform. There is complete information on the side of voters and parties. This sequence (revelation of employment or unemployment across individuals, followed by voting) is repeated at the start of each period.

Assume that $p < .5$, so that the median voter is employed. What level of t will the median voter choose? If the employed individual receives a pretax income of 1, then the expected utility of an individual at time $\tau = 0$ *before* the individual knows whether or not he is unemployed is

$$\overline{V}_0 \equiv \sum_{\tau=0}^{\infty} \delta^\tau \left[(1 - p) \cdot u(1 - t_\tau) + p \cdot u(t_\tau \cdot (1 - p)/p) \right] \tag{4.1}$$

where $\delta \in [0, 1]$ is the discount factor and $u(x)$ is the utility derived from net receipts (income or unemployment benefit). Define t^{**} as the value of t, which maximizes (4.1) under the assumption that t_τ has the same value for all $\tau = 0, \ldots, \infty$. Assume the conditions exist on $u(\cdot)$ to guarantee an interior maximum. The example used in this chapter is $u(x) = \log x$. In this case, $t^{**} = p$.[1] So the preferred level of taxation is directly proportional to the risk of being unemployed.

Now consider a median voter at $\tau = 0$ who knows that he or she is *employed*. His or her expected utility is given by

$$V_0 \equiv u(1 - t_0) + \sum_{\tau=1}^{\infty} \delta^\tau \left[(1 - p) \cdot u(1 - t_\tau) + p \cdot u(t_\tau \cdot (1 - p)/p) \right] \tag{4.2}$$

---

[1] If t is constant for all τ, $\overline{V}_0 = \delta^{-1}[(1 - p)\log(1 - t) + p \log((1 - p)t/p))]$, which implies

$$\frac{\partial \overline{V}_0}{\partial t} \Rightarrow \frac{1 - p}{1 - t} = \frac{p}{[(1 - p) \cdot t]/p} \cdot \frac{1 - p}{p} \quad \text{or} \quad t^{**} = p$$

Define t^* as the value of t that maximizes (4.2) under the same assumptions as before, and we find that $t^* = \delta p$. Note that $t^* < t^{**}$ because there is no possibility that the employed median voter requires an unemployment benefit in $\tau = 0$. For example, if the probability of unemployment is, say, 5 percent, and the length of office is 4 years, δ (the discount factor) would be around 0.8 and, hence, t^* would be 80% of t^{**}.

Yet, the real problem arises because *the median voter only chooses the unemployment benefit for the current electoral period*, $\tau = 0$, that is t_0. For the next period $\tau = 1$, there will be a new median voter choosing t_1. If the median voter in any one period is sincere, the vote in that period has no effect on the votes of median voters in subsequent periods; current voters cannot commit future voters. Hence, the median voter must take all future tax rates as given. It can then be seen from (4.2) that the employed median voter at $\tau = 0$ chooses t_0 to maximize

$$V_0 \equiv \log(1 - t_0) \tag{4.3}$$

implying an optimal choice of $t_0 = 0$. And because each subsequent median voter will also be employed, we see that the electoral system will produce $t_\tau = 0$, for all $\tau \geq 0$, if parties are short-term vote maximizers or there is free entry of parties. This is the fundamental time-inconsistency problem of majoritarian democracy with periodic elections to which this chapter draws attention. Although it would be optimal for the current and for all future median voters to set $t = t^* = \partial p$ (or $t^{**} = p$ behind the veil), the lack of any mechanism whereby the current median voter can commit future median voters implies that each median voter will vote for t = 0.

Proposition 1. The time-inconsistency problem. Given (i) the preferences of individuals defined by (4.1), (4.2), and (4.3); (ii) sincere voting; and (iii) free candidate entry and/or short-term parties: (a) the optimal ex-ante tax rate is p, (b) the optimal tax rate at any point in time for the current and all future median voters is δp, and (c) the equilibrium tax rate is 0.

The time-inconsistency problem as defined here is related to overlapping generations models of public goods provision. In a standard overlapping generations setup, public goods in these models are provided in such a manner that noncontributing older generations benefit from the contributions of younger generations. This would be similar to a situation in the current model where an employed median voter supported transfers to those currently unemployed. Yet, all existing overlapping generations models fail to offer solutions to the key time-inconsistency problem of interest. In Browning (1975), median voters choose the level of social insurance, but because the insurance scheme is in effect for the rest of their lives, time inconsistency is assumed away. Hu (1982) presents a three-period overlapping generations model of social security where the current median voter has some uncertainty about the future level of insurance. But because uncertainty is a random variable with a mean that depends on past levels, the median voter is in effect always making choices for both present and future generations. Likewise, while Broadway and Wildasin (1989) correctly note that the current median voter's choice depends on the choice of future median voters, they then go on to assume that the median voter chooses a level of insurance that will remain in place for the rest of his or her lifetime. Other ways around the problem have been to assume that different generations can write binding contracts with one another, as in Kotlikoff, Persson, and Svensson (1988), or that governments weigh the preferences of each generation regardless of which generation contains the median voter, as in Grossman and Helpman (1998).

A more satisfactory class of models derives the solution endogenously by allowing a possibility of punishment for noncooperation. In this setup, members of a group in the overlapping generations model make continuous decisions about whether to contribute to the public good or not, and this creates opportunities for decentrally enforced cooperation in infinitely lived groups (Dickson and Shepsle 2001; Rangel 2003). Yet, while this solution makes sense in the context of some overlapping generations problems, it makes little sense in our context. The reasons are that a voter is unlikely to choose the level of insurance more than once in a lifetime and that present and future median voters do not know the identity of one another. Because of this, the decision of the median voter is equivalent to a member deciding whether to cooperate in the last period of a finitely lived group in an overlapping generations model.[2] We, thus, need an entirely different solution. In the following, I focus on the key role played by political party organizations and electoral systems.

---

[2] A similar problem applies to the model proposed by Bawn (1999). Analogously to an overlapping generations model, she considers a situation where some members of a group are benefiting from the effort of others, and where the game is repeated indefinitely. In this game, cooperation by reciprocity is a possibility, but the solution is again highly implausible for my purposes because it requires present and future median voters to know each other and to transition repeatedly in and out of the median voter position.

4.2. Two Qualifications

In reality, the problem is not as stark as stated in Proposition 1 for two reasons. First, because the median voter at $\tau = 0$ has a risk of unemployment in the next electoral period, *even* if the voter knows that he or she is currently employed, that voter will demand insurance against *that* risk from the currently elected government. That implies a positive tax rate. Yet, there is still a time-inconsistency problem so long as $p|E < p|U$, where $p|E$ is the probability of unemployment in the next electoral period *when currently employed* and $p|U$ is the probability of unemployment in the next electoral period *when currently unemployed*. The reason is that the optimal level of insurance is chosen for a situation when the voter does not know whether he or she is employed or unemployed (i.e., is behind the veil), which is defined by a probability somewhere between $p|E$ and $p|U$. In general, the difference between the risk before and after the veil is removed defines the severity of the time-inconsistency problem, and it will vary by policy area. In the case of old-age insurance, for example, the median voter, who is likely to be a middle-aged person, will know for certain that the condition for collecting the benefits will be zero in the following electoral period. For most other types of social insurance, including unemployment insurance, the risk is lower unveiled than behind the veil.

Second, and importantly, many benefits are going to those who are both employed and unemployed. Even when benefits are targeted to the employed, to the extent that they reduce variability of earned income, what I have referred to as *income protection*, they serve insurance purposes. Behind the veil, spending on such insurance suffers from exactly the same time-inconsistency problem as identified earlier. Unveiled, however, income protection can be supported for redistributive reasons. The reason is simple and goes back to the preference model in Chapter 3. If workers discount insurance as a result of the time-inconsistency problem, the demand for spending is equal to the demand for redistribution. In the Meltzer-Richard model, this demand is represented by the median voter's preference for redistributive spending and is given by Equation (3.10). The lower the relative income of the median voter is, the greater the demand for spending is.

If the translation of the median voter preferences were direct, we would know from the asset model in Chapter 3 that spending would rise with higher risk of unemployment and more skill specificity. The time-inconsistency problem cuts into this type of spending, while leaving redistribution-motivated spending intact. The difference between the optimal level of spending desired by the median voter and the actual level of spending depends on the probability of unemployment and skills of the median voter. But as this discussion illustrates, there are two potential solutions to the problem: One is to bind the hands of the government across time, the other is to shift the locus of political power from high to lower income groups. I consider each in turn.

4.3. Institutionalized Parties

Assume that there is majoritarian voting and that voters vote sincerely. Furthermore, assume that voters have assets that are at risk of becoming unemployed and for which they seek protection. As in previous chapters, workers' main asset is their skills, and voters are indexed by the specificity of these skills, s, precisely as in Chapter 3. Because this section focuses exclusively on the insurance motive and the intertemporal tradeoff to which it gives rise, differences in income are ignored. In the next section, variability in skills and the risk of unemployment is ignored, and only relative income, and, hence, contemporaneous redistribution, is considered. This enables a clear focus on each of the two problems described in the introduction.

Skill specificity is uniformly distributed across voters on the interval $[s_{min}, s_{max}]$,[3] with s_m being the skill level of the median voter. Individual voters will be referred to by their skill level s. Voters are divided into Low and High (L and H) risk where $s \in L$ when $s < s_m$ and $s \in H$ when $s > s_m$. s is known throughout the game and cannot be changed. As before, the probability that voters will be unemployed during the coming period of governmental office is p; whether they are employed or unemployed is revealed to them at the start of the period; and after it has been revealed, they vote. Again, it is assumed that $p < .5$ so that the median voter is employed.[4]

There are two parties at the start of each period. If a third party can enter and win, that will occur. With sincere voting, an implication of this is that tax-financed unemployment benefits will always be zero if that is the only policy dimension (as demonstrated in the previous section).

---

[3] We can, thus, classify the average degree of skill specificity in a polity by $s_m = (s_{max} + s_{min} / 2$.

[4] Instead of speaking of workers being unemployed, one could more generally talk about assets being unemployed. In terms of developing the logic of the argument, it does not matter.

129

However, governments do not only provide protection against unemployment of assets. They also seek to produce a variety of public goods – including training for workers, wage restraint, and international competitiveness – that are neither guaranteed by the market nor produced by simple tax and spend policies. For the provision of these public goods, governments depend on the cooperation of private economic agents.[5] It is assumed, therefore, that the provision of a public good, a, can only be effective if subsets of voters give the parties adequate support to do so. The way this is accomplished, it is argued, is through a process that will be referred to as *party institutionalization*.

4.3.1. Party Institutionalization

The key intuition behind the argument is that an institutionalized party has a long-term relationship with some group in the electorate characterized by a common set of interests. In exchange for contributions and other resources from the group, which are critical for the production of public goods, the group has an influence on the policy platform of the party enshrined in the party's explicit or implicit constitution. The party also has a leader who can, in principle, impose his or her will on the party's platform. But in compensation, the group has a say in the election and reelection of leaders. The degree of institutionalization can, thus, be seen as the relative power of leader and group. This is essential to the solution of the time-inconsistency problem because, without power over platforms and party leaders, the time-inconsistency problem would always tempt parties to offer lower tax rates.

This conception of party institutionalization is quite similar to the existing literature on parties and corresponds to what is usually referred to as responsible and programmatic parties. For example, in a classic analysis of party organizations, Schlesinger (1984) conceives of parties as voluntary organizations producing collective goods. To be electorally successful, parties rely on the work of rank-and-file members, and these in turn must be "compensated" through influence over policy and leadership selection. Platform control, in other words, is traded for rank-and-file support. In Schlesinger's conceptualization, however, the incentives of individual members to contribute is problematic because policies represent collective goods. In the

---

[5] There may be other types of public goods, such as a civil service or even a general educational system, that do not require cooperation from private groups. The provision of these are theoretically unproblematic and not considered here.

present model, the supporters are collective actors with the ability to use selective incentives to solve internal collective action problems. This conception of parties is very close to that in Aldrich (1995).

To provide greater precision to the argument, assume that institutionalized parties have a constitution. The constitution lays down that members pay a fee in exchange for which they can nominate the party's platform. "Fee" is used here in the broad sense of any sacrifices made by a party's constituency to facilitate the provision of a public good in exchange for policy influence. The party leader is not bound to accept this platform, but if it is rejected, the event $\mathfrak{R}$, the leader's probability of reselection, $q_{\mathfrak{R}}$, at the end of the period is lower than the probability of reselection if the leader accepts the platform, which is assumed to be 1. The difference $1 - q_{\mathfrak{R}}$ is called the *degree of institutionalization* of the party because it measures the degree to which the party constituency can control the leader – or inversely the leader's degree of discretion over policy.

Assume that $1 - q_{\mathfrak{R}}$ is an increasing function of membership fees (again, in the broad sense suggested earlier) and that these are determined by the costs of the public goods provision, $c(a)$. Because specific skills require an infrastructure of institutions to ensure the provision of such skills (in particular vocational training systems) as well as to cope with the hold-up problems endemic to specific asset investments (the wage bargaining system), the choice of a_i is a function of the s level of the median member of group $i = L, H$.[6] The simplest way to think about this is in terms of wage restraint. Union leaders, on behalf of their members, may underexploit their negotiation power in collective bargaining in order to encourage investment and employment. The greater the control over specific assets is, the greater is the potential collective good to be achieved. But if unions have no guarantees that the government will keep its promise of future insurance, the expected value of future earnings falls, and the attraction of maximization in the present increases.

Stated slightly more formally, in order for the expected value of current pay to be equal to the expected value of future pay, future pay must be greater than the current pay. This follows trivially from discounting of future consumption, but on top of that there must be a future pay premium

[6] The implication is not that those with general skills have no interests in public goods but that, insofar as this is the case – as with general education – they tend to be of a nature that makes it possible for the government to provide it without the cooperation of private groups.

to compensate for the riskiness of future pay. Everything else being equal, a worker with specific assets (high s) will face greater risks and, therefore, value current over future pay more than a worker with general assets. This difference disappears, however, as income protection reduces the riskiness of future pay for high-s workers. For risk-averse workers, the expected utility of future income rises as the protection of future income goes up, keeping the expected value constant.

Using this logic, if R^* is the optimal level of social protection, as defined previosuly, a government that can credibly make a promise to provide this level of R will encourage current restraint compared to a government that cannot credibly commit. In other words, a political party able to make credible offers of future protection is in a better position to offer certain collective goods such as wage restraint. Because collective goods provision is a valuable electoral asset, there is an incentive for a party to yield power to unions over platform and leadership selection in order to raise the credibility of its social insurance commitments. Of course, this comes at the cost of lower electoral flexibility and a more constrained party leader.

4.3.2. The Game between Parties, Voters, and Groups

The preferences of groups and voters are essentially variations of the utility functions presented in the previous section, except the costs and benefits of public goods provision are taken into account. *The key is whether decisions are made behind the veil or not.* The group choosing the party platform makes its decisions behind the veil because choosing a platform has long-term consequences if party leaders are made to accept the platform. The employed median group member does not know whether he or she will be unemployed in the future. The relative durability of party platforms matters here; if party platforms are chosen infrequently or if they are subject to only incremental change, there is a clear difference between choosing a platform and choosing a policy. Voters are not choosing platforms but only a party to govern for the next electoral term. The veil behind which voters are making decisions is, therefore, very thin: They can only project policies into the next electoral period. This is a critical distinction.

More specifically, the group's utility function is analogous to Equation (4.1), except that there is a positive term representing the net utility derived from the public good a (Appendix 4.A contains the details). The preferences of s_m, the median employed voter, *after the veil has been raised* is analogous to Equation (4.3) (see Appendix 4.A for details). With these assumptions, the party leader faces the following tradeoff. On the one hand, there is an incentive to follow the nominated strategy because it guarantees reselection. On the other hand, the leader would like to have total policy flexibility because it makes it more likely that he or she can win the next election and become head of government (or prime minister, PM). Also, it is more difficult to control leaders as head of government because prime ministers can make use of institutionalized resources, including ample media access, that they do not enjoy to the same extent as party leaders.

To capture this logic, let B be the benefits of office and L the benefits of leadership of the party. The more institutionalized the party is, the greater are the constraints put on the leader and PM.

These constraints diminish the attractiveness of both leadership and PM positions, especially as a increases, because a is exchanged for greater party institutionalization. Because the preferred level of a is a positive function of s, leaders of parties representing specific assets are more constrained than parties representing general assets, which also means that they are constrained to accept a higher t. More specifically, the period utility for the leader can be written as

$$U_{pol} = e \cdot B(s) + L(s) \tag{4.4}$$

where e is the probability of becoming a PM. To capture the idea that it is easier to control leaders when they are not heads of governments, assume that

$$\frac{\partial \ln B}{\partial \ln s} > \frac{\partial \ln L}{\partial \ln s}$$

4.3.3. Solving the Game

The chosen levels of t and a is the solution to the following stage game.

Stage i: The median voter in each of the two groups, s_{ML} and s_{MH}, chooses contribution levels and nominating platforms (behind the veil).

Stage ii: Party leaders choose electoral platforms.

Stage iii: Voters vote (unveiled).

Stage iv: Leaders are reselected with a certain probability.

Because a new subgame that does not depend on the history up to that point begins at the start of the next period, all we need to do is analyze the choices in the current period through backward induction. The solution is characterized next, with the mathematical details explained in Appendix 4.A.

Stage iv: Reselection of Leaders. At the end of the period, the leaders are reselected with certain contingent probabilities [1 if the leader accepted the platform and $(1 - q_{\Re})$ if the leader did not]. This involves no choices.

Stage iii: Voting. Assume that no new party has entered (an assumption that is demonstrated to hold in Appendix 4.A) and that leaders have accepted platforms that differentiate their party from the other. L will then vote for L and H will vote for H because they vote sincerely and because L offers an a closer to all voters in L than the a offered by H and similarly for members in H. The median voter will choose the party with a combination of t and a that comes closest to the median voter's ideal combination of policies: $t = 0$ and $a = \alpha s_m$. If the two parties are equally attractive, then the median voter will vote for each party with equal probability.

Stage ii: Party Leader's Choice. The leader has to choose t and face two opposing incentives. On the one hand, the leader would like to win the election (and thereby become prime minister) by choosing a low t. On the other hand, he or she wants to remain the leader of the party and produce a high level of public goods (a), which requires the leader to pay attention to the preferences of his or her constituent group (given by Equation (4.4)). To model this choice, we assume that the base cannot monitor perfectly what the leader does. In other words, there is a possibility that the leader can "cheat" and get away with it. This may arise, for example, because an unexpected recession makes a tax cut a prudent policy.

How high does $1 - q_{\Re}$ (the probability of non-reelection) have to be to ensure leader i cooperates? Appendix 4.A derives the exact condition, but the key variables affecting whether the condition is satisfied can be easily summarized. Institutionalization $(1 - q_{\Re})$ would need to be higher (i) the greater is B (the benefits of office), which raises the temptation to defect for the leader; (ii) the lower is L (the benefits of being party leader), which again raises the temptation to defect; (iii) the higher is s (which raises the group's preferred tax level); (iv) the lower is the discount rate, λ; and (v) the higher is the probability that there are no shocks requiring a lower tax rate.

The group or party base would obviously want to choose a level of institutionalization that ensures the cooperation of the leader. But whether it can accomplish this cooperation depends on the resources that are at the disposal of the group. Being able to extract a high fee, which is equivalent to being able to influence significantly the ability of the party to offer a high level of the public good a, accords more group power over leadership selection. Well-organized and encompassing groups will therefore tend to be associated with more institutionalized parties, and effective organization is in turn partly a function of the specificity of member assets, which confers hold-up power.

But whether the leader cooperates also depends critically on his or her temptation to defect. When winning government power carries a very high reward (high B), it is harder for the party base to prevent leadership defection. In an analogous manner, given a fixed prize of winning office, the greater the effect of getting an additional vote on the probability of winning is, the greater the temptation to cheat is. Both factors are positively correlated with having a two-party majoritarian electoral system. Because a single party wins the election outright, being the prime minister is likely to be associated with considerably more power than in multiparty PR systems with minority and/or multiparty governments. In addition, as argued by Rogowski and Kayser (2002), majoritarian elections produce a very high "vote-seat elasticity," where winning a few more votes can have a big effect on the prospect of winning office. Party leaders, therefore, have a relatively greater incentive to pay attention to the median voter than to their base compared to PR systems. Majoritarianinsm, in other words, makes it more likely that the leader will fall for the "populist" temptation of cutting taxes.

Stage i: The Choice of Party Platforms. The groups sponsoring each party choose the contribution levels and tax rates to maximize their welfare function, which is given by Equation (A4.1) in the appendix [analogous to Equation (4.1)]. Using a simple cost function, Appendix 4.A shows that the optimal tax rate is

$$t^*(s) = p \cdot (1 + \gamma(s)) \tag{4.5}$$

where $\gamma(s)$ is a search cost for finding a new job in the event of unemployment. It is assumed that it is harder for those with more specific skills to find jobs that are suitable to their skills The optimal tax rate, $t^*(s)$, is, thus, positively related to the probability of unemployment p and also positively related to search costs, $\gamma(s)$. Note that if there are no search costs, Equation (4.5) reduces to $t^* = p$, which is the optimal long-term level of taxation preferred by the median voter as initially identified. Introducing s and search costs, $\gamma(s)$, implies policy differentiation. The optimal contribution

135

level, a^*, is also directly proportional to s (details are provided in Appendix 4.A).

Whether the contribution level is sufficiently high to induce leadership cooperation cannot be determined a priori. To some extent, we have to treat party organizations, and hence the ability of groups to influence policies, as historically given. The same is true for the incentives of leaders to cooperate. However, the comparative statics is clear because as the specificity of assets rises, so does the ability and willingness of groups to pay higher "fees," which in turn gives parties and their leaders a greater incentive to yield influence over party policies. Asset specificity and party institutionalization, therefore, will tend to go hand in hand. In addition, because the prize of winning a majority is very high in a two-party majoritarian systems, the temptation of the party leader to present a short-sighted platform should be expected to be greater than in multiparty PR systems where the marginal effect of an additional vote on power tends to be lower.

4.4. Redistribution

As argued previously, there are two dimensions to the provision of social insurance. One is an intertemporal dimension where current payment is exchanged for (potential) future receipts. The second is a contemporaneous redistributive dimension where income is transferred from one group to another. The two dimensions are intertwined because transfers motivated by redistribution can serve insurance purposes, and transfers motived by insurance can have redistributive consequences. Current unemployed may in the past have supported unemployment benefits for purely insurance reasons, but they now have a redistributive motive to continue supporting it. And if unemployment benefits exist only because of political pressure from the unemployed, that does not mean that those currently employed are not benefiting from the insurance effects of such benefits. Hence, if distributive politics produces continuous pressure for redistribution, it can help overcome the time-inconsistency problem. To understand the politics of social insurance, we, therefore, need to understand the politics of redistribution. This section seeks to provide such an understanding.

As noted in Chapter 1, most of the literature on redistribution focuses on the effects of politics being dominated by the left or the right but does not offer a convincing account of the source of such partisan dominance. Identifying this source is key to explaining redistribtuion. This section argues that the source of partisan dominance is the electoral system.

The model is a special version of a very general model of redistribution proposed in Iversen and Soskice (2004). That model assumes that (i) parties represent groups, or classes; (ii) that parties maximize the distributive preferences of their members (but subject to a time-inconsistency problem); and (iii) that the net effect of government taxation and spending is nonregressive in the sense that those with lower incomes need to benefit from government policies as much as those with higher incomes. I present here a simple version of this model that is easy to explain and relate to existing work on the welfare state. The model makes specific assumptions about the structure of benefits, but the conclusions hold for any tax-benefit structure that is nonregressive and not strictly one-dimensional (the Meltzer-Richard model is nonregressive but also unidimensional).

The model has two key results. First, in a two-party majoritarian system, the center-right party has an electoral advantage whenever there is a nonzero probability that the winning party will deviate from its electoral platform once in power. The reason is that left party leaders under majoritarianism need to compromise the ideal redistributive policies of their members more than right party leaders and, therefore, face a greater postelection incentive to adopt policies that are unattractive to the median voter. In a multiparty PR system, by contrast, where each party represents a distinct class and must ally with another party to govern, the typical pattern is that the middle class (or center) party will ally with the lower class (or left) party. The reason here is that the middle-class party can use taxes that fall disproportionately on the rich to bargain with the lower-class party for a level of social insurance (and hence taxation) that is closer to its ideal point. The implications are that (i) center-left governments will be more frequent under PR, (ii) center-right governments will be more frequent under majoritarian rules, and (iii) redistribution will be greater under PR than under majoritarianism.

4.4.1. The Politics of Redistribution

There is a huge empirical literature on the welfare state based on Esping-Andersen's (1990) classic study. Whatever the specific aims of these studies, there is broad agreement that Esping-Andersen's depiction of the distributive dimensions of social policy describes the policy space of advanced democracies rather well. Most systems combine a universalistic or flat-rate benefit with a means-tested benefit targeted at the poor, although the relative weights of these benefits vary across countries. Esping-Andersen also distinguishes earnings-related benefits, but if these benefits are directly proportional to income, they are equivalent for our analytical purposes to people keeping their market income. Although such benefits may serve important insurance purposes, I deliberately ignore these in this section.

Assume that the flat-rate benefit, which is called f, is fully financed by a proportional tax, t. This makes it equivalent to the Meltzer-Richard model. But even though the Meltzer-Richard model is convenient, it is not descriptively accurate and precludes us from understanding the multidimensional politics of redistribution that give rise to coalitional politics. This is where the means-tested benefit, g, enters. To make it maximally redistributive in nature, I assume that it is financed by a progressive tax, which falls disproportionately on those with higher incomes. Still, a small but nonnegligible share of g, $\varepsilon \cdot g$, is paid by the middle class (as is the case for most progressive taxes).

It is easy to see that these assumptions satisfy the nonregressivity constraint (i.e., the poor will not be made worse off), and although they are more restrictive than necessary, combining f and g, and their associated taxes, yields a redistributive policy space that is flexible enough to describe most actual social benefit systems. Again the key is nonregressivity, which can be defended on many grounds. The marginal utility of money may be higher among the poor than among the rich; or the costs of extracting one tax dollar from a poor person may be higher than extracting a dollar from a rich person. Most fundamentally, "reverse" redistribution may be inconsistent with the underlying conditions that gave rise to democracy, namely the need to attend to the distributive preferences of the poor and the middle classes (Acemoglu and Robinson 2005). An argument along these lines is spelled out in detail in Iversen and Soskice (2004). Whatever the reason, data for advanced democracies, which are discussed later in this chapter, show no case where taxes and transfer result in a more *dispersed* distribution of income. To the extent that the democratic governments redistribute money, it flows from higher to lower incomes, and no analysis of the welfare state implies otherwise. The two best-known analyses, that of Meltzer-Richard and that of Esping-Andersen, are cases in point.

More specifically, the model follows Persson and Tabellini (1999) and assumes that there are three equally sized income classes in the population: L (low), M (middle), and H (high). Majoritarian systems are assumed to be dominated by two parties (Duverger's law), but under PR each group is assumed to be represented by its own party.[7] In both cases, parties represent income classes in the population (i.e., they are "class parties"). In the majoritarian case, the middle class is split between a center-right and a center-left party, making the median voter pivotal.

The transfer g (and corresponding tax) has a cost that includes expenses for administration, rents to politicians who provide tax "loopholes" to the rich, and the costs of paying lawyers to take advantage of these loopholes – where the cost of g to H is αg with $\alpha > 0$. In addition, it is assumed that $0 \leq g \leq g^*$, where g^* is a constitutionally guaranteed upper limit that can be thought of as a basic property right protection preventing complete expropriation of property. For specificity, assume that this constitutional protection can only be overturned by three quarters of the legislature. In this case, H (assuming it has one third of the seats in the legislature) can always block any attempt to raise g^*, and H voters will have an incentive to vote under PR regardless of whether they can anticipate H to be in government or not. Loosely speaking, one can think of g^* as measuring the power of (high-income) veto players in the system.

It is possible to present the model with preferences over taxation that are endogenously determined by the relative income of each group and the efficiency costs of taxation.[8] However, one can derive all the key comparative statics from a simple indirect utility function model, in which each group has preferences over t and g. The main difference is that, in the model with endogenous policy preferences, relative income is an independent cause of redistribution. But because relative income turns out not to have much of an empirical effect, I omit the variable in the current presentation.

In this simple model, L is interested in maximizing g and t; H, in minimizing both g and t; and M, in setting t as close as possible to some intermediate level of t, which is assumed to be 0.5, and in minimizing g. In terms of t, this is the structure of preferences across income groups implied by the Meltzer-Richard model. Also note that M would be equally distanced

---

[7] Persson and Tabellini (1999) assume only two parties under PR, but they acknowledge that it plainly does not make much sense: "We hold the party structure fixed, ignoring theoretical arguments as well as empirical evidence for a larger number of parties under proportional elections" (p. 706). They go on to say that "our excuse is pragmatic; we simply do not know how to analyze multi-dimensional policy consequences of electoral competition in a multi-party setting" (p. 706).

[8] The model is available from the author upon request.

from L and H if f (or t) were the only policy dimension. The preferences over g follow trivially from the assumptions made. The goals of the three groups, therefore, are

$$u_L = g + t$$
$$u_M = -|t - 0.5| - g \cdot (1 + \alpha) \cdot \varepsilon$$
$$u_H = -t - g \cdot (1 + \alpha) \cdot (1 - \varepsilon)$$

4.4.2. Majoritarian Elections

There are two parties, CL (center-left) and CR (center-right), which organize voters on either side of the median income. One party, thus, "represents" the center-left; the other, the center-right. Each will have different ideal policies as a result. Given that the middle income group is a minority in both parties, if these are characterized by the preferences of the median constituent in each party, the center-left party will want $\{g, t\} = \{g^*, 1\}$ while the center-right party will want $\{g, t\} = \{0, 0\}$. However, in a majoritarian system, no party can affect policy without winning a majority of the vote, so the platform presented in the election will clearly need to deviate from the policy preferences of the median constituent in each party.

What is the vote-maximizing platform? It turns out that this is given by a simple median voter result. Because there are two policy dimensions, it is not obvious why this should be so, but Appendix 4.B proves that it is. Essentially, if CR proposes taxes that are below 0.5, CL will offer a policy of $(0, 0.5)$; if CL proposes a $g > 0$, CR will offer a policy of $(0.5, 0)$, and the preferences of L and H are too misaligned to make it possible that both would prefer a platform that is different than $(0, 0.5)$.

Before proceeding, it is useful to characterize the median voter platform briefly in left–right terms. Compared to the ideal policies of L and H, the median voter platform is closer to the preferences of H than to the preferences of L, and in that sense the median voter platform may be thought of as right-of-center. The reason is that although the middle class deviates from both the lower and upper class in terms of preferences over the level of taxation and spending, it shares an interest with the latter in restricting redistributive transfers to the poor. This is an old insight in the welfare state literature, emphasized by Esping-Andersen in his discussion of means-tested benefits (1990, Chapter 1). It arises in the model because of the two-dimensional nature of social spending.

Given that the two parties in a majoritarian system represent different constituencies, is it realistic that they will converge on the median voter platform? Most existing answers in the party literature suggest that even though there is significant pressure on parties to present moderate platforms in general elections, it is hard for party leaders to ignore the policy preferences of their core constituents completely. One argument is that leaders need to mobilize their base in order to maximize voter turnout among their prospective supporters. This involves appeals to the policy preferences of the median activist and emphasis on policy differences with the other party (Schlesinger 1984; Aldrich 1993, 1995, Chapter 6).

An alternative formulation with similar results is that parties cannot make binding commitments to electoral platforms (Downs 1957; Persson and Tabellini 1999). This is the generic time-inconsistency problem identified in the previous section. Once in office, there is an incentive for both parties to adopt policies that reflect the preferences of their median constituents. This incentive is tempered by the concern for cultivating a reputation among voters for reliability, but reputation is an imperfect commitment mechanism in a world with short-sighted politicians. As a result, the median voter has reason to worry that whoever wins the election will give in to the temptation of pursuing policies that appeal to the party's internal core constituents. Thus, the temptation for the center-right party, if it wins, is to put the policies $\{0, 0\}$ into operation and for the center-left party to carry out the policies $\{1, g^*\}$. This affects the voting behavior of the median voter in a subtle, but important way.

To understand this, assume that whether or not a party yields to the temptation if elected depends on whether the costs outweigh the temptation benefits, T_{CL} and T_{CR}. These variables are straightforwardly calculated – $T_{CL} = g^* + 0.5$, $T_{CR} = 0.5$ – in each case the gain from switching from the median voter's ideal point $(0.5, 0)$ to $(1, g^*)$ and $(0, 0)$, respectively. The cost of adopting more extreme policies is the loss of reputation. The loss of reputation for trustworthiness matters to a government because, without such a reputation, governing is less effective because it is harder for the government to make deals with other agents.[9] This is modeled by assuming that the loss of effectiveness is a cost, c_{CL} and c_{CR}, respectively, which restricts government effectiveness if a defection to more extreme policies takes place. Thus, the payoff to the left party from

---

[9] An additional possibility is that voters punish defecting governments in future elections, but this adds to the complexity of the model without altering its insights.

defecting is $T_{CL} - c_{CL} = g^* + 0.5 - c_{CL}$ and the payoff to the right party is $T_{CR} - c_{CR} = 0.5 - c_{CR}$.

Next, assume that c_{CL} and c_{CR} are random variables independently drawn at each election from the same uniform distribution, normalized for convenience to [0, 1], with $1 > \max[T_{CL}, T_{CR}]$. Thus, in the election campaign, the median voter forms an idea of how trustworthy each of the party leaders are after they have set out their platforms; because this trustworthiness can be valuably used by the executive if it carried out the median voter policies, the loss of this attribute would be the cost of yielding to the temptation of switching to left or right policies once in power.

The median voter would be indifferent to which party he or she voted for if $T_{CL} < c_{CL}$ and $T_{CR} < c_{CR}$. But if $T_{CL} > c_{CL}$ and $T_{CR} < c_{CR}$ or if $T_{CL} > c_{CL}$ and $T_{CR} > c_{CR}$, the median voter would vote center-right; if $T_{CL} < c_{CL}$ and $T_{CR} > c_{CR}$, the median voter would vote center-left. Using the joint cumulative distribution function of c_{CL} and c_{CR}, it is not difficult to see that the center-right would win a proportion

$$\pi_{CR} = T_L \cdot (1 - T_R) + T_L \cdot T_R + \frac{(1 - T_L) \cdot (1 - T_R)}{2}$$

of elections against

$$\pi_{CL} = T_R \cdot (1 - T_L) + \frac{(1 - T_L) \cdot (1 - T_R)}{2}$$

won by the center-left. It follows that

$$\pi_{CR} - \pi_{CL} = T_L - T_R + T_L T_R > 0$$

In other words, the center-right party wins more of the time. The intuition behind the result is simple and goes back to the observation that the median voter shares an interest with the well-off to avoid means-tested transfers to the poor. Even though both parties may fall to the temptation to adopt tax policies that are unattractive to the median voter, it is only the center-left party that has an incentive to adopt policies of means-tested transfers to the poor. This makes the median voter more likely to vote for the center-right party.

Whether a center-right party would also win against a center party depends on the exact interpretation of what a center party is. This matters only because some parties in the empirical analysis are classified as "center parties," specifically, if the center party represents middle-class voters, then it would be more attractive to the median voter than the center-right party.

But if the center party is really a center-left party with a platform mirroring the preferences of the median voter, whereas the center-right party has a platform that deviates to the right, then the prediction is ambiguous since the center party is closer to the median voter, yet faces a greater incentive to defect. Because no existing data clearly distinguish between these different "types" of center parties, we cannot form any clear predictions about the performance of center parties in majoritarian systems. The predictions for center-left and center-right parties, however, are unambiguous: The latter win more of the time.

4.4.3. Proportional Representation

For simplicity, assume here that there are three representative parties under PR – L, M, and H – none of which have an absolute majority in the electorate. It is furthermore assumed to be common knowledge that each party seeks to promote the welfare of the class it represents. Because there is no imperative under PR to win the median voter, a party does not have the incentive to adopt a platform that is different from the optimal policies of its class. If it did, it would not be credible. Indeed, this distinction between the credible commitment of representative parties under PR and the difficulty of such commitment under majoritarian arrangements is one of the central differences between the two types of electoral systems. Recall from the previous section that this difference was also important for the provision of insurance.

On the face of it, coalitions between M and H would seem as likely as coalitions between L and M. When t is the only policy dimension, and if a "split-the-difference" rule determines the policy a coalition will adopt, M will indeed be indifferent between a coalition with H and a tax rate of 0.25 and a coalition with L and a tax rate of 0.75. Both imply utility of -0.25 to M.

But this conclusion no longer holds when g is added. The reason is that M can now offer concessions to L on g at a low cost that reflects the progressive nature of the tax (i.e., most of the cost is paid by H). In exchange for such concessions, M can demand a tax rate that is closer to its preferred rate. Specifically, for a suitably low ε, the Rubinstein bargaining solution is $0.75 - g^*/2$ (see Appendix 4.C). Thus, a bargain with L will always be closer to M's preferred policy than 0.75. M has no such bargaining leverage over H, and the outcome of that bargain would, therefore, be a simple split between preferred tax rates (0.25). Consequently, M prefers to be in a center-left coalition. Appendix 4.C demonstrates this conclusion more formally and addresses the objection that *H* can always break an *LM* coalition by offering *M* a deal that is closer to *M*'s ideal policy. This cannot happen, it turns out, if there is *any* cost of coalition breakup because that prevents H from making a credible offer to *M*.

Combining the results for PR with those for majoritarian institutions, the analysis has yielded an unambiguous and stark insight that has not been articulated in any of the existing literature: Majoritarian electoral systems tend to produce center-right governments, whereas proportional electoral systems tend to produce center-left governments. The former will redistribute less than the latter. The key to understanding redistribution is the long-time political dominance of the left or right, and a key to understanding long-term partisan dominance is the electoral rule.

4.5. Empirics

The theory is explored in two parts. The first examines the party institutionalization argument using cross-sectional data for twenty-one countries. Because time-series data are not available, the emphasis here is on establishing stable equilibrium couplings, although I will go as far as is possible to establish causality using quantitative data. The second part explores the redistribution argument. One section uses partisanship as the explanatory variable to account for differences in the level of redistribution. Another uses partisanship as the dependent variable to test the proposition that the electoral system shapes coalition behavior and, therefore, the composition of governments. The results of the analysis reinforce each other because institutionalized parties are associated with more social insurance spending, and such parties are more likely to be found in PR systems, in which redistribution tends to be greater.

4.5.1. Party Institutionalization

Insofar as party institutionalization varies systematically across countries, the argument has two macro-level implications. The first is that we should expect more young people to acquire specific skills in countries where party institutionalization is high. On the one hand, public goods provision, which includes vocational training systems, is expected to be higher in countries with highly institutionalized party systems. On the other hand, more young people are likely to invest in specific skills when such investments are backed by credible institutional guarantees. Second, one would expect the skill profiles of national labor markets to be associated with higher social transfers. When a large portion of the electorate have highly specific skills, the preferred level of social insurance will be high. If parties are capable of credible commitment, such preferences will get translated into actual protection. In turn, protection encourages further investment in specific skills.

It is important to point out that this is an argument about institutional equilibria. If the median voter is pivotal, for example, we would not expect this voter to have skills that are inconsistent with the institutional capacity of commitment or the level of social protection. If institutionalization dropped below what is required to sustain confidence in the future viability of public goods provision, and in the future of social protection, we should see adjustments in peoples' skill investments toward greater emphasis on general skills until the point where institutionalization, skills, and social protection are once again aligned in a steady-state equilibrium. When we look at national systems over longer periods of time, we therefore expect to observe a high degree of collinearity between these variables. Only if there is a shock to one of the variables, or to the level of risks in the labor market, would that variable become a causal agent triggering changes in the other variables.

Chapter 5 examines what happens to social spending in different institutional settings when the system is exposed to exogenous shocks. Here I simply examine if the observed covariation between variables across countries is consistent with the equilibria implied by the model. That is, I look at whether heavy investment in specific skills is in fact associated with high capacity of the party system for institutional commitment and whether these variables in turn are linked to government spending. To this end, twenty-one OECD countries are compared for the period 1980–95, which is the period for which comparable figures for the age cohort going through vocational training exist.[10] Vocational training activity serves as the macro-level proxy for the importance of specific skills in the labor force (corresponding to average level of s in the theoretical model). As an indicator for the extent to which the government engages in social spending – the variable t in the

---

[10] The countries are Australia, Austria, Belgium, Canada, Denmark, Finland, France, Germany, Ireland, Italy, Japan, the Netherlands, Norway, Portugal, Spain, Sweden, Switzerland, the United Kingdom, and the the United States.

theoretical model – the sum of government consumption and transfers as a share of GDP is used.[11]

The measure of the institutionalization of the party system is based on two sources of data. One concerns the centralization and discipline of political party systems; the other, the extent to which interests are organized in a corporatist manner. We need the first because a necessary condition for parties to be able to credibly commit to a policy is that elected leaders have individual incentives to run their campaigns on the policy platform of the party rather than on personal resources and policy appeals. A necessary, and potentially sufficient, condition is that such centralized control is coupled with close ties to well-organized and centralized private groups, and a measure of corporatism is used to capture this aspect. The combination of these variables constitutes the, admittedly crude, variable for party system institutionalization.

The data are adapted from Carey and Shugart's (1995) path-breaking analysis of electoral systems in terms of the incentives they provide politicians to either run on the party platform and toe the party line or to cultivate their own personal following without regard to the preferences of the party. The classification of party systems in this analysis is coupled with Siaroff's (1998) measure of corporatism, which measures both the organizational centralization of private interests and their ties with the state and political parties. The exact procedures for creating the combined index are explained in Appendix 4.D.

Figure 4.1 shows the relationships between the three variables. Figure 4.1a suggests a fairly tight linkage between institutionalization of the party system and vocational training activity, with a familiar clustering of Anglo-Saxon countries at one end and the continental European countries at the other (with France in a somewhat precarious intermediate position). It is also notable that Japan is much closer to the Anglo-Saxon cluster than to the continental European cluster. In addition to low institutional capacity for commitment, the Japanese welfare state is underdeveloped, which would imply underinvestment in specific skills. In the Japanese system, however, extensive training in highly firm-specific skills, which is not fully captured

---

[11] Specifically, the measure refers to all government payments to the civilian household sector, including social security transfers, government grants, public employee pensions, and transfers to nonprofit institutions serving the household sector as a percent of GDP (1980–95). *Sources:* Cusack (1991) and OECD, *National Accounts, Part II: Detailed Tables* (various years).

by the UNESCO educational categories, is made possible by very high job security and protection of future earnings for skilled workers at the firm level.

Figures 4.1.b and 4.1c show the relationship between government transfers and vocational training and institutionalization. Again, the covariances are relatively strong and in the expected direction. Countries with high levels of vocational training also have high government spending, and spending is likewise rising with the degree of institutionalization of the party system. Switzerland is a bit of an outlier because it is coded as having high

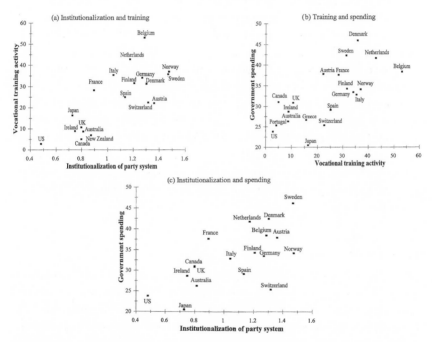

Figure 4.1 The relationship between institutionalization of the party system, vocational training intensity, and government spending. *Vocational training*: The share of an age cohort in either secondary or postsecondary (ISCED5) vocational training.

Source: UNESCO (1999). *Government spending*: Government civilian consumption plus government transfers in the form of payments to the civilian household sector (including social security transfers, government grants, public employee pensions, and transfers to nonprofit institutions serving the household sector) as a percent of GDP. *Sources:* Cusack (1991) and OECD, *National Accounts, Part II: Detailed Tables* (various years). *Institutionalization*: Average (after standardization) of Siaroff's (1999) corporatism index and Carey and Shugart's (1995) classification of electoral systems. See Appendix 4.D for details.

institutional capacity, yet it does not train or spend at a commensurable level. The reasons, similar to those in Japan, could be the relatively high protection built into the industrial relations system. It may also be that the institutionalization variable gives an exaggerated measure of capacity for commitment given that unions are much weaker in Switzerland than they are in other corporatist countries.

Whatever the exact explanation for the somewhat aberrant positions of Japan and Switzerland, the correlations between the variables are high (ranging between .68 and .77). Again, this says nothing about causality, and the three variables are best considered part of an institutional equilibrium without a clear causal order. During particular historical periods, each can be either a dependent or an independent variable. This complementarity logic is one that has taken root in economics (see Aoki 1994; Cooper 1999), and it is central to the varieties of capitalism. What this section has attempted to show is that party institutionalization is an integral component of the welfare production regimes that we observe.

However, we go beyond the identification of institutional complementarities in two ways. The first is to investigate the causal effects of partisan governments on redistribution, as well as the effects of electoral systems on partisanship. This is the task in the next section. Second, we want to investigate the extent to which countries with different institutional equilibria respond differently to external shocks in terms of social spending. This task is left for Chapter 5.

4.5.2. Redistribution

Most existing work on redistribution relies on indirect measures such as government transfers, social spending, or some other indicator of welfare state effort. Such measures are not entirely satisfactory because the data come in a form that typically tell us very little about the extent of redistribution as opposed to the level of spending.

Fortunately, relying on spending data to measure redistribution is no longer necessary. During the past three decades, the Luxembourg Income Study has been compiling a significant database on pre- and posttax and transfer income inequality. The LIS data used for this study cover fourteen countries over a period that runs from the late 1960s (the first observation is 1967) to the late 1990s (the last observation is 1997). All fourteen countries have been democracies since the Second World War. There are a total of sixty-one observations, with the number of observations for each country ranging from two to seven. About one fifth of the observations are from the 1970s and late 1960s, about 40 percent are from the 1980s, and the remainder are from the 1990s. The data are collected from separate national surveys, but considerable effort has gone into harmonizing the data (or "Lissifying" them) to ensure they are comparable across countries and time. The LIS data are widely considered to be of high quality and the best available for the purposes of studying distribution and redistribution (see OECD 1995; Brady 2003).

I use the data specifically to explore the determinants of redistribution as measured by the percentage reduction in the Gini coefficient from before to after taxes and transfers. The Gini coefficient is a summary measure of inequality, which falls as income is shifted from those with higher to those with lower incomes. It varies from 0 (when there is a perfectly even distribution of income) to 1 (when all income goes to the top decile). Using an adjusted version of the LIS data – constructed by Huber, Stephens, and their associates (Bradley et al. in press)[12] – I include only working age families, primarily because generous public pension systems (especially in Scandinavia) discourage private savings and, therefore, exaggerate the degree of redistribution among older people. Furthermore, because data are only available at the household level, income is adjusted for household size using a standard square root divisor (see OECD 1995).

On the independent side, the key variable for explaining redistribution is government partisanship, which is an index of the partisan left–right "center of gravity" of the cabinet based on (i) the average of three expert classifications of government parties' placement on a left–right scale, weighted by (ii) their decimal share of cabinet portfolios. The index was conceived by Thomas Cusack who generously shared all the data from a new comprehensive source on parties and partisanship (see Cusack and Fuchs 2002 and Cusack and Engelhardt 2002 for details). The expert codings are from Castles and Mair (1984), Huber and Inglehart (1995), and Laver and Hunt (1992). For the purpose of explaining partisanship, the key variable is electoral system. I use several different measures that are explained in detail in the partisanship section later in this chapter.

I also controlled for variables that are commonly assumed to affect redistribution, most notably income inequality. These variables, with definitions,

---

[12] I am grateful to the authors for letting us use their data.

sources, and a short discussion of causal logic, are listed here. Country means and a variable correlation matrix are provided in Tables A4.3 and A4.4 in Appendix 4.E.

Pretax and transfer inequality. This variable is included to capture the Meltzer-Richard logic that more inequality will lead to more pressure for redistribution. It is measured as the earnings of a worker in the ninetieth percentile of the earnings distribution as a share of the earnings of the worker with a median income. The data are from OECD's wage dispersion data set (unpublished electronic data).

Constitutional veto points. This variable is Huber et al.'s (1993) composite measure of federalism, presidentialism, bicameralism, and the frequency of referenda. The more independent decision nodes available, the more veto points there are. One can raise definitional objections to the inclusion of referenda as a veto point, but it is clearly the case that referenda are typically used to block legislation that would otherwise have passed by a majority (see Lijphart 1999, pp. 230–1).

Unionization. According to power resource arguments, high union density should lead to more political pressure for redistribution while simultaneously affecting the primary income distribution (see Huber and Stephens 2001 and Bradley et al. 2003). The data are from Visser (1989, 1996).

Voter turnout. Meltzer and Richard (1981) argue that the extension of the franchise reduced the income of the median voter and raised the demand for redistribution. A similar logic may apply to voter turnout if non-turnout is concentrated among the poor as some research suggests (Lijphart 1997). The data are from annual records in Mackie and Rose (1991) and International Institute for Democracy and Electoral Assistance (1997).

Vocational training. Iversen and Soskice (2001) argue that people with specific skills are more likely to support social insurance with a redistributive component. As an indicator of the extent to which workers are schooled in specific vocational skills, as opposed to general academic skills, I use the share of an age cohort that goes through a secondary or short-term postsecondary vocational training. The data are from the *UNESCO Statistical Yearbook* (UNESCO, 1999).

Unemployment. Because the unemployed receive no wage income, they are typically poor without transfers. Because all countries have public unemployment insurance, higher unemployment will "automatically" be linked to more redistribution. The unemployment figures are standardized rates from OECD, *Labour Force Statistics* (various years).

Real per capita income. This variable is a standard control to capture "Wagner's law," which says that demand for social insurance is income elastic and, therefore, will tend to raise spending and redistribution. The data are expressed in constant 1985 dollars and are from the World Bank's Global Development Network Growth Database (*http://www.worldbank.org/research/growth/GDNdata.htm*) – itself based on *Penn World Table*, *Global Development Finance*, and *World Development* Indicators.

Female labor force participation. Women's participation in the job market varies considerably across countries and time, and it is likely that such participation matters for redistribution because it entitles some women to benefits (unemployment insurance, health insurance, etc.) that they would otherwise not get. Whether this leads to more redistribution depends on the position of working women in the income distribution as well as their family status, but there is a common presumption that women are more likely to be in low-paid jobs and from low-income (single-parent) households. The measure is female labor force participation as a percentage of the working age population and is taken from OECD, *Labour Force Statistics* (various years).

4.5.3. Statistical Model

The starting point is a simple error correction model. In this model, current redistribution is equal to past redistribution plus a contribution from redistributive partisan policies that deviate from policies that would preserve the status quo level of redistribution:

$$R_{i,t} = \lambda \cdot [\alpha + \beta \cdot P_{i,t} - R_{t,t-1}] + R_{i,t-1} + u_{i,t}$$

where u is identically and independently distributed with mean 0 and variance s_u^2.

With the available data on redistribution, however, one cannot estimate this model directly because the observations on the dependent variable for each country are unequally spaced, varying between 2 and as many as 10 years. To deal with this problem, I use a modified version of the model where I substitute the preceding expression for $R_{i,t-1}$, $R_{i,t-2}$, and so on, until one gets to another observation of the lagged dependent variable. This procedure yields the following expression:

$$R_{i,t} = \lambda \cdot \alpha \cdot \sum_{s=0}^{N} (1 - \lambda)^s + \lambda \cdot \beta \cdot \sum_{s=0}^{N} (1 - \lambda)^s \cdot P_{i,t-s}$$

$$+ (1 - \lambda)^{N+1} \cdot R_{i,t-N+1} + \sum_{s=0}^{N} (1 - \lambda)^s \cdot u_{i,t-s}$$

or

$$R_{i,t} - (1 - \lambda)^{N+1} \cdot R_{i,t-N+1}$$

$$= \lambda \cdot \alpha \cdot \sum_{s=0}^{N} (1 - \lambda)^s + \lambda \cdot \beta \cdot \sum_{s=0}^{N} (1 - \lambda)^s \cdot P_{i,t-s} + \sum_{s=0}^{N} (1 - \lambda)^s \cdot u_{i,t-s}$$

The second term in the last expression is a measure of the cumulative effect of partisanship over a period of N years, where N is the gap between the current and previous observation. Of course, insofar as other variables affect redistribution, we need to calculate the cumulative effects of these in precisely the same manner as for partisanship. Because there are annual observations for partisanship and all control variables, the estimated model is based on complete time series except for the dependent variable. The model is estimated by choosing a value for λ that maximizes the explained variance.

Given the assumption that the composite errors are serially uncorrelated,[13] but because the error term depends on N, there is heteroscedasticity. To adjust for this, as well as contemporaneous correlation of errors, I use panel corrected standard errors as is common when analyzing pooled cross-sectional time-series data (see Beck and Katz 1995).

The model used to explain partisanship in the second part of the analysis is a simple ordinary least squares regression that is explained later.

4.5.4. Findings

4.5.4.1. Redistribution I begin the presentation with the results from estimating a simple baseline model with economic variables only (column 1 in Table 4.1). As expected, female labor force participation and

---

[13] $E(\sum_{s=1}^{N_1} [(1 - \lambda)^s u_{i,t-s}] \cdot \sum_{s=1}^{N_2} [(1 - \lambda)^s u_{i,t-(N_1+1)-s}]) = 0$ since the errors in the first square bracket run from $u_{i,t}$ to $u_{i,t-N_1}$ and in the second from $u_{i,t-(N_1+1)}$ to $u_{i,t-(N_1+1)-N_2}$.

Table 4.1. *Regression Results for Reduction in Inequality (standard errors in parentheses)*

	1	2
Inequality	−16.75***	8.94
	(5.68)	(7.87)
Political-institutional variables:		
Partisanship (right)	–	−9.63***
		(3.35)
Voter turnout	–	0.00
		(0.01)
Unionization	–	0.18**
		(0.08)
Number of veto points	–	−1.01*
		(0.58)
Vocational training	–	0.10***
		(0.03)
Controls:		
Per capita income	−0.0014***	−0.0005
	(0.0005)	(0.0006)
Female labor force participation	0.73***	0.39**
	(0.11)	(0.18)
Unemployment	0.81***	0.90***
	(0.27)	(0.26)
λ	.4	.7
Adjusted R-squared	0.61	0.73
N	47	47

Significance levels: *** <.01; ** <.05; * <.10 (two-tailed tests).
Note: All independent variables are measures of the cumulative effect of these variables between observations on the dependent variable. See regression equation and text for details.

unemployment are associated with more redistribution. Contrary to Wagner's law, higher per capita income slightly reduces redistribution. With the exception of unemployment, none of these effects are robust across model specifications.

As in other studies, I also find that inequality of pretax and transfer income has a *negative* effect on redistribution, contrary to the theoretical expectation of Meltzer and Richard. This negative effect is statistically significant at a .01 level, and the substantive impact is also strong; a 1-standard-deviation increase in inequality is associated with a 0.3-standard-deviation reduction in redistribution.

Model 2 introduces five political-institutional variables: government partisanship, voter turnout, unionization, veto points, and vocational training. All variables carry the expected sign, and all but voter turnout have statistically significant effects. The effects of partisanship and vocational training are the strongest both substantively and statistically. Thus, a 1-standard-deviation change in either partisanship or vocational training is associated with a 0.25-standard-deviation reduction in redistribution.

Another notable change in moving from the baseline model to the full model is that the effect of inequality *reverses* (though the positive effect is not significant). One likely reason for this change is that left governments (and strong unions) not only increase redistribution but also reduce inequality. For example, partisan differences in educational policies are likely to have an effect on before tax and transfer inequality. If so, excluding partisanship produces an omitted variable bias on the coefficient for inequality.

Such a bias may also be caused by other variables. Experimentation with including one variable at a time shows that vocational training and the number of veto points also contribute to the shift in the sign for the inequality variable. In the case of vocational training, the likely reason is that emphasis on specific skills simultaneously produces a more compressed skill and wage structure *and* increases electoral support for spending. Similarly, multiple veto points are likely to impede policies to both redistribute and reduce inequality, thereby contributing to a negative sign on inequality when the veto points variable is excluded. Obviously, these conjectures need to be substantiated by further empirical analysis. For my purposes, the key result is the one for partisanship, which is strong and consistent across model specifications. This finding is largely confirmation of previous research, especially Bradley et al. (in press).

To check the robustness of the results, I also estimated the model using reduction in the poverty rate instead of reduction in the Gini coefficient as the dependent variable. Redistribution in the poverty rate is the percentage change in the share of families below 50 percent of the median income, from before to after taxes and transfers. The results by and large confirm those in Table 4.1. Partisanship and vocational training continue to be the strongest predictors (and significant at a .01 level). However, the effect of turnout is now significant, while the sign on unionization turns negative and is borderline significant. Some of the negative effect of inequality also remains after inclusion of all controls. Clearly, one must be cautious interpreting the effect of inequality given how unstable it is across measures and model specifications.

4.5.4.2. Partisanship While government partisanship is important in explaining redistribution, partisanship itself is a function of coalitional politics, which is shaped by the electoral system. A key implication of the argument is that center-left governments tend to dominate over long periods of time under PR, whereas center-right governments tend to dominate under majoritarianism. Put differently, partisanship is the mechanism through which electoral systems exert an effect on redistribution.

To test this implication, I use the partisan center of gravity (CoG) index as a dependent variable and indicators for party and electoral systems as independent variables. There are data for eighteen countries that have been democracies since the Second World War, beginning with the first democratic election after the war and ending in 1998. One country – Switzerland – has a collective executive that prevents coalition politics from having any influence on the composition of the government. I, therefore, exclude this case from the analysis, although every result reported in this section holds even when Switzerland is included.

In the theoretical analysis, a distinction was made between majoritarian two-party systems and proportional multiparty systems. In the former, only one party can win the election, which determines who forms government, whereas in the latter no party can form the government without the support of one or more other parties. The distinction underscores the importance of whether governments are formed through postelection coalitions or as direct outcomes of elections. Yet, in practice, the dichotomy is complicated by the fact that voters' expectations about government formation affect the partisan distribution of support. Where a single party can reasonably be expected to form a government alone, the model implies that strategic voting will favor the right and, thus, government composition, *even* if the government is ultimately formed as a coalition. One, therefore, cannot simply look at the number of parties in government at any given moment in time but must take into account the institutionally mediated expectations of voters.

There are no direct measures of voter expectations, but we do know the nature of national electoral systems, which are distinguished in the first column of Table 4.2. The strategy is simply to link electoral rules to the expectation voters can reasonably be assumed to have concerning the nature of the government formation process. With the possible exception of Austria (because of the strong position of the two main parties), all PR systems clearly give rise to expectations of governments based on support from more than one party. This is not the case in any of the non-PR systems,

155

Table 4.2. *Key Indicators of Party and Electoral Systems*

		Electoral System	Expectation That Single-Party Government Forms without Need for Third-Party Support	Effective Number of Legislative Parties	Proportionality of Electoral System
Majoritarian	Australia	Majoritarity[a]	Yes	2.5	0.19
	Canada	SMP	Yes	2.2	0.13
	France	Run-off[b]	Yes	3.8	0.16
	Ireland	STV[c]	Ambiguous	2.8	0.70
	Japan	SNTV[d]	Yes	2.7	0.61
	New Zealand	SMP	Yes	2.0	0.00
	United Kingdom	SMP	Yes	2.1	0.16
	United States	SMP	Yes	1.9	0.39
	Average			*2.5*	*0.30*
Proportional	Austria	PR	Ambiguous	2.4	0.89
	Belgium	PR	No	5.2	0.86
	Denmark	PR	No	4.4	0.96
	Finland	PR	No	5.1	0.87
	Germany	PR	No	2.6	0.91
	Italy	PR	No	4.0	0.91
	Netherlands	PR	No	4.6	1.00
	Norway	PR	No	3.3	0.76
	Sweden	PR	No	3.3	0.90
	Average			*3.9*	*0.90*

[a] The use of the single transferable vote in single-member constituencies makes the Australian electoral system a majority rather than plurality system.

[b] The two-round run-off system has been in place for most of the postwar period with short interruptions of PR (1945 until early 1950s and 1986–8).

[c] The Irish single transferable vote system (STV) is unique. Although sometimes classified as a PR system, the low constituency size (five or less) and the strong centripetal incentives for parties in the system makes it similar to a median voter-dominated SMP system.

[d] The single nontransferable voting (SNTV) in Japan (until 1994) deviates from SMP in that more than one candidate is elected from each district, but small district size and nontransferability make it clearly distinct from PR list systems.

although Australia and Ireland *have* experienced several instances of coalition governments. Ireland is perhaps the most ambiguous case, but the inclusion or exclusion of these cases makes little difference to the results.

The division into PR and majoritarian systems is buttressed by quantitative measures of party and electoral systems. First, countries with

Table 4.3. *Electoral System and the Number of Years with Left and Right Governments, 1945–1998*

| | | Government Partisanship | | Proportion of |
		Left	Right	Right Governments
	Proportional	342	120	0.26
Electoral system		(8)	(1)	
	Majoritarian	86	256	0.75
		(0)	(8)	

Note: Excludes centrist governments (see text for details).

majoritarian systems tend to have fewer parties than countries with PR systems. This is indicated in the third column of Table 4.2 using Laasko and Taagepera's (1979) measure of the effective number of parties in parliament.[14] France is somewhat of an outlier, but at least in presidential elections the second round of voting in the French run-off system typically involves only candidates from two parties.

The second quantitative indicator, the proportionality of the electoral system, is a composite index of two widely used indices of electoral system. One is Lijphart's measure of the effective threshold of representation based on national election laws. It indicates the actual threshold of electoral support that a party must get in order to secure representation. The other is Gallagher's measure of the disproportionality between votes and seats, which is an indication of the extent to which smaller parties are being represented at their full strength. Both indicators were standardized to have a mean of 0 and a standard deviation of 1 before averaged into an index that varies from low proportionality (0) to high proportionality (1). The data are from Lijphart (1994).

The proportionality index is consistent with the division into a majoritarian and a proportional group. There are no cases that should be "switched" based on their value on the index, although Ireland and Japan have relatively high scores among the majoritarian countries. Coupled with the other information in Table 4.2, the dichotomus division of countries into two types, thus, seems reasonable.

Table 4.3 is a simple cross-tabulation of electoral system and government partisanship using annual observations as the unit of analysis (the table is

[14] The effective number of parties is defined as one divided by the sum of the square root of the shares of seats held by different parties (or one divided by the Hilferding index).

157

identical to Table 1.2, but reproduced here for convenience). Governments are coded as being left-of-center if their position on the composite left–right index is to the left of the overall mean. This is somewhat arbitrary because the mean may not correspond to a centrist position. An alternative would be to define the center as the middle of the scale. But in two of the three expert surveys, the middle of the scale is not explicitly defined as centrist in terms of a common standard, and experts may well equate it instead with the *observed* center of a party system, whether or not this center is shifted to the left or right. In practice, the choice has little effect on the results.

Identifying a centrist position, however, is important for a different reason. If a CL leadership party in a majoritarian system is centrist, then the model implies that it stands a good chance of winning. Observing such a party in government is therefore consistent with the model. At the same time, it cannot be counted as confirmatory evidence because we do not have any measure to determine whether the party platform is credible. The relative frequency of center and center-right governments therefore cannot be hypothesized a priori. Moreover, because the theory implies that the political space in majoritarian systems is tilted to the right (owing to strategic voting in a setting of incomplete platform commitment), *if* we include governments that are centrist in an absolute sense, these would be counted as center-left in terms of their relative position. Using a scale such as the composite CoG index, the results would therefore be biased against the theory because the center on this scale is almost certainly affected by relative assessments. The solution is to use one of the component measures in the CoG index by Castles and Mair to exclude governments that are centrist in the absolute sense. The Castles-Mair measure is the only one that explicitly defines the middle value (3) as a party having a centrist left–right ideology. An alternative strategy of measuring the left–right leanings of governments against the position of the median legislator is discussed later in this chapter.

Only one country, Germany, does not conform to the predicted pattern. In this case, there were 34 years with center-right governments and only 16 years with center-left governments. There is an interesting potential explanation for this. If a center-right party can appeal to voters on grounds other than class, especially religion, and thereby capture some support among middle- and lower-income people, such a party can credibly claim to be closer to the center than when it represents only high-income voters. This makes the party a more attractive coalition partner for center parties. This could be why the small pivotal liberal party (FDP) for most of the postwar period chose to ally with the Christian Democratic Party (CDU/CSU) instead of the Social Democratic Party (SPD). The resulting equilibrium is still heavily influenced by PR because the right must be moderate and prepared to accept some redistribution. The space is thus shifted to the left compared to majoritarian systems. But it does produce less redistribution than in a typical PR system based entirely on class.

Germany aside, it can be objected to the evidence in Table 4.3 that it does not take into account that the left–right balance of governments is also affected by the left–right balance of power in the legislature. It may be that whole electorates are shifted to the left or right for reasons that are outside the model and that this, not party politics, explains why the composition of the government varies across countries. Note again, however, that the theoretical model implies strategic voting in majoritarian systems that *does* shift the legislative center to the right. Also, the distribution of seats in PR systems does not matter in principle as long as coalitions that are either to the left or to the right of the center can be formed. Still, we cannot exclude the possibility that the distribution of *prestrategic* voter preferences differs across countries and affects government partisanship.

To test the possibility, I computed the position of the median legislator, defined as the left–right location of the median legislative party. If policies were decided by majority voting, not bargaining, the preference of the median party would be the Condorcet winner. I therefore calculated the difference between the government position, as measured by the CoG index, and the position of the median party in the legislature. Governments to the left of the median are called center-left; governments to the right, center-right. This procedure, however, does not work for single-party governments with a majority in the legislature. If the Conservatives in Britain control government power, for example, they will also command a majority in the lower house. In such instances, the median in the legislature will be identical to the government's position. Yet, clearly, the government can still sensibly be counted as either left or right. In these cases, I therefore compared the government position to the *average* of party position, in the legislature, weighted by the parties' share of seats. The results are reported in Table 4.4

As one would expect, the results are somewhat weaker than in Table 4.1, yet they are entirely consistent with these. About two thirds of governments under PR are to the left of the legislative median, whereas two thirds of governments under majoritarian institutions are to the right. All but one country conforms to this pattern. The "outlier" is no longer Germany

Table 4.4. *Electoral System and the Number of Years with Governments Farther to the Left or to the Right Than the Median Legislator, 1945–1998*

		Government Partisanship		Proportion of Right Governments
		Left	Right	
Electoral system	Proportional	291	171	0.37
		(9)	(0)	
	Majoritarian	116	226	0.66
		(1)	(7)	

Note: Excludes governments coded as centrist on the Castles-Mair scale.

because most governments were in fact to the left of the median, even as they tended to be right compared to other PR systems. Instead, the deviant case is France where twenty-nine of fifty-two observations are to the left of the legislative median. But this is hardly disconfirming evidence since the government CoG is based on the distribution of cabinet portfolios, which in the French system is decided through coalition bargaining between parties in the National Assembly. Clearly, such a system does not preclude governments forming to the left of the median – indeed, we should expect it. The French president, on the other hand, is chosen through a two-candidate contest (barring an outright majority in the first round), and here the argument implies that the center-right will win more of the time. This has indeed been the case (the sole exception is the Socialist Presidency of Mitterran). Hence, if the position of the presidential party were used instead of the CoG cabinet measure, the results would clearly support the argument. Also note that because French political parties take policy positions that are at least partly adopted with an eye to winning the presidency, the rightist bias in the presidential election will also tilt the legislature to the right. This is why France conforms to the predicted when we use the absolute CoG measure (Table 4.1).

What alternative explanations might there be for the pattern observed in Table 4.4? Because I use the difference between the position of the government and the median legislator, I have limited such alternatives to variables that affect the *postelection* partisan composition of governments. I thus implicitly "control" for all variables that may affect the left–right balance in the legislature. Although there are obviously a plethora of situationally specific factors that shape each instance of government formation, variables that would *systematically* bias the composition of governments in one ideological direction or the other are in fact not easy to think of.

One important exception is the extent of party fractionalization on either side of the center. Where the left (right) is relatively more divided than the right (left), we would expect government formation between left (right) parties to be more complicated under PR rules. Similarly, as argued by Powell (2002), we would expect such fragmentation to produce more electoral defeats under majoritarian rules. If so, this could confound the relationship between electoral system and government partisanship. Specifically, Rokkan (1970) and Boix (1999) have argued that at the time of the extension of the franchise, when a united right faced a rising but divided left, the governing right chose to retain majoritarian institutions. Conversely, when a divided right faced a rising and united left, the response was to opt for PR. If this pattern of fractionalization persisted in the postwar period, the right would tend to have an advantage in majoritarian systems, whereas the left would tend to have an advantage under PR. This is precisely the pattern that our model predicts, but for different reasons.

Testing this alternative requires us to use multiple regression. Because there is little meaningful variance in electoral systems over time, I ran a simple cross-sectional regression on the averages from 1950 to 1996 (for which complete data exist on several control variables). The results are shown in Table 4.5. The fractionalization variable is the difference between party fractionalization on the left and right, where fractionalization is defined as one minus the sum of the squared seat shares held by parties to the left or to the right of center (Rae 1967).

As expected, both electoral system (PR) and fractionalization on the left significantly reduce the likelihood of getting a government that is to the left of the legislative median, and both effects remain when the variables are entered simultaneously (column 3). In substantive terms, going from a majoritarian to a PR system reduces the predicted center of gravity of the government by 0.15 (relative to the legislative median). This difference is roughly equivalent to the difference between a typical social democratic and a typical Christian democratic government, or between the latter and a typical conservative government. Another way to convey the finding is that the effect is roughly equal to a one standard deviation on the government CoG variable – a large impact by any standard. The effect of a one-standard-deviation increase in left fractionalization is about one third of this effect. Note also that including both variables simultaneously does not notably affect the estimated parameter for electoral system.

Table 4.5. *Regression Results for Government Partisanship, 1950–1996 (standard errors in parentheses)*

	(1) Government CoG Minus Legislative Median	(2) Government CoG Minus Legislative Median	(3) Government CoG Minus Legislative Median	(4) Government CoG	(5) Government CoG
Constant	0.653*** (0.039)	0.593*** (0.031)	0.664*** (0.033)	0.163*** (0.018)	−0.085 (0.529)
Electoral system (PR)	−0.173*** (0.054)	–	−0.147*** (0.047)	−0.202*** (0.050)	−0.242*** (0.086)
Fragmentation (left minus right)	–	0.303** (0.115)	−0.241** (0.094)	0.159 (0.099)	0.011 (0.171)
Electoral participation	–	–	–	–	0.007 (0.006)
Unionization	–	–	–	–	−0.005 (0.004)
Female labor force participation	–	–	–	–	0.007 (0.005)
Adjusted R-squared	0.37	0.27	0.54	0.56	0.54
N	17	17	17	17	17

Significance levels: *** < .01; ** < .05; * < .10 (two-tailed tests).

In column (4), I use the absolute government CoG measure as the dependent variable. The effect of left fractionalization on this measure is weaker and no longer statistically significant. The effect of electoral system, however, increases, mirroring the observed differences in strength between the results presented in columns (1) and (4). This continues to be the case if we control for other variables that may reasonably be expected to affect the political center (column 5). Predictably, high unionization rates are associated with most left-leaning governments, but the effect is weak and statistically insignificant. Electoral participation and female labor force participation do not have the effects one might have predicted, but, again, the coefficients are not significantly different from zero. The only strong predictor continues to be the electoral system, and the fact that the effect is stronger than when using the position of the government relative to the median suggests that the electoral system affects not only government formation but also the center of the political space.

4.6. Conclusion

This chapter has explored an overlooked problem in the politics of social policy making: The inability of current voters to commit future voters to particular policies, even when these policies are in their common interest. This time-inconsistency problem is particularly notable in the area of social insurance because those who are pivotal in electoral politics ("the median voters") tend to be employed and unlikely to benefit from social spending, except at some time in the future when they will no longer be pivotal. The implication of this problem is a serious underprovision of social protection compared to (long-term) voter preferences. And that in turn undermines the institutional foundations for specific skills systems, including coordinated wage bargaining and well-functioning vocational training systems.

There are two related solutions to the problem. One is disciplined and responsible parties with close ties to private groups representing workers with specific skills. If parties offer a set of public goods that cannot be provided efficiently without support from private actors – a vocational training system, for example, requires information and sponsorship by unions and employer associations to work efficiently, and incomes policies cannot succeed without the cooperation of workers and their unions – the groups whose cooperation is required can gain influence over policy. In the institutionalized party model, resources come in the form of "fees" to political parties, broadly conceived, that are exchanged for influence over party platforms and leadership selection. When the incentives of party leaders to defect are not too great, as may be the case in winner-take-all electoral systems, party organization can alleviate the time-inconsistency problem.

The second institutional mechanism is electoral systems and the distributive politics to which they give rise. Redistributive transfers not only shift income between groups but also provide insurance against income loss in the event of unemployment, sickness, and so on (Moene and Wallerstein 2001). Insofar as there is a strategic complementarity between such insurance and individuals' decisions to invest in particular types of skills, the ability of the government to credibly commit to redistributive spending serves as insurance against the loss of income when specific skills are rendered obsolete by technological and other forces of change. Because PR promotes left party dominance and redistribution, it serves as a key commitment mechanism in political economies that depend on workers making heavy investments in highly specific skills. It is probably no accident, therefore, that PR and vocational training are highly correlated $(r = .7)$.

The key insight of this analysis is that political institutions – the electoral system and political party organizations – support, and are being supported by, economic as well as social institutions. Although the historical interplay between these institutions is a major topic for future research, the clustering into two institutional configurations – one characterized by PR, disciplined and responsible parties, generous welfare states, and specific skills production and the other by majoritarianism, leadership-dominated parties, small welfare states, and general skills – should not come as a surprise. They reflect, in Hall and Soskice's (2001), conceptional framework, extensive institutional complementarities.

Appendix 4.A: Mathematical Proofs for the Party Institutionalization Model

Definition of Utility Functions

The Group Utility Function   Given that platforms are chosen behind the veil, if the employed group member receives a pretax income of 1, then the expected utility of an individual is at $\tau = 0$ *before* the individual knows whether or not he is unemployed. Compared to the group utility function there is no probability of unemployment.

$$\overline{V}_0 \equiv \sum_{\tau=0}^{\infty} \delta^\tau \left[(1 - p) \cdot \log(1 - t_\tau + \alpha(s \cdot a_\tau - c(a_\tau))) \right.$$
$$\left. + p \cdot \log(t_\tau \cdot (1 - p)/p + \alpha(s \cdot a_\tau - c(a_\tau)) - \gamma(s)) \right] \qquad (A4.1)$$

where $\delta \in [0, 1]$ is the discount factor and where $u(x)$ is the utility derived from net receipts (income or unemployment benefit), as before. The negative skill-specificity contingent cost $\gamma(s)$ is incurred in the event of unemployment because it is harder for those with more specific skills to find jobs that are suitable to their skills. $\gamma(s)$, in other words, can be conceived as a *search cost*.

164

The Median Voter Utility Function The preferences of s_m, the median employed voter, *after the veil has been raised*, are given by

$$V_{sm} = \log(1 - t + \alpha(s_m a - \bar{c})) \tag{A4.2}$$

where $\bar{c}$ is whatever contributions the median voter has already paid to one or the other of the two parties; since that has already been paid, it will not influence his or her vote.

The Condition for Party Leader Cooperation in Stage ii of Game

The condition for party leader cooperation is derived as follows. The base can observe if the leader sets the nominated platform t_L or not, but the leader may not always have the power to set t_L and may instead be forced to set a lower tax rate of $t_L - \bar{\varepsilon}$ (because of, say, an unexpected recession). If the base observes the platform $t_L - \bar{\varepsilon}$, it does not know whether the leader has been forced to choose this platform or whether the leader has done it deliberately to undercut the other party's platform and win the election.

Concretely assume there is a random variable $\varepsilon_i = \{0, \bar{\varepsilon}\}$, $i = L, H$; only the leader i knows the value of ε_i. A leader then has two possible strategies: Cooperate with the party base by always setting $t = t_i - \varepsilon_i$ or defect by setting $t = t_i - \bar{\varepsilon}$. Assuming the other leader opts for a cooperative strategy, how high does $1 - q$ (the probability of non-reelection) have to be to ensure that leader i cooperates? The answer is given by the following inequality:

$$(1 - q_{\Re}) \geq \frac{r \cdot (1 - \lambda)}{\lambda} \cdot \frac{B(s)/2}{B(s)/2 + L(s)} \tag{A4.3}$$

where r is the probability that the random variables take the values $(0, 0)$. From this follows the substantive interpretation of the condition provided in the body of the text.

Proof of (A4.3). Let V be the present value of the maximum utility for a reselected politician at the start of the current period. Because the game is stationary, we have

$$B \cdot [q^2/2 + q \cdot (1 - q) + (1 - q)^2/2] + L + \lambda V$$
$$\geq B \cdot [q^2 + q \cdot (1 - q)/2 + q \cdot (1 - q) + (1 - q)^2/2] + L + \lambda \gamma V \tag{A4.4}$$

The left-hand side is the present value of cooperation: q^2 is the probability that the random variables take the values $(0, 0)$, and $\frac{1}{2}$ is the probability of the leader winning in that case, and so on. The right-hand side is the present value of defection: Thus, when the random variables take the values $(0, 0)$ with probability q^2, the leader sets the platform $t = t_i - \bar{\varepsilon}$ and thus wins with probability 1 and so on. In both cases, the other leader pursues the cooperative strategy. Because the square-bracketed term on the left-hand side is $\frac{1}{2}$ and that on the right-hand side is $(1 + q)/2$, this implies

$$\lambda \cdot (1 - \gamma)V \geq q\,B/2 \tag{A4.5a}$$

We also have from the left-hand side

$$V = B/2 + L + \lambda V = (B/2 + L)/(1 - \lambda) \tag{A4.5b}$$

which together imply Equation (A4.3). Q.E.D.

The relation between s and the probability of dismissal can likewise be deduced from this equation. We have

$$\frac{\partial \ln B}{\partial \ln s} > \frac{\partial \ln L}{\partial \ln s} \Leftrightarrow \frac{\partial (1 - \gamma)}{\partial s} > 0 \tag{A4.6}$$

which is assumed to hold in (A4.3). Thus, as the level of specific assets of the median voter in the party base grows, so does the leader's punishment for not following the party platform. This is the key behavioral mechanism in this stage of the game because it implies that leaders in H parties will go along with higher rates of taxation than leaders in L parties. Given that the leader incentives to defect are known to the groups who propose platforms, it is assumed in the following that the platforms chosen by the groups satisfy the constraint in (A4.3).[15]

Derivation of Equation (4.5) in Stage i of Game

Assuming that t_τ and a_τ have the same values $\forall \tau = 0, \ldots, \infty$, we can find the utility-maximizing values, t^* and a^*, from Equation (4.4). For simplicity, define

$$c(a) \equiv -a^2/2 \tag{A4.7}$$

---

[15] In a more complete model, institutionalization would be determined endogenously as the outcome of a bargaining game over a and $(1 - \gamma)$. Yet, all that is needed for the logic of the argument to go through is that $(1 - \gamma)$ is a rising function of membership fees, $c(a)$, which are in turn rising in s. As long as $(1 - \gamma)$ is valuable to the group, and a is valuable to the party, this condition will hold in any reasonable bargaining game.

which yields the following optimal tax rate:

$$\frac{\partial \overline{V}_0}{\partial t} = -\frac{1-p}{1-t+\alpha(sa-a^2/2)}$$

$$+\frac{p}{(1-p)t/p+\alpha(sa-a^2/2)-\gamma(s)}\cdot\frac{1-p}{p}=0$$

$$\Rightarrow p\cdot(1-t)=(1-p)\cdot t-\gamma(s)$$

$$\Rightarrow t^*(s)=p\cdot(1+\gamma(s)) \tag{A4.8}$$

which is equivalent to Equation (4.5).

To find a^*, it is assumed, without serious loss of generality, that $\gamma(s) = s/2$. It follows that

$$\frac{\partial \overline{V}_0}{\partial a} = s-a=0 \Rightarrow a^*(s)=s \tag{A4.9}$$

so that the preferred level of a rises in s.

The resulting equilibrium is robust to the possibility of third-party entry as shown later. However, depending on the values of s_{ML} and s_{MH} compared to the median voter, the median voter may always prefer one party over the other. For the losing party to avoid this, it would have to adjust the nominated platform so that it had an equal chance of winning. Such a "contingency" requirement would still produce a subgame perfect equilibrium. More importantly, this is a problem that arises only in majoritarian systems, and it is not endemic to the time-inconsistency problem.[16]

Proof That No Third Party Will Enter

The model equilibrium of the model is robust to the possibility of third-party entry. Such entry will happen if the entrant can win outright. The median voter will prefer a new entrant with a platform of $t = a = 0$ to the platform of the L or H parties unless:

$$\log(1-\overline{c}) \le \log(1-p\cdot(1+s_{ML}/2)+\alpha s_M s_{ML}-\overline{c})$$

where the left-hand side of the inequality is the payoff from the new entrant's platform with a zero tax rate and level of a, and the right-hand side is the

---

[16] Alternatively, one can allow uncertainty about the election outcome. If parties seek to maximize expected policy outcomes, party platforms will diverge (Whitman 1973).

payoff from the platform of the L party. This inequality implies that there is a level of s_M below which a new entrant will enter; this is given implicitly by

$$s_M^2 - s_M \left(\frac{\alpha L + 2}{\alpha 4} \right) > \left(p - \frac{L}{8} \right) \alpha^{-1}$$

Taking a Taylor expansion of the left-hand side around implies

$$s_M > \frac{1}{2} + \frac{8p - L}{\alpha L + 2}$$

This says that (i) the larger p is, the higher the tax rate will be and, therefore, the greater s_M will have to be for this to be compensated by the public good (the value of which increases with s_M; (ii) the larger α is, the smaller s_M can be consistently with the new entrant being kept out because the greater is the value of the public good. This is a critical condition because its failure to hold means that an institutional party system – even with relatively low degrees of institutionalization – will cease to be viable. Still, it is clear that it is perfectly possible to have two parties that set tax rates above zero, despite the ability of new entrants to enter and do so. Under many circumstances, if they did enter, they would not win.

Appendix 4.B: Proof That the Win-set of m^* Is Empty

Refer to Figure A4.1. The transfer g is on the horizontal axis, and the tax t is on the vertical axis. The indifference curves for L and H are drawn through $m^* = \{g, t\} = \{0, 0.5\}$, the median voter's ideal point. The relevant indifference curve of L, $u_L(m^*)$, is downward sloping with a gradient of -1. That of H, $u_H(m^*)$, is downward sloping with a gradient of $-(1 + \alpha)(1 - \varepsilon) \cdot u_H(m^*)$ that is steeper than $u_L(m^*)$ if $\alpha > \varepsilon/(1 - \varepsilon)$, which is assumed to be the case. Utility for L improves in a northeasterly direction with increasing g and t; for H the opposite is the case. Thus, it can be seen that the LH win-set of m^* is empty so that no alternative platform will attract the votes for both L and H. Hence, m^* is the Condorcet winner.

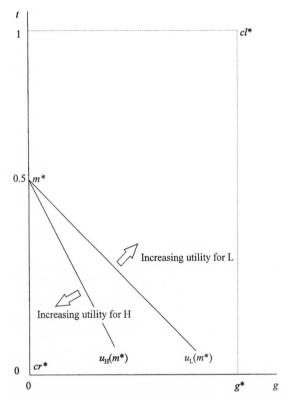

Figure A4.1 The indifference curves for L and H and the empty LH win-set of m^*.

Appendix 4.C: Rubinstein Bargaining Solution for *LM* and *MH* Coalitions

LM Coalition

The Rubinstein solution is derived in the absence of outside options. The bargaining over t ranges from $\frac{1}{2}$ to 1 and the bargain over g ranges from 0 to g^*. The normalized utility functions for L and M can be written as

$$\hat{u}_L = u_L(t, g) - u_L(.5, 0) = t + g - 0.5$$

and

$$\hat{u}_M = u_M(t) - u_M(1) = -|t - 0.5| + |0.5|$$

169

In the following proof it is assumed that $\varepsilon = 0$, but the result holds for small enough ε.[17] Two conditions need to be satisfied in a multidimensional bargain (Kreps, 1990, p. 561, Proposition 2): First, L's offer to M must be worth at least as much to M now as M's offer to L next period will be worth to M now:

$$\hat{u}m(t^L) = \delta \cdot \hat{u}m(t^M) \qquad (A4.10)$$

This implies

$$-|t^L - 0.5| + 0.5 = -\delta|t^M - 0.5| + 0.5\delta$$
$$\Rightarrow t^L = (1 - \delta) + \delta t^M$$

And, second, M's offer to L must be worth at least as much to L now as L's offer to M next period will be worth to L now:

$$\hat{u}_L(t^M, g^M) = \delta \cdot \hat{u}_L(t^L, g^L) \qquad (A4.11)$$

which implies

$$t^M + g^M - 0.5 = \delta \cdot (t^L + g^M - 0.5)$$

Solving for t^M in terms of g^M and g^L gives

$$t^M = \frac{1 + 0.5\delta}{1 + \delta} - \frac{(\delta g^M - \delta^2 g^L)}{(1 - \delta) \cdot (1 + \delta)}$$

As $\delta \to 1$, so the difference between first and second mover offers goes to zero, so that

$$t = 0.75 - g/2 \qquad (A4.12)$$

(A4.12) is a necessary condition for the unique subgame perfect equilibrium (SGPE) of this bargaining game. If (A4.12) is substituted into $\hat{u}_M$ and $\hat{u}_L$ so that both are functions of g alone, the assumption of Pareto optimality implies that g is maximized so that

$$t_{LM} = 0.75 - g^*/2$$

---

[17] Follow the proof through using $\hat{u}_M = -|t - 0.5| + |1 - 0.5| + (1 + \alpha)\varepsilon(g^* - g)$. This generates the necessary condition $t = 0.75 - g/2 + (1 + \alpha) \cdot \varepsilon \cdot (g^* - g)/2$. The condition for $\partial \hat{u}_M / \partial g > 0$ is $\varepsilon < 1/(1 + \alpha)$.

MH Coalition

Bargaining is over t in the range $[0, 0.5]$. It is in the common interest of both parties to agree on $g = 0$. The normalized utility functions are $\hat{u}_M = -|t - 0.5|$ and $\hat{u}_H = -t$. The conditions for a SGPE are

$$-|t^H - 0.5| = -\delta|t^M - 0.5| \tag{A4.13}$$

and

$$-t^M = -\delta t^H \tag{A4.14}$$

and these imply

$$t^H = 0.5/(1 + \delta) \tag{A4.15}$$

or as $\delta \to 1$, $t_{HM} \to 0.25$.

Can H break an LM coalition by offering M a deal that is closer to M's ideal policy? Figure A4.2 shows the argument that it cannot as an extensive game with complete and perfect information. Without serious loss

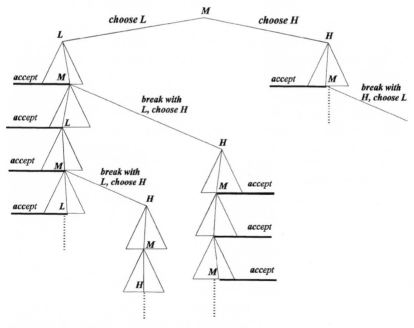

Figure A4.2 The structure of the coalition game.

of generality, M is charged with coalition formation (the decision node at the top of the game) and can either choose L or H to enter into coalition bargaining.[18] Suppose M chooses L. At that point, a Rubinstein-type alternative offers infinite-move bargaining, and the subgame begins. During the subgame, there is a discount factor, δ^s, attached to the payoff after s bargaining rounds. Without significant loss of generality, it is assumed that the party to whom the proposal is made has the first move. Thus, we are at the top-left L decision node. It is assumed that $g = g^*$ as part of the ML bargaining[19] so that the bargaining subgame entails alternating offers of the tax rate. Starting with L's first move, the closed interval of possible tax rates, $t \, \varepsilon \, [0, 1]$, is given by the base line of the triangle at the apex, which is L's decision node. L's choice of a tax rate offer is indicated by a line from L's decision node to the base of the triangle. M now has the move and three alternatives: (1) to accept L's offer, in which case the game ends and an ML coalition is established with $g = g^*$ and the tax rate being that offered by L; (2) to reject L's offer and to make a counteroffer to L (the line from M's decision node down to the base of the triangle); or (3) to break off negotiations with L and enter into negotiations with H. If (2), L can then choose whether to accept M's offer, so that the game ends, or to reject it and make a counteroffer. M again has the threefold options of acceptance, of rejection and making a new offer, or of breaking off negotiations with L. And so on. It is assumed that whenever the game ends with the establishment of a coalition, a discount factor δ^S is applied to the utility of the parties where S is the number of bargaining rounds that have elapsed.

It is further assumed, realistically, that if M enters into and then breaks a coalition, M incurs a cost of $C > 0$. This cost can be interpreted as a transaction cost of negotiations after they have started, or it can be interpreted as the cost of breaking up a coalition government after it has formed. The key is that negotiators can anticipate that M cannot defect with impunity from a coalition that it has agreed to enter into. Coalition breakups are accompanied by discord and put on public display the inability of parties to bargain and govern effectively. Whatever the magnitude of the cost, *any* positive cost of breaking off negotiations will prevent H from underbidding a coalition of L and M that is based on a Rubinstein solution.

[18] Again for simplicity, it is assumed that parties do not reject an offer of coalition bargaining.

[19] Which implies from the solution to the Rubinstein subgame that the equilibrium tax rate will be lower (in M's favor).

For simplicity, also assume that M can only break off negotiations once. If M, for instance, breaks off negotiations with L, then M must continue bargaining with H until a coalition agreement has been reached. In fact, the results go through in a model in which M can break off negotiations an infinite number of times, so long as C is strictly positive and incurred on each break-off situation. The proof is available from the authors on request.

The subgame perfect equilibrium can be worked out through backward induction.

1. The SGPE solution to the bargaining subgame between M and L, *absent* M's outside option of breaking off negotiations and switching to negotiate with H, is for L at its first move to offer $t = 0.75 - g^*/2$ to M and for M to accept this offer, as δ goes to unity. This is the standard Rubinstein result (see Appendix 4.A).

2. Similarly, the SGPE solution to the bargaining subgame between M and H as a result of M breaking with L is $t = 0.25$, as δ goes to unity.

3. The SGPE of the bargaining subgame between M and L, *including* M's outside option to switch to bargaining with H is the same as the solution without the outside option (i.e., that in step 1). This follows from a minor modification of Proposition 5.1 of Muthoo [1999]: If the value to M of the outside option is less than the value of the subgame without it, the outside option is irrelevant.

4. The SGPE of the bargaining subgame between M and H, *including* M's outside option to switch to bargaining with L requires us to evaluate the payoff to M if M responds to an offer by H by breaking negotiations and switching to L. From step 1, the outcome of the subsequent bargaining subgame between M and L is $t_{ML} = 0.75 - g^*/2$. However, this result can now be incurred only at a cost of C. H will therefore offer M a deal that is worse than $0.75\, t_{ML} = 0.75 - g^*/2$ by an amount equal to C, and M will accept this deal.

In combination, steps 1–4 imply that M chooses initially to negotiate with L. This is because an initial negotiation with L results in $u_M(t_{ML}, g^*)$ where $t_{ML} = 0.75 - g^*/2$ (from step 1), but an initial negotiation with H results in $u_M(t_{ML}, g^*) - C$ (from step 4). Hence, an ML coalition will result with $t_{ML} = .75 - g^*/2$ and $g = g^*$. The intuition is simple; because g falls disproportionately on H, M can use g as a bargaining chip in negotiations with L to get a better deal. Although H would then have an incentive to offer M an even better deal, after an HM coalition had formed, H would have an incentive to exploit its bargaining power to the point where the deal offered M was exactly the same as the one M could get from L *minus* the cost to M of breaking up the coalition. H, thus, faces a time-inconsistency problem, and M will, therefore, prefer L as the coalition partner.

Appendix 4.D: The Measurement of Party System Institutionalization

Centralized Parties

Carey and Shugart (1995) analyzed the conditions under which parties can control their candidates. Confirming a long-standing intuition among students of political parties, the incentives for politicians to campaign on the party platform is critically dependent on the ability of parties' to control politicians' reelection chances.

The best known means to accomplish such control is a closed party list system where a candidate's rank on the list determines that candidate's likelihood of reelection. In closed list systems like the Norwegian or the Swedish, failure to adhere to the party platform during or after the election can severely curtail a politician's reelection chances. In open list systems like the Finnish or the Dutch, the party controls who gets on the list, but voters can choose among the candidates on the list, thereby reducing the party's control over who gets elected. This furnishes politicians with a reason to take advantage of electoral opportunities even when these require them to deviate from the party platform. This problem, however, is magnified in systems with primaries, such as elections to the U.S. Congress, because political parties do not control who gets on the ballot. Politicians, thus, have incentives to run their campaigns with little regard for the party platform, although after the primaries are over and the candidates face an opponent from another party, the party label still carries some value. In an extreme electoral system like that of the Japanese before the reforms in 1994, even this incentive to use the party label is dissipated because an open nomination process is coupled with elections where candidates from the same party compete against each other for a single nontransferable

Table A4.1. *Electoral Systems and Incentives of Politicians to Campaign on the Party Platform*

Electoral System	Countries	Incentives to Campaign on Party Platform (rank score)
Closed list	Norway, Spain, Sweden	6
Flexible lists	Denmark, Germany, Greece, Italy, Austria, Belgium, Switzerland	5
Single member district plurality	Britain, Canada, New Zealand	4
Single member district majority with run-off	France	4
Open lists	Finland, Netherlands	4
Single transferable vote, party endorsements	Australia, Ireland	3
Primary system	United States	2
Single nontransferable vote, open endorsement	Japan (pre-1993)	1

Source: Adapted from Carey and Shugart (1995).

vote. Policy differentiation, not coordination, within the party is the result.

Table A4.1 shows the classification of electoral systems according to the incentives of politicians to campaign on the platform of their parties. Higher numbers indicate greater incentives to toe the party line. The classification follows Carey and Shugart's, with a few qualifications. First, Carey and Shugart only distinguish between open and closed list systems, but as Cox (1997) points out, many countries have "flexible" list systems where the voter can cast a vote for both individual candidates and for the list as a whole. In these systems, voters have some capacity to "break" the list, but the party retains considerable control over who receives the list votes and hence who gets elected (Cox 1997, p. 61). In practice, flexible list systems function very similarly to closed list systems, and they have been ranked just below closed list systems in terms of the incentives they create for politicians to campaign on a party platform as opposed to other appeals.

Second, it is not clear that open lists can be unambiguously ranked below single member plurality systems as Carey and Shugart (1995) do. Their justification for doing so is that the party in single member plurality (SMP) systems controls the list, whereas in open list systems the voter has discretion over who on the list is picked. Yet, in SMP systems the total

175

number of listed candidates is large – as large as the number of seats in the legislature if a party fields candidates in each district – and each candidate must appeal to local constituencies where strict adherence to the party platform is often not conducive to electoral success. By contrast, larger districts in open list systems create greater competition for a smaller number of nominations, thereby increasing the leverage of the party leadership. On the other hand, open list systems generate competition between candidates from a single party that are absent under SMP voting. It is unclear which of these effects dominates, and the two systems are, therefore, ranked similarly. The same has been done for run-off majority systems (France) because, as Carey and Shugart acknowledge, the incentives are only marginally different from SMP systems. The rest of the classification follows Carey and Shugart's scheme.

Corporatism

Turning to corporatism, by and large Schmitter's conceptualization is used, which includes (a) the capacity of interests groups to aggregate and articulate demands on behalf of their members and to implement policy commitments ("intermediation"), and (b) the extent to which there is coordination of demands between groups and political parties ("concertation"). In the theoretical model, corporatist intermediation refers to the capacity of groups to commit resources to parties, while concertation concerns the potential influence over party platforms. Specifically, a recent composite index developed by Siaroff (1998), which Lijphart (1999) considers to be the most encompassing in terms of my concerns with policy influence and capacity for implementation, is used. The index values are listed in Table A4.2 along with the electoral system numbers. To get a composite measure of party institutionalization, we simply add the two measures together after standardization (column 3).

Table A4.2. *Political Institutions and Capacity for Commitment*

	(1) Corporatism Index	(2) Incentives to Campaign on Party Platform	(3) Institutional Capacity for Commitment[a]
Norway	4.6	6.0	1.5
Sweden	4.5	6.0	1.5
Austria	4.4	5.0	1.4
Germany	3.6	5.0	1.3
Switzerland	4.0	5.0	1.3
Belgium	3.8	5.0	1.3
Denmark	3.9	5.0	1.3
Netherlands	3.8	4.0	1.2
Finland	4.0	4.0	1.2
Spain	1.8	6.0	1.1
Italy	2.0	5.0	1.0
France	2.0	4.0	0.9
United Kingdom	1.5	4.0	0.9
Canada	1.5	4.0	0.8
New Zealand	1.9	4.0	0.8
Australia	2.4	3.0	0.8
Ireland	2.1	3.0	0.7
Japan	3.8	1.0	0.7
United States	1.9	2.0	0.5

[a] Calculated as the sum of (1) and (2) after standardization.

Appendix 4E. Summary Statistics for Section 4.5.2

Table A4.3. *Country Means for Variables Used in Regression Analysis*

	Redistribution (% reduction in Gini coefficient)	Inequality (p90/p50 ratio)	Partisanship (left–right CoG index)	Voter Turnout (%)	Unionization (%)	Veto Points	Vocational Training (%)	Electoral System	Effective Number of Parties	Fragmentation	Per Capita Income (1985 dollars)	Female Labor Force Participation (%)	Unemployment (%)	Manufacturing Work Force (%)
Australia	23.97	1.70	0.59	84	46	3	0.9	0.20	2.5	−0.39	10,909	46	4.63	21
Austria	–	–	0.37	87	54	–	–	0.90	2.4	−0.18	8,311	51	2.76	26
Belgium	35.56	1.64	0.46	88	48	1	56.3	0.87	5.2	−0.34	8,949	43	7.89	23
Canada	21.26	1.82	0.45	68	30	2	4.6	0.14	2.2	0.18	11,670	48	6.91	18
Denmark	37.89	1.58	0.44	84	67	0	31.8	0.96	4.4	−0.40	9,982	63	6.83	24
Finland	35.17	1.68	0.37	79	53	1	32.9	0.87	5.1	−0.18	8,661	66	4.48	23
France	25.36	1.94	0.50	66	18	1	27.9	0.18	3.8	0.10	9,485	51	4.57	23
Germany	18.70	1.70	0.49	81	34	4	34.9	0.91	2.6	−0.13	9,729	51	4.86	29
Ireland	–	–	0.53	75	48	–	–	0.70	2.8	−0.33	5,807	37	9.09	16
Japan	–	–	0.98	71	31	–	–	0.61	2.6	0.22	7,918	56	1.77	23
Italy	12.13	1.63	0.46	93	34	1	37.5	0.92	3.8	0.20	7,777	38	8.12	20
Netherlands	30.59	1.64	0.38	85	33	1	42.5	1.00	4.6	0.18	9,269	35	4.62	20
New Zealand	–	–	0.54	–	–	0	37.4	−0.00	2.0	−0.40	–	–	–	–
Norway	27.52	1.50	0.19	80	54	0	–	0.77	3.3	−0.02	9,863	52	2.28	22
Sweden	37.89	1.58	0.44	84	67	0	33.2	0.96	4.4	−0.40	9,982	63	6.83	24
Switzerland	8.84	1.68	0.32	35	32	6	35.5	0.86	5.3	0.16	12,377	53	0.78	32
United Kingdom	22.67	1.78	0.65	76	42	0	10.4	0.17	2.1	0.08	9,282	54	5.01	28
United States	17.60	2.07	0.50	56	23	5	2.9	0.39	1.9	0.00	13,651	53	5.74	20

Note: Time coverage is 1950–96 except for redistribution and inequality, which are restricted to the LIS observations. Excludes Switzerland.

Table A4.4. *Correlation Matrix*

	(1)	(2)	(3)	(4)	(5)	(6)	(7)	(8)	(9)	(10)	(11)	(12)	(13)
(1) Redistribution	1.00												
(2) Inequality	-0.47	1.00											
(3) Partisanship	-0.58	0.48	1.00										
(4) Voter turnout	0.32	-0.76	-0.05	1.00									
(5) Unionization	0.67	-0.71	-0.42	0.49	1.00								
(6) Electoral system	0.38	-0.70	-0.42	0.31	0.47	1.00							
(7) Effective number of parties	-0.66	0.56	-0.39	-0.03	0.18	0.57	1.00						
(8) Left fragmentation	–	–	0.27	-0.40	-0.78	-0.24	-0.07	1.00					
(9) Number of veto points	-0.55	0.64	0.45	-0.56	-0.53	-0.27	0.58	–	1.00				
(10) Vocational training	0.32	-0.6	-0.46	0.52	0.23	0.79	-0.83	–	-0.29	1			
(11) Per capita income	-0.20	0.39	-0.27	-0.56	-0.21	-0.30	-0.08	0.10	0.53	-0.43	1.00		
(12) Female labor force part	0.51	-0.22	-0.07	-0.19	0.41	0.03	0.05	-0.26	-0.31	-0.12	0.31	1.00	
(13) Unemployment	-0.11	0.09	0.11	0.38	-0.04	-0.09	-0.03	-0.21	-0.04	0.15	-0.31	-0.49	1.00
(14) Manufacturing work force	–	–	-0.11	-0.30	0.12	0.22	0.16	-0.00	–	–	0.25	0.50	-0.63

Note: Correlations based on period averages.

179

PART III

Forces of Change

5

Coping with Risk

THE EXPANSION OF SOCIAL PROTECTION

One of the most remarkable facts about welfare spending in advanced democracies is its rapid and almost uninterrupted expansion since the 1950s. Figure 5.1 illustrates this expansion for two broad categories of spending: government consumption of services and government transfers, both expressed as shares of GDP. Although the very rapid expansion beginning in the mid-1960s slowed down in the 1980s, and the fiscal retrenchment associated with the reining in of public deficits in the late 1980s seems to have caused a temporary reduction in public consumption, there are no signs of any broad-scale retrenchment. This continued growth of the welfare state presents an intriguing puzzle for political economy since the traditional blue-collar working class, the supposed pillar of the welfare state, has everywhere declined during the past four decades (cf. Piven 1991).

One of the solutions to this puzzle proposed in the literature is that growing exposure to the international economy has increased labor market insecurities and propelled demands for social protection. Thus, Cameron (1978) and Katzenstein (1985), and more recently Garrett (1998) and Rodrik (1998), argue that even though integration into the international economy promises large potential welfare gains, such integration comes at the cost of exposure to the ups and downs of global markets and reduced capacity for governments to counteract these cycles. The way governments solve this dilemma, so the argument goes, is to accept high trade exposure while simultaneously adopting comprehensive social programs to compensate people for increased levels of risk (see also Ruggie 1983).

Figure 5.1 shows that the growth in government spending does indeed track the expansion in trade, and the thesis is logically consistent with the argument presented in this book. Although never linked explicitly to limited mobility of skills, if globalization leads to greater labor market volatility, one *should* expect demand for social protection to rise. Globalization is, however, probably only one piece in the welfare state expansion puzzle. The reason is that participation in international trade opens opportunities to escape excessive dependence on small home markets and to diversify risks, much the same way as mutual stock funds spread the risks across industries and, increasingly, across national markets. Although trade implies greater specialization, and hence more concentrated risks, the bulk of the trade between advanced economies is intra-industry and does not lead to excessive dependence on one or a few industries. Indeed, many industries in countries with small home markets can prosper *only* by taking advantage of the production of scale that global markets enable. As I show later in this chapter, with appropriate controls, the relationship between trade and spending depicted in Figure 5.1 is weak and sometimes disappears altogether.

As Tom Cusack and I have argued (Iversen and Cusack 2000), a more important source of welfare expansion has been deindustrialization. As

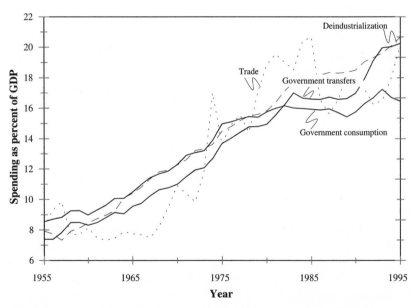

Figure 5.1 Spending, trade, and deindustrialization in seventeen OECD countries, 1952–1995.
Notes: Government consumption is all spending on public services less military spending; transfers are all government transfers less interest payments and subsidies; trade is exports plus imports divided by the GDP.
Sources: OECD, *National Accounts, Part II: Detailed Tables* (various years).

indicated in Figure 5.1, this variable, which is explained in detail later in this chapter, is (like trade) also closely related to the evolution of spending, and the relationship (unlike trade) turns out to hold up with control for a large number of potentially confounding factors. There are good reasons why this would be the case. The labor market dislocations associated with deindustrialization are considerable and compare in magnitude to the movement of workers from the countryside to the city during the industrial revolution. In 1960, for example, about 60 percent of the labor force in the OECD area was employed in the primary sectors; thirty-five years later this figure is down to about 30 percent. This massive shift in employment is the outgrowth of deep forces of technological change coupled with progressive market saturation in manufactured goods and shifts in demand toward services – structural-technological conditions that also characterized the great transformation from agriculture to industry.

Perhaps more surprisingly, there is also considerable variance in the speed of deindustrialization across countries.[1] For example, in an early industrializing country like the United States, industrial employment as a percentage of the adult population declined by only 3 percentage points between 1960 and 1995, whereas for a late industrializer like Sweden, the figure is 13 percent. If we add to these figures the decline of agricultural employment, the numbers increase to 6 and 22 percent, respectively. The difference in these numbers would translate into 23 million lost jobs if the United States had gone through the same process of deindustrialization as Sweden did from 1960 to 1995. The reason for this difference is that the United States industrialized earlier than Sweden, did so at a slower pace, and never became as heavily dominated by industry as did Sweden.

But even though it is sensible to assume that shifts in the employment structure, proxied by deindustrialization, raise the demand for social protection, the argument in this book implies that the effect is conditional on the skill system and on the electoral system. The more an economy emphasizes specific skills through the training system, the less portable skills will be, and the greater the effects of shocks such as deindustrialization on demand for protection. In addition, because the aggregation of preferences is mediated by political institutions – in particular electoral systems as argued

---

[1] There seems to be a misconception that deindustrialization is uniform across countries, and therefore cannot explain cross-national variance in the speed of welfare state expansion. At least, this is one of the only reasons I can imagine for why not a single large-N, cross-national study of the welfare state has focused on the effects of deindustrialization.

in detail in Chapter 4 – we expect the effects of shocks to be conditional on these institutions. Electoral systems shape the capacity of governments credibly to commit to social protection and affect the ideological hue of the government. The magnitude of the effect of shocks should therefore be rising in the proportionality of the electoral system.

This chapter is organized into three sections. The first elaborates on the argument, presents some background data, and specifies the empirical hypotheses to be tested. The second tests the argument using time-series data for sixteen advanced democracies, while the final section discusses the long-term political consequences of the fact that the occupational structure has been gradually stabilizing in the last couple of decades.

5.1. Deindustrialization and the Role of Institutions

The importance of changes in the occupational structure depends on the transferability of skills and social benefits. A main argument of this book is that transferable skills protect workers against market vagaries, whereas specific skills expose them to risks. Labor market risks therefore arise across the interfaces between economic sectors requiring very different types of skills. This logic is reinforced when we consider that privately provided social benefits, such as health insurance and pensions, also tend to be constrained by the transferability of skills. The reason is that when skills are firm-specific, employers only have an incentive to provide nontransferable benefits, both as a tool of control over the workforce and as an incentive for their employees to acquire additional firm-specific skills (Mares 1998). Correspondingly, if skills are industry-wide, there is a rationale for employers in that industry to provide benefits that are transferable across firms – but only *within* the industry. The latter clearly depends on the ability of employers to collude in the provision of both skills and benefits. The point is simply that *the transferability of benefits will never exceed the transferability of skills in the absence of state intervention.*

The approximate correspondence between the scope of employer-sponsored insurance and the transferability of skills means that if a worker loses his or her job and must either transgress a skill boundary or remain nonemployed, labor market power and benefits will be forfeited or downgraded. In some cases, this implies that workers are left outside employment with few or no means of support; in other cases, it means that workers find new jobs at substantially reduced wages and benefits. It is therefore only through the mediation of the state that workers can protect themselves

186

against the risks of major shifts in the economic and occupational structure. Such protection comes in the form of state-guaranteed health and old-age insurance (which makes it possible to move across sectoral interfaces without losing benefits), as well as through early retirement and certain forms of disability insurance that facilitate a relatively painless exit from the labor market (and therefore make it possible *not* to have to move across the skill interfaces). Even though transfer income is usually related to past earnings, there is unambiguous evidence for all OECD countries that posttax and transfer income is more equally distributed than the pretax and transfer income. We already saw this in Chapter 1 (see especially Figure 1.4), and it was further documented in the analysis of redistribution in Chapter 4. This is even more true for government services, which are usually not income related, although public services do not always serve protection purposes.

It is important to point out that state accommodation of demands for protection against labor market risks is not necessarily opposed by employers, as commonly assumed in the welfare state literature. Without assurances from the state, workers will be less inclined to make risky investments in nontransferable skills, and many employers depend on workers making precisely such investments. Especially with the transition to more knowledge-intensive forms of production, firms that rely on firm- and industry-specific skills share with their employees an interest in strengthening the aspects of the welfare state that reduce the riskiness for workers of making investments in specific skills. While this implication is clearly at odds with the standard assumption that business always opposes social spending, it is consistent with an emerging new body of scholarship that documents the supportive and often proactive role of employers in developing and shaping the modern welfare state (Martin 1995, 2003; Mares 1998, 2003; Swenson 2002).

Like the distinction between agriculture and industry in the latter half of the previous century, the distinction between manufacturing and services represents one of the most important economic interfaces affecting the transferability of skills in the latter half of the 20th century. Even low-skilled blue-color workers, almost all males, find it exceedingly hard to adjust to similarly low-skilled service sector jobs because they lack something that, for want of a better word, may be thought of as a form of social skills. In addition, employers in the two sectors are usually organized into different associations and do not cooperate in the provision of training or benefits. In addition, a switch in employment across the two sectors typically requires workers to change their membership in unions and unemployment insurance funds.

But the growth of the welfare state is not an automatic response to deindustrialization (or to other shocks such as trade for that matter). As I showed in Part II, the translation of sectoral shifts in the economy into social policy depends on two key institutional variables: the skill system and the electoral system. When skills can be unemployed to different degrees, and the risk of skills being unemployed depends on the specificity of those skills, shocks to the labor market will affect those with specific skills more than those with general skills. In turn, this translates into different pressure on the welfare state in countries with different skill regimes.

Going back to the model of preferences presented in Chapter 3, if we treat the long-term probability of entering the state of the world where specific skills are unemployed (State II in Figure 3.1) as a variable, an individual's demand for social protection is the interaction between this variable and the specificity of his or her skills. Let us therefore recall the expression for the probability of being in the "general skills only state" (State II – i.e., a state of the work where specific skills are worthless):

$$\beta = (1 - r) \cdot e$$

Assume now that the (equilibrium) level of employment, e, is constant. Then β is a positive function of $(1 - r)$, which is the probability of unemployed workers being reemployed into a state of the world where their specific skills are unutilized. The harder it is for unemployed to find jobs where their specific skills are used, the higher the probability of some day experiencing a drop in income, and the greater the demand for income protection, R. The central claim is therefore that deindustrialization, and other major shocks to the labor market, have the effect of raising $(1 - r)$ and hence the demand for social protection. The magnitude of the effect depends on the specificity of skills as illustrated in Figure 5.2.

The effect of exogenous shocks is also likely to depend on the electoral system. There are two arguments. The first concerns the demand for insurance. As argued in Chapter 4, the fundamental problem in the provision of social insurance is that when a shock hits, those who are affected will not likely be the ones setting policy. Those who have not been directly affected will update their subjective assessment of risks, but they only have an interest in compensatory policies if such policies can be seen as a premium for protection against *future* shocks. Yet, current voters can only commit the government for one term at a time, and there is no way to bind future voters to the policy preferences of current voters. The time-inconsistency problem means that shocks that would raise demand for protection will not necessarily be translated into actual policies.

As argued in Chapter 4, there are two institutional remedies for the time-inconsistency problem. The first is that political parties with detailed policy programs and highly developed party organizations, especially links to unions, limit the ability of leaders to give in to short-term electoral incentives and constrain the choice set of voters to alternatives that are optimal in the long run. However, this solution does not eliminate the temptation for party leaders to offer tax cuts and to shun long-term investment in social protection. And this temptation is particularly high in majoritarian systems where the reward for winning the next election is great.

The second argument goes back to the idea that PR electoral systems give centrist parties an incentive to ally with left parties for current redistributive purposes. If left parties tend to represent voters who are at greater risk, the preferences of these voters will be represented in coalition bargaining. The same is not true in a majoritarian system where the median voter will

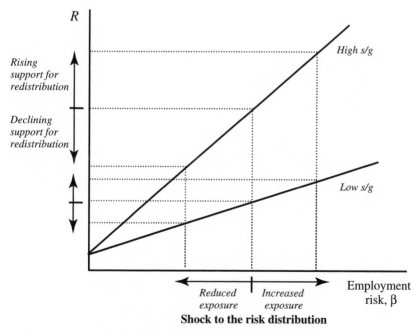

Figure 5.2 Support for redistribution as a function of risk.

ignore the distributive preferences of those with little income. Indeed, these preferences present a threat to the interests of the median voter, who might become more prone to vote for the center-right as a result.

But a shock to the income distribution may also negatively affect the median voter and hence drive up demand for redistributive spending. Still, the difference between PR and majoritarian systems remains. To see this, imagine a means-preserving increase in inequality. In this situation, both the poor and the median voter will prefer more redistribution. In a PR system, this will come about as a compromise between the center and left parties, where those who have lost the most in the "tail" of the distribution will have as much influence as those in the center who are likely to have lost the least. In a majoritarian system, by contrast, although the median voter will prefer more spending, he or she will also be more fearful of a center-left party where the poor set policy. The first effect will make the median voter more likely to vote center-left, the second effect less likely to do so. The net effect is a less significant shift in policies than under PR as illustrated in Figure 5.3. As in the case of skill systems,

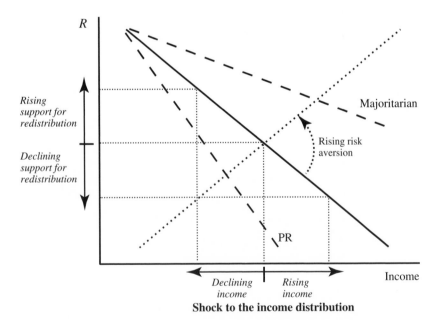

Figure 5.3   Support for redistribution as a function of shocks to income.

190

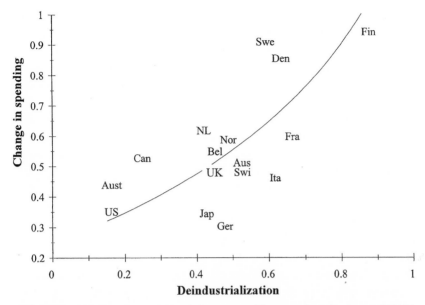

Figure 5.4 Deindustrialization and change in welfare spending for sixteen OECD countries, 1960–93.

Notes: Government spending is the average annual change in civilian government consumption plus social transfers as a percentage of GDP; deindustrialization is the average annual reduction in employment in industry plus agriculture as a percentage of the working age population.
Sources: OECD, *Labour Force Statistics* (various years); OECD, *National Accounts, Part II: Detailed Tables* (1997).

the elasticity of government spending to shocks depends on the type of electoral system.

5.2. Empirical Evidence[2]

Figure 5.4 shows the association between the average annual figures for deindustrialization – in the sense of the joint employment losses in industry and agriculture – and the comparable figure for the expansion in total government spending. As expected, there is a positive association that is of about the same strength as the cross-national correlation between openness and spending. There is some clustering around the mean, but this is mainly the result of averaging over a thirty-five-year period (as will become

---

[2] This section builds on Iversen and Cusack (2000).

apparent later). Most of the countries have gone through periods of both relatively slow and relatively rapid deindustrialization, and the temporal order of these swings varies. In addition, the effects of deindustrialization are institutionally mediated, and similar magnitudes can, therefore, have different effects in different countries. All this can be captured through multiple regression analyses of time-series data, to which I turn next.

The evidence covers sixteen OECD countries over a thirty-five-year period from 1960 to 1995.[3] This period represents the historically most dramatic phase of growth in welfare spending with transfer payments more than doubling from 8.5 percent of GDP in 1960 to over 20 percent in 1995, and government consumption increasing from about 9 percent of GDP in 1960 to over 16 percent in 1995. The cross-national variance in transfers (measured by the coefficient of variation) declined somewhat over time, but it rose for government consumption. Measured in terms of the difference between the smallest and biggest "spenders," divergence increased in both categories of spending. More precisely, the transfers payment gap increased from 10 to 15 percent of GDP, and the government consumption gap, from 6 to 15 percent of GDP. The data thus represents not only considerable intertemporal variance but also large cross-national differences – a good testing ground for competing explanations of welfare state expansion.

In addition to overall spending on transfers and services, the analysis also examines spending that is specifically targeted for purposes of social protection. Specifically, I use data on consolidated central government spending on social security, health, and welfare as a percent of GDP, which the International Monetary Fund (IMF) has compiled since 1970 for fourteen of these sixteen cases (IMF, *Government Finance Statistics Yearbook*, various years). The OECD collects similar data, but they only go back to 1980, thereby missing a critical phase of deindustrialization and welfare state expansion. The IMF data does have one important limitation: It excludes spending that is financed locally (as opposed to spending financed by central government grants). Nevertheless, it captures core social expenditures that can be expected to respond to pressures for more social protection. As it turns out, total transfers and IMF's measure have a correlation of .9, so the first is a good proxy for the latter.

---

[3] The countries are Australia, Austria, Belgium, Canada, Denmark, Finland, France, West Germany, Italy, Japan, Netherlands, Norway, Sweden, Switzerland, United Kingdom, and United States.

5.2.1. Model Specification

The empirical analysis falls into two parts. In the first, I focus on the effects of deindustrialization, ignoring interactive institutional effects. This allows for a fairly detailed analysis of the intertemporal properties of the effects of deindustrialization and other potential explanatory variables using an error correction model. The second part focuses on the effects of training systems and electoral systems, using a methodology developed by Blanchard and Wolfers (2000).

The error correction model uses changes in government spending (defined below) as the dependent variables and has the following form:

$$\Delta Y_{i,t} = \alpha_i + \beta_1 \cdot Y_{i,t-1} + \sum \beta^j \cdot X_{i,t-1}^j + \sum \beta_\Delta^j \cdot \Delta X_{i,t}^j + \epsilon_{i,t} \qquad (5.1)$$

where Y is a spending variable (transfers, consumption, or social spending), and X is an independent variable. The subscripts i and t index countries and time periods, respectively, while the superscript j indexes a particular independent variable. Δ is the first difference operator. Note that the model uses country-specific intercepts ("country dummies").

This model has a number of useful properties (see Beck and Katz 1996). First, the parameter for the lagged dependent level variable, β_1, provides an easy check on equilibrium properties. β_1 should be between -1 and 0 to ensure that the incremental effects of a shock to any exogenous variable are progressively reduced over time, causing spending to converge to a long-term equilibrium. For readers more familiar with models that use the *level* of spending on the left-hand side, the current model can be reformulated into such a model by simply adding $Y_{i,t-1}$ on both sides of the equal sign. This yields $Y_{t,i} = \alpha + (1 + \beta_1) \cdot Y_{i,t-1} + \cdots$, where $(1 + \beta_1)$ is the new parameter for the lagged dependent level variable. There is a small advantage for using first differences, however, because the model yields estimates of R^2 that are more informative of the variance explained by the independent variables of interest.[4]

The other useful feature of the present model is that it enables us to separate out the permanent and transitory effects of any independent variable. Although not intuitively obvious, it can be shown that the parameter for a lagged independent *level* variable, X_{t-1}, is a measure of the permanent (or lasting) effect of a one-off change in that variable, while the parameter for

---

[4] The reason for the advantage is that in the model using levels of spending on the left-hand side, much of the variance will be accounted for by the lagged dependent variable, showing simply that current spending depends on past spending.

a *change* variable, ΔX_t, is a measure of the transitory (or passing) effect of a one-off change in that variable (see Beck 1992). The long-term permanent effect of an independent variable can be calculated by dividing the parameter for the lagged level of that variable by minus the parameter for the lagged dependent level variable: $\beta^j / - \beta_1$ (assuming that β_1 between 0 and -1). If a variable exhibits *only* transitory effects (i.e., if only the parameter for its first difference is different from zero), spending will eventually revert back to its original level unless the independent variable changes continuously (assuming again that β_1 is between 0 and -1). Because all the theoretical variables are defined as proportions (either of GDP or of the working age population), they cannot grow (or fall) indefinitely and will therefore have no lasting effect on spending *unless* the parameters for the their lagged levels are significant.[5] In the interactive institutional model presented later in this chapter, I focus on levels, and hence permanent effects only (basically to keep the model manageable).

As noted, all regressions were run with a full set of *country dummies* (or country-specific intercepts) to control for nationally specific effects. For example, Esping-Andersen (1990) has forcefully argued that the institutional blueprints for many of today's welfare states were established in the pre–World War II period, and that these institutional characteristics keep reproducing the contemporary development of the welfare state. Likewise, the argument by Huber et al. (1993) that the greater the opportunities for minorities to block new spending bills (i.e., the greater the number of veto points in the political system), the less likely it is that new legislation will be passed or implemented. Since their index of government structures varies across my sixteen cases, but not across time, the effect will be picked up by the country dummies.

This estimation strategy, however, leaves out one question of considerable theoretical interest, namely whether countries with different institutions respond differently to exogenous shocks. Again, the two institutional features that I have emphasized are the skill system and the electoral system. The problem with including these variables in the analysis is that they exhibit little meaningful variance across time and, therefore, are perfectly (or nearly perfectly) collinear with the country dummies. To overcome this problem, I subsequently adopt an estimation strategy developed by Blanchard and Wolfers (2000) that involves entering the institutional

---

[5] This does not *have* to be the case. One of the control variables, unexpected GDP growth, can in principle rise indefinitely.

variables only as interactions with the shocks that they are supposed to condition the affect of.[6]

Blanchard and Wolfers propose two versions of the model, and I estimate both. The first assumes that countries are exposed to uniform, and unobservable, exogenous shocks. Because the nature of the shocks are left entirely unspecified, the purpose is simply to determine whether countries with different institutions respond differently to them. The shocks are proxied by a set of year dummies, D_t, that are interacted with the institutional variables, I_i:

$$Y_{i,t} = \alpha_i + D_t \cdot (1 + \beta \cdot I_i) + \sum \beta^j \cdot X_{i,t}^j + \varepsilon_{i,t} \tag{5.2}$$

The common unobserved shocks in this formulation are captured by the time dummies, and the institutional effect is captured by the parameter β. If β is zero, it means that the effects of the shocks are identical across institutional configurations. If it is positive, it means that the relevant institutional feature (skill specificity or PR in our case) magnifies the effect of the common shocks.

The second formulation identifies the nature of the shock and allows it to vary across countries. Our shock variable, of course, is deindustrialization, $E_{i,t}$, which is simply substituted in for the time dummies:

$$Y_{i,t} = \alpha_i + E_{i,t} \cdot (1 + \beta \cdot I_i) + \sum \beta^j \cdot X_{i,,t}^j + \varepsilon_{i,t} \tag{5.3}$$

Explanatory Variables *Deindustrialization* is defined as 100 minus the sum of manufacturing and agricultural employment as a percentage of the working-age population. The base of 100 is arbitrary. For example, one could have used the peak of employment in agriculture and manufacturing as the base instead, and this is a number that varies across countries. It is in fact not easy to theoretically justify the use of a particular base, but it turns out not to be necessary. The reasons is that the statistical analysis includes a full set of country dummies.[7] As a result, if each country has a unique base, it simply alters the nationally specific intercepts, and the dummies permit these to take on any value.

Again, the *institutional variables* are skill specificity and electoral system. For the latter, I use the simple classification of electoral systems into

---

[6] The dependent variable in Blanchard and Wolfer's analysis is unemployment.

[7] An F-test indicates that the country dummies belong in the model.

majoritarian (0) and PR (1) that was used in Chapter 4. For the former, I use the share of an age cohort going through a vocational training. This measure, which starts in 1980s, exhibits little meaningful variation over time and is treated as an institutional variable. As such, it was simply extrapolated back in time.

In addition to these variables, the analysis contains the following set of controls.

Government center of gravity. This variable is the same as that used in Chapter 4 and is based on three expert surveys of the left–right position of parties (weighted by the share of parties' seats in government). Source: Cusack and Fuchs (2002).

Trade openness. This variable includes total exports and imports of goods and services as a percentage of GDP. Source: OECD, *National Accounts, Part II: Detailed Tables* (various years).

Capital market openness. The index is taken from Quinn and Inclan (1997) and measures the extent to which capital markets are liberalized.

Electoral participation. The measure is voter turnout rates as recorded on an annual basis in Mackie and Rose (1991), *European Journal of Political Research*, and International Institute for Democracy and Electoral Assistance (1997).

Unexpected growth. This is a variable emphasized in Roubini and Sachs (1989) and is defined as per capita real GDP growth at time t minus average real per capita growth in the preceding three years. It is intended to capture the logic that budgeting relies on GDP forecasts based on performance in the recent past. If growth is unexpectedly high, it reduces spending as a proportion of GDP. Sources: Cusack (1991) and OECD, *National Accounts, Part II : Detailed Tables* (various years).

Two additional variables deserve particular emphasis. Both are designed to remove nondiscretionary elements of government spending, and they are essential to get a well-specified model.[8] The first relates transfer payments to changes in unemployment and demographics that generate "automatic" disbursements of payments according to rules that cannot be readily altered in the short run. It is standard pratice to control for such effects by

---

[8] In my view, too little care is often taken in controlling for nondiscretionary spending, which creates potential problems of omitted variable bias. See Iversen and Cusack (2000) for an example.

including variables for unemployment and the number of people above the pension age; however, Cusack (1997) has developed a more satisfactory measure that takes account of the fact that the generosity of transfers varies across countries. The measure is referred to as *automatic transfers* and defined as

Automatic transfers
$$= \text{Generosity}\,(t-1) \cdot \Delta \frac{\text{Unemployed} + \text{Population} > 65}{\text{Population}}(t)$$

where generosity is the percentage share of transfers in GDP relative to the percentage share of the dependent population in the total population at time $t - 1$. In other words, changes in size of the dependent population – the unemployed and the retired – causes an automatic increase in transfers at time t, the size of which depends on the generosity of transfers in the previous period (according to prevailing rules). The source for the unemployment and population figures is OECD, *Labour Force Statistics* (various years).

Another nondiscretionary element of spending concerns government consumption. Because productivity increases in public services are generally lower than in the rest of the economy, while wage and other costs tend to follow productivity increases in the rest of the economy, the price level of government services will "automatically" grow at a faster rate than the general price level (the "Baumol effect"). Even at constant provision levels, government consumption will therefore increase as a share of GDP. This nondiscretionary effect can be removed by another measure developed by Cusack (1997). It is here called *automatic consumption* and is defined as

$$\text{Automatic consumption} = \frac{\text{Gov consumption}}{\text{GDP}}(t-1)$$
$$\cdot \left(\frac{\Delta Gov\ deflator\ (t)}{Gov\ deflator\ (t-1)} \right) \bigg/ \left(\frac{\Delta \text{GDP def}}{\text{GDP def}} \right)$$

where Gov deflator is the price deflator for government services, and GDP deflator is the price deflator for the whole GDP. The equation simply says that if prices on government services grow faster than the general price level, government consumption will automatically increase by a proportional amount.

5.2.2. Findings

5.2.2.1. Effects of Deindustrialization

The results for each category of spending are presented in Table 5.1.[9] First note the effects of deindustrialization. For each percent decline in employment in the traditional sectors, the long-term equilibrium for social transfer spending increases by approximately 0.65 percent. The corresponding effect for government consumption is somewhat smaller, 0.55 percent, while the short-term impact is to elevate the actual spending level by 1 percent for every percent decrease in employment in the traditional sectors. The effect on equilibrium spending on healthcare, social security, and welfare is .40 percent. In other words, a standard deviation change in deindustrialization is associated with at roughly 0.5 standard deviation change in spending, which implies that about half of the variance in spending is explained by the deindustrialization variable. All effects of deindustrialization are statistically significant at a .01 level or better.

It is also noteworthy that the effect of deindustrialization *persists* over time. Apparently spending gets "locked in" by organizational and institutional factors that are exogenous to the model. As argued by Pierson, spending itself creates political clienteles that will press for further spending and resist attempts at retrenchment (Pierson 1994; 1996). Hence, even though the process of deindustrialization is the causal agent in the expansion of the welfare state, the disappearance of this causal agent will not necessarily lead to retrenchment – it will "merely" retard further expansion. However, the character of the political game over welfare policies is likely to change when compromises involving overall expansion are no longer feasible; this conjecture deserves closer attention considering that the process of deindustrialization is coming to a halt in many countries.

Not surprisingly, the automatic transfers variable also has a strong effect. A parameter of .87 means that a 1 percent increase in the dependent population is turned into additional spending amounting to .87 percent of GDP. There is a similar effect on government consumption of changes in relative prices (automatic consumption). Roughly speaking, if wages and productivity in the private sector rise by 1 percent, wages in the public sector are also expected to rise by .89 percent even when productivity remains constant.

---

[9] Tests for heteroskedasticity in both pooled regressions suggested the need to correct for this problem, so I employed Beck and Katz's (1995) method for deriving panel-corrected standard errors. Separate runs using robust regression techniques (not shown) yield almost identical results, so the findings are not driven by outliers.

Table 5.1. *Regression Results for Government Spending (t-scores in parentheses)*

	Transfers	Consumption	Social Spending
Lagged dependent level	−0.071***	−0.049***	−0.186***
	(0.022)	(0.015)	(0.036)
Deindustrialization$_{t-1}$	0.046***	0.027***	0.072***
	(0.015)	(0.010)	(0.026)
Δ Deindustrialization$_t$	0.120***	0.081***	0.096*
	(0.033)	(0.027)	(0.053)
Partisanship$_{t-1}$	0.297*	−0.140	0.159
	(0.159)	(0.134)	(0.196)
Δ Partisanship$_t$	−0.201	−0.020	−0.106
	(0.200)	(0.147)	(0.288)
Turnout$_{t-1}$	−0.005	0.011*	0.009
	(0.006)	(0.006)	(0.009)
Δ Turnout$_t$	−0.005	0.002	−0.000
	(0.007)	(0.009)	(0.010)
Trade openness$_{t-1}$	−0.005	−0.004*	−0.012
	(0.005)	(0.002)	(0.006)
Δ Trade openness$_t$	0.018*	−0.006	−0.022
	(0.010)	(0.005)	(0.011)
Capital openness$_{t-1}$	0.007	−0.020	0.022
	(0.028)	(0.018)	(0.055)
Δ Capital openness$_t$	0.045	−0.078*	−0.038
	(0.053)	(0.037)	(0.102)
Unexpected growth$_t$	−0.077***	−0.092***	−0.091***
	(0.011)	(0.007)	(0.018)
Automatic transfers$_t$	0.865***	−	0.596***
	(0.097)		(0.086)
Automatic consumption$_t$	−	0.875***	−
		(0.069)	
Adjusted R-squared	0.48	0.56	0.49
Number of observations	508	508	267

Significance levels: * <0.10; ** <0.05; *** <0.01.
Note: The results for country dummies are not shown.

No other variable appears to have a strong and statistically significant effect. Most surprisingly, perhaps, is the fact that none of the globalization measures have much of an impact. There are no statistically significant effects on government transfers, and the small effect of trade openness on government consumption has the "wrong" sign. It is conceivable that this reflects a differential welfare effect of trade. Thus, while growing exposure to competition from low-wage countries raises the uncertainty for those already at high risk (Wood 1994; Leamer 1996), trade may well be welfare improving for all others (Rodrik 1997, Chapter 4). Whatever the explanation, the magnitude of the effect is small and only borderline significant. For each percentage point increase in openness, the long-term equilibrium level of civilian government consumption declines by .07 percent. All other effects of globalization are transitory in nature.

The absence of strong effects of government partisanship is also noteworthy. Indeed, the one effect that is borderline significant (for transfers) is opposite of the expectation (right-of-center governments spend marginally *more* than left-of-center governments). But we must be careful in how we interpret this finding. Because the dependent variable is first differences, and because the model includes a full set of country dummies, the variance to be explained is entirely intertemporal. Some of the cross-country differences may be attributable to the effect of past partisan policies. Indeed, if the country dummies are left out of the model, the positive effect right partisanship has on transfers disappears, and the negative effect on consumption becomes strong and significant.[10] Both effects are further magnified if we exclude the variable automatic consumption, which depends on the extent to which public and private sector wages are coordinated – an attribute we normally associate with solidaristic wage policies of the left.

Most importantly, the additive nature of the model does not allow us to answer a key dynamic question about partisanship: Do left-leaning governments expand social protection more than right-leaning governments in response to exogenous shocks such as deindustrialization? This question cannot be answered by looking only at the direct effects of partisanship. We need an interactive specification that is outlined in Section 5.2.2.4 and is further developed in the next chapter.

More generally, the results imply that deindustrialization has an augmenting effect on spending, but they cannot help us answer questions about whether the effects of deindustrialization, and potentially other forces of change, are mediated by nationally specific political-economic institutions. In addition to the role of partisanship, we have theoretical reasons to believe that the nature of both the skill system and the electoral system

---

[10] It is also problematic to remove the dummies because it is very easy to run into omitted variable bias. Here one also cannot do it because omitting the dummies will potentially render the deindustrialization variable meaningless (the problem of having an arbitrary base).

affect national responses to deindustrialization. To explore this issue, the next section borrows the Blanchard-Wolfers approach and uses national institutions as econometric "prisms" for the effects of exogenous shocks.

5.2.2.2. Potential Objections Before turning to the institutional story, it is perhaps helpful to address a couple of common objections to the deindustrialization argument that the reader may also harbor. The first is that the effect of deindustrialization reflects some sort of accounting relationship. The argument is that increasing public consumption means employing more people in the public sector, and because public employment is an element in the denominator of the deindustrialization variable, there must necessarily be a relationship between spending and deindustrialization. This is simply wrong. The denominator is defined as the total working-age population, not the labor force; therefore, it cannot be affected by spending except through the birth rate. So although it is true that public employment affects an element in the denominator, it is *not true* that this affects the total size of the denominator. The only logically valid argument about reversed causality is that government spending causes employment in industry and agriculture to decline – a possibility that will be considered in Section 5.3.

Another objection is that as long as the natural movement of people into retirement – "natural attrition" – is sufficiently large, deindustrialization need not have any effect on the level of labor market risks. Yet, this argument confuses the net effect of a set of variables with the independent effect of these variables. Natural attrition in any market segment will increase the job security of workers by reducing supply relative to demand, just as new entry into a segment will increase job insecurity by raising supply relative to demand. This is why early retirement, as a public policy, is a way to ameliorate such insecurities, and this is why spending on early retirement schemes is causally linked to deindustrialization. But this does not alter the thesis that reduction in the labor force as a result of deindustrialization has an the independent, risk-augmenting effect on the labor market. Regardless of the level of natural attrition, we always expect deindustrialization to increase job insecurity.

5.2.2.3. Institutional Effects Table 5.2 shows the results of estimating Equation (5.2) using nonlinear least squares regression. The dependent variables are levels of spending; the time dummies serve as proxies for the

Table 5.2. *Common Shocks, National Institutions, and Government Spending (standard errors in parentheses)*

	Transfers	Consumption	Transfers	Consumption	Transfers	Consumption
Time effect	7.20***	7.844***	7.67***	7.92***	7.55***	7.93***
	(0.86)	(0.604)	(0.87)	(0.61)	(0.86)	(0.61)
Vocational training* time dummies	0.013***	0.004***	—	—	0.006***	0.001
	(0.002)	(0.001)			(0.002)	(0.002)
PR* time dummies	—	—	0.53***	0.18***	0.36***	0.15***
			(0.08)	(0.05)	(0.10)	(0.06)
Partisanship	0.93**	0.086	0.81**	0.04	0.81**	0.04
	(0.40)	(0.345)	(0.40)	(0.34)	(0.39)	(0.35)
Dependency ratio$_t$	0.54***	—	0.58***	—	0.56***	—
	(0.07)		(0.07)		(0.07)	
Relative prices$_t$	—	-1.509*	—	-1.53*	—	-1.56
		(0.780)		(0.78)		(0.78)
Minimum	5.17	7.19	5.16	7.04	4.85	6.98
Maximum	11.72	9.29	9.20	8.46	10.85	8.87
Effect	*6.56*	*2.09*	*4.04*	*1.46*	*6.00*	*1.89*
Adjusted R-squared	0.92	0.9	0.92	0.91	0.92	0.9
Number of observations	564	564	564	564	564	564

Significance levels: * < 0.10;** < 0.05; *** < 0.01.
Notes: The results for the interactive terms correspond to β in the statistical model. The results for country and time dummies are not shown.

exogenous shocks. Because small changes in the balance between local and central government spending can significantly affect the estimated effects of period by period shocks, Table 5.2 only reports results for total government transfers and consumption.[11] To reflect that the dependent variable refers to levels, the two automatic spending variables used earlier have also been redefined as levels. One is the ratio of the dependent population (unemployed and those over 65) to the working-age population; the other is the price index for public services divided by the GDP price index. Several of the variables that either did not produce notable effects in the previous regressions or referred to change were omitted. Most of these, globalization in particular, can also be seen as elements in the exogenous shocks that produce the fiscal responses and, therefore, should not be included in principle. As noted previously, the time dummies are deliberately designed not to identify the nature of the shocks.

The key issue, of course, is whether governments in countries with strong vocational training systems, or with PR electoral systems, react differently to shocks than governments in countries with weak vocational training systems and majoritaritarian institutions. The parameter β on the interaction term provides the answer. If it is positive, it means that shocks cause spending to increase *more* in countries with high values on the institutional variable. With this in mind, it is easy to see that countries with strong vocational training institutions and PR electoral systems responded to shocks by increasing spending by a greater amount than in countries with weak vocational training institutions and majoritarian electoral systems. The effects are positive across all spending categories and statistically significant at a .01 level in five of the six regressions.

To gauge the substantive impact of institutions, I again follow Blanchard and Wolfers's methodology. The institutional variables have been defined as deviations from their cross-country means so that the effects of the time dummies refer to a country with average values on the institutional (and control) variables. In this way, the total time effect, shown in the first line of Table 5.2, is the difference between the parameter on the 1995 time dummy and parameter on the 1960 time dummy. By adding to and subtracting from the time effect, the product between this effect and β times the minimum and maximum values on the institutional variables, respectively, we can differentiate the spending effects of the shocks in countries with extreme

---

[11] The results for the IMF variable are unstable and sometimes insignificant. The significant results are consistent with those reported in this section.

values on the institutional variables. For example, the first column shows that the effect on transfers of the exogenous shocks occurring between 1960 and 1995 has been to raise spending as a percentage of GDP by 5 percent in a country with the weakest vocational training system but by nearly 12 percent in a country with the strongest vocational training system. These numbers are referred to as the minimum and the maximum at the end of the table, and what is referred to as the effect is the difference between the two. The effect can be read as a summary measure of the impact of an institution on any particular spending variable.

Again, both intensive vocational training and PR are associated with notably higher levels of spending. This is particularly true of transfers where the institutional effect, when measured separately, is about 5 percent of GDP. For government consumption, it is smaller, between 1 and 2 percent. The effects of institutions are more impressive when they are used jointly to account for differences in the effects of shocks (the last two columns). Even though there is quite strong collinearity between the variables ($r = .7$), all parameters are in the right direction and statistically significant *except* for vocational training in the case of government consumption. When entered together, PR clearly does most of the explanatory work for consumption. The likely explanation is that public service provision often does not serve a clear insurance function. Daycare services and elderly care are examples. And we know from the theoretical model that skills only matter for insurance preferences. Still, public employment often serves an employment protection function, and public health care and a range of other free or low-cost services can be seen as a form of income protection. Be that as it may, the combined effects are large and clearly support the conclusion that institutions powerfully shape countries' responses to exogenous shocks. And they do so in a way that is anticipated by the institutional argument.

Did governments respond differently to the changing economic environment during the 1980s and 1990s than they did during the 1960s and 1970s? The question is difficult to answer with precision because government spending did not change very much in the second period, leaving very little variance to be explained. In itself, this suggests that governments either became more constrained or reached an equilibrium level of spending by the early 1980s where shocks were adequately addressed through automatic disbursements of transfers. Either way, it has the implication that small measurement errors can have big effects on the results. With that caveat, Table 5.3 reports the results by period (omitting the controls for presentational economy).

204

Table 5.3. *Shocks and Spending in Two Subperiods*

		Transfers	Consumption
1960–79	Vocational training	0.015***	0.004*
	Time effect	7.45***	6.89***
	PR	0.364***	0.221***
	Time effect	6.76***	6.96***
1980–95	Vocational training	0.055***	0.009
	Time effect	0.70**	−0.02
	PR	1.51***	0.239
	Time effect	1.45***	−0.16

Significance levels: * < 0.10; ** < 0.05; *** < 0.01.

The high stability of government consumption in the second period makes it difficult to say anything with confidence about changes in the effects of institutions on this category of spending. But looking at the parameters for the institutional variables across spending categories gives no indication that the distinctiveness of government responses across institutional systems has diminished. In fact, all the parameters are larger in the second period. Bear in mind, however, that because the time effect is dramatically smaller in the second period (in the case of government consumption it is slightly negative), the overall effect is small. Coupled with the measurement error issue, one is well advised not to draw strong conclusions about changes in the relative responsiveness of governments over time. But certainly there is no evidence of convergence.

What the results presented thus far cannot tell us is anything about the nature of the shocks. This is a virtue in the sense that the results do not depend on any particular conceptualization of the forces of change. On the other hand, we do care about the identity of these forces. Also, because the model treats shocks as common, we do not allow for the possibility that some countries have been more exposed to shocks than others. If the extent of shocks is correlated with the institutions, the shocks rather than the institutions could explain the divergence in policies.

Our shock variable is, of course, deindustrialization. To examine the effects of this variable, I substitute it for the time dummies in the estimating equation (5.3). The results are shown in Table 5.4. The presentation is similar to that in Table 5.3, but the minimum and maximum (and the effect) are now referring to the effects of the average deindustrialization that occurred between 1960 and 1995 (about 18 percent) in countries with extreme

Table 5.4. *Deindustrialization, National Institutions, and Government Spending (standard errors in parentheses)*

	Transfers	Consumption	Transfers	Consumption	Transfers	Consumption
Deindustrialization effect	4.48***	6.95***	4.14***	6.67***	4.04***	6.74***
	(0.51)	(0.38)	(0.51)	(0.37)	(0.51)	(0.38)
Vocational training* deindustrialization	0.002***	−0.000	—	—	0.002*	−0.000
	(0.001)	(0.000)			(0.001)	(0.001)
PR* deindustrialization	—	—	0.64***	0.21***	0.62***	0.22***
			(0.16)	(0.08)	(0.16)	(0.08)
Partisanship	0.39	−0.77*	0.24	−0.89**	0.21	−0.88
	(0.41)	(0.40)	(0.40)	(0.40)	(0.40)	(0.40)
Dependency ratio$_t$	0.79***	—	0.83***	—	0.83***	—
	(0.06)		(0.06)		(0.06)	
Relative prices$_t$	—	1.36	—	1.74*	—	1.71*
		(0.20)		(0.94)		(0.95)
Minimum	3.66	6.80	2.49	5.81	2.35	5.90
Maximum	6.31	7.03	5.15	7.20	5.31	7.15
Effect	2.65	−0.23	2.67	1.37	2.97	1.25
Adjusted R-squared	0.91	0.83	0.92	0.86	0.92	0.86
Number of observations	564	564	564	564	564	564

Significance levels: * < 0.10; ** < 0.05; *** < 0.01
Notes: The results for the interactive terms correspond to β in the statistical model. The results for country and time dummies are not shown.

values on the institutional variables.[12] The average effect of deindustrialization (shown at the top of the table) is about 4 percent for transfers, and 6 percent for consumption, which accounts for between 60 and 80 percent of the total time effect (refer to Table 5.2).[13]

The results for the institutional variables are comfortingly similar to those for the time dummies. Countries with extensive vocational training systems and PR always respond to the effects of deindustrialization by increasing transfer much more than countries with general skills systems and majoritarian institutions. Countries with PR also tend to increase government consumption more than countries with majoritarian institutions, whereas there is no effect of vocational training. If we assume that transfers serve both insurance and redistributive purposes, while government consumption is mainly redistributive, this is precisely the pattern we should observe. People with specific skills demand insurance while PR promote alliances behind more spending for both insurance and redistribution.

5.2.2.4. Partisan Effects   The final question to be answered is whether left and right governments react differently to the employment shocks produced by deindustrialization. Clearly, we would expect left governments to show more sensitivity to social needs, and we know from Chapter 4 that if the electoral system matters for spending, as we just saw, chances are that partisanship does as well.

The previous analysis included controls for partisanship (higher values indicate more right-wing governments), but the results were not strong. In the common shocks version (using time dummies), there is a hint of right governments spending more than left governments on transfers but not on consumption. In the deindustrialization version, there is some indication of left governments spending more on consumption but not on transfers. Again, if government consumption is more redistributive than transfers, this is the pattern we should observe. But the more interesting question is whether left and right governments respond differently to shocks, and that is indeed what the results in Table 5.5 imply. Left governments are far more prone to react to deindustrialization by expanding spending than right governments.

---

[12] Recall that this number is a percentage of the working-age population. As a percentage of employment, it is more than 10 percent larger.

[13] Note that the effect of deindustrialization is not directly comparable to that estimated for the error correction model. The latter refers to the simulated effect on equilibrium levels of spending, whereas the former refers to the actual effect in a particular time period.

Table 5.5. *Deindustrialization, Partisanship, and Government Spending (standard errors in parentheses)*

	Transfers	Consumption
Deindustrialization effect	3.90***	5.17***
	(0.56)	(0.45)
Partisanship × deindustrialization	−0.92***	−0.59***
	(0.30)	(0.19)
Partisanship	14.98***	11.91***
	(3.77)	(3.59)
GDP per capita$_t$	0.99*	3.44***
	(0.57)	(0.57)
Dependency ratio$_t$	0.81***	−
	(0.07)	
Relative prices$_t$	−	−1.15
		(1.03)
Minimum	0.56	3.85
Maximum	3.90	6.29
Range	2.86	2.43
Adjusted R-squared	0.91	0.86
Number of observations	564	564

Significance levels: * < 0.10; ** < 0.05; *** < 0.01.
Notes: The results for the interactive terms correspond to β in the statistical model. The results for country and time dummies are not shown.

At the same time, it must be noted that when shocks are small, the results suggest that right governments actually spend more than left ones. Why this is so is an intriguing question. Bear in mind, however, that this is a fixed effects model where the evidence is based entirely on cross-time variation, and where the temporal relationship between partisanship and spending is difficult to determine. Chapter 6 will provide a much more detailed account of partisan responses to deindustrialization.

5.3. The Sources of Deindustrialization

If deindustrialization appears to be such an important force of change, it naturally raises the question of the sources of deindustrialization. Economists are divided on this question. On one side of the debate, reflecting not only a particular economic theory but also a generally popular view (the "giant sucking sound"), is the idea that the sources of deindustrialization in the West during recent decades lay in the competitive pressures emanating from Third World producers (Wood 1994; Saeger 1996, 1997). From this perspective, changes in the North-South trade have been estimated to account on average for 50 percent of the reduction in manufacturing that occurred between 1970 and 1990 (Saeger 1997, p. 604). In addition, it can be argued that the removal of restrictions on capital makes it increasingly easy for businesses to relocate production facilities to countries with lower wage costs, and that this in turn diminishes the demand for labor within the industrial sectors of the advanced market economies (Saeger 1997).

The alternative school, while not denying that trade has played a role in deindustrialization, sees the principal causes as residing in domestic sources (Krugman 1996; Rowthorn and Ramaswamy 1997). Among these are changing preference patterns away from manufactured goods and toward services, high productivity growth in the face of inelastic demand, as well as the associated changes in investment in new productive capacity (Rowthorn and Ramaswamy 1999, p. 19). North-South trade accounts for at most one sixth of the loss in manufacturing employment in these studies.

Furthermore, it may indeed be the case that the welfare state is itself responsible for the decline in employment in the traditional sectors. As Bacon and Eltis (1976) have argued, both the costs posed by taxation and the generosity of the modern welfare state, including the opportunity to work for at least equivalent if not higher wages in the public sector, have had a tremendous negative effect on competitiveness and industrial employment (see also Alesina and Perotti 1997). This is, of course, also a view that is popular with political parties and governments of a neoliberal bent, but the discussion in Chapter 4 challenges this idea, and there is little systematic empirical evidence to support it.

Figure 5.5 provides some descriptive evidence on the question of whether trade causes deindustrialization. It plots the loss of employment in the traditional sectors from 1962 through 1991 against the average trade openness for the same period. There is little hint of any relationship. Indeed the correlation between the two series is about 0.17.

Alternatively, if one were to adopt the hypothesis that deindustrialization has more to do with internal processes (processes of productivity gain and shifting tastes), then one would expect that a process of convergence has been underway. Thus, early industrializers, which had pretty much gone through this transformation by the beginning of this period, would have suffered the least loss of employment in the traditional sectors, while late industrializers would have experienced more rapid decline.

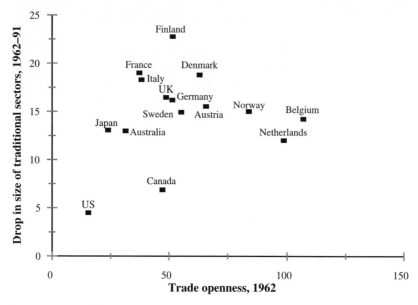

Figure 5.5 Trade openness and losses in traditional sectors.

As Figure 5.6 demonstrates, there seems to be a fair amount of support for this position. The correlation between employment intensity in the traditional sectors in the year 1962 and the loss of employment in these sectors over the three succeeding decades is about .85. Thus, the United States, which had the smallest traditional sectors (about 24 percent), experienced the smallest loss (less than 5 percent), while Finland, lagging well behind the United States and having nearly 50 percent of its working-age population engaged in the traditional sectors, experienced the largest loss in the sample of fifteen countries, well over 20 percent.

But descriptive, and indirect, evidence of this nature can be misleading, and I have therefore estimated a pooled cross-sectional time-series model that uses the change in the log of the number of people employed in manufacturing and agriculture as a share of the working-age population as the dependent variable (see Table 5.6).[14] This is a standard setup in the existing literature except that I have included agricultural employment on the left-hand side to make the results speak directly to the deindustrialization variable. However, the results are very similar if one focuses exclusively on

[14] As in the previous analysis, problems of heteroskedasticity led us to employ Beck and Katz's (1995) method for deriving panel corrected standard errors.

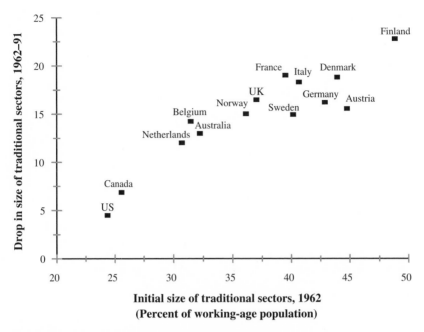

Figure 5.6 Initial size and losses in traditional sectors.

manufacturing employment. The analysis includes fourteen OECD countries for which there are complete data in the period from 1964 through 1990.[15]

For presentational ease, Table 5.6 divides the independent variables into a group of "domestic" variables and a group of "international" variables. Following the existing economic literature, the domestic-structural variables include (i) a measure of productivity growth, (ii) the log of income per capita and the square of this variable to capture changing consumption preferences, (iii) the growth in per capita income as a measure of demand effects, (iv) gross capital formation as a share of GDP, and (v) the two spending variables. For the exogenous variables the regression includes (vi) the balance of trade with OECD, the Organization of Petroleum Exporting Countries (OPEC), and less-developed countries (LDCs), and (vii) the Quinn-Inclan capital market openness variable.

[15] The countries include Austria, Belgium, Canada, Denmark, Finland, France, Germany, Italy, Japan, Netherlands, Norway, Sweden, the United Kingdom, and the United States. Missing data problems precluded adding Switzerland. The time frame is the maximum possible given the availability of data.

Table 5.6. *Regression Results for Industrialization (t-scores in parentheses)*

Endogenous Variables		Exogenous Variables	
[Lagged level]	−0.113***	Capital openness	0.001
	(−5.27)		(0.30)
Productivity growth	−0.353***	Δ Capital openness	0.001
	(9.09)		(0.50)
Income	0.523**	OECD trade balance	0.002***
	(2.18)		(3.47)
Income squared	−0.30**	Δ OECD trade balance	0.004***
	(2.24)		(4.43)
Growth in income	0.585***	OPEC trade balance	−0.004*
	(8.50)		(−1.96)
Capital formation	0.032***	Δ OPEC trade balance	−0.003
	(5.53)		(−1.35)
Government transfers	−0.001	LDC trade balance	−0.003**
	(−0.99)		(−2.12)
Government	0.001	Δ LDC trade balance	−0.002
	(0.30)		(−1.19)
Consumption	(0.30)		(−1.19)
Increase in explained variance	35%		5%
Adjusted R-squared			0.52
Number of observations	378		378

Significance levels: * < 0.10; ** < 0.05; *** < 0.01.
Notes: The increase in explained variance is the change in R-squared when the set of endogenous and exogenous variables are added to a model where these variables are excluded. The results for country dummies are not shown.

The productivity measure is meant to capture the tendency for firms to shed workers as productivity increases. Note that there is some theoretical ambiguity with respect to the impact of this variable. Even though faster productivity growth makes goods relatively cheaper, and therefore boosts demand, less labor is required to produce the same amount of output. The net effect on employment depends on the price and income elasticity of demand, as well as on real wage changes. Research, however, has shown that the labor-saving effect tends to dominate the demand effect in the period of interest (Appelbaum and Schettkat 1994, 1995). For the income terms, the expectation is that the parameter on the first term will be positive while that on the second term will be negative, signifying that as income passes beyond a certain level, the relative demand for goods in both the agricultural and manufacturing sectors will begin to decline. The effects of capital formation and growth in income are expected to be positive because both will boost production and demand for labor.[16]

The results show that deindustrialization appears to be driven mostly by domestic factors *other* than the welfare state. Technological progress, demand conditions, and shifting consumption patterns cause employment in industry and agriculture to decline. There is no evidence that government spending has "crowded out" employment in the traditional sectors; every indication is that the causal arrow goes in the opposite direction. Nor does trade appear to be a particularly important source of deindustrialization. A negative trade balance with other industrialized countries (and the first difference in that trade balance) *does* hurt industrial employment, but the effect is substantively small and cannot have been a major cause of deindustrialization across the OECD area for the simple reason that intra-OECD trade is relatively balanced over time.

The crucial question with respect to trade is whether growing trade with less-developed countries has priced out a substantial number of workers in agriculture and industry in the advanced countries. There is no evidence to that effect. The coefficients on the lagged levels of the trade balances with OPEC countries and with Third World countries are both negative and statistically significant, while both of the coefficients on the first differences are statistically insignificant. Note that these results, which suggest that positive trade balances with the OPEC and Third World countries *lower* employment, while negative balances promote employment, are not the consequence of multicollinearity. Nor do their effects change in substantive terms when one uses alternative specifications of the model. A large number of regressions using a variety of combinations of trade balances and import penetration measures were run, and the results are *all* contrary to the "trade leads to deindustrialization" hypothesis. In fact, the results presented in Table 5.6 are the strongest possible in *support* of the popular perception. The same is the case for the capital market openness variable, which consistently fails to produce effects that are statistically distinguishable from zero.

Though somewhat surprising given popular views, the results essentially replicate those in an IMF study by Rowthorn and Ramaswamy (1999), even though data and model specification vary somewhat. As in the Rowthorn-Ramaswamy study, deindustrialization is driven primarily by economic

---

[16] Investment is measured as a percentage share of GDP. It is taken from Robert Summers and Alan Heston, *Penn World Tables*, Version 5.5, data file (Cambridge, MA: National Bureau of Economic Research, 1993).

processes that are unrelated to either openness or spending. Productivity growth in the traditional sectors leads to a loss in employment, whereas rising demand through growing investment or incomes has a positive effect. Consistent with Engel's law, the results also indicate that demand for agricultural and manufacturing first rises with income and then falls at higher levels, thereby eventually diminishing the level of traditional employment. Hence, the argument and results for spending appear quite robust to both the charge that deindustrialization is merely a mediating variable and the charge that its association with spending is a result of reversed causality.

One caveat is that technological change and productivity growth are affected by international competition. Undoubtedly, there is some truth to this. German and Japanese car makers pushed Americans ones to adopt more flexible and efficient production methods, while competition from American high-tech firms triggered massive investments in information technology everywhere else. But competition and innovation is a general feature of capitalism and would surely have occurred in large measure even in the absence of growing trade and capital mobility.

5.4. Conclusion: The Welfare State at the End of Industrial Society

Based on data for sixteen OECD countries over a thirty-five-year period, there is little evidence that trade, or capital mobility for that matter, has played an important role in the expansion of the modern welfare state. Correspondingly, there is little support for the idea, proposed by Katzenstein (1985), that large countries will become more akin to small corporatist welfare states as they grow increasingly exposed to the vagaries of international markets. On the other hand there is also little evidence that globalization is a major threat to the welfare state. Instead, what has propelled much of the expansion of the welfare state since the early 1960s is a dynamic process of technological progress in manufacturing combined with the saturation of markets for agricultural and industrial products.

Somewhat paradoxically, therefore, the very process that has decimated the traditional industrial working class underpins the growth of the welfare state. However, it does not mean that partisan politics has played no role. By and large, left governments have been more prone to raise spending in response to deindustrialization than have right governments. Likewise, institutions that tend to be associated with "left" politics, namely elaborate vocational training and proportional representation, have greatly magnified the spending effects of deindustrialization.

214

Perhaps the most pressing political question flowing from the results is what happens when the deindustrialization process comes to a halt. Figure 5.7, which shows the relationship between the share of the working age population outside industry and the speed of deindustrialization, clearly suggests that such a slowdown is occurring. From very different starting points in the early 1960s (the labeled entries to the left of the dotted line), all countries have been converging on a "postindustrial" equilibrium in the 1990s (the labeled entries to the right of the dotted line), albeit at very different speeds. This process of convergence has been accompanied by a slowdown in the pace of deindustrialization (the vertical axis). If the insecurities associated with past deindustrialization spread demands for compensation and for socialization of risks well into the middle classes, will the stabilization of the sectoral employment structure reverse the process?

As already noted, this is unlikely to happen. The costs of retrenchment are concentrated on vocal constituencies, and most people have simply

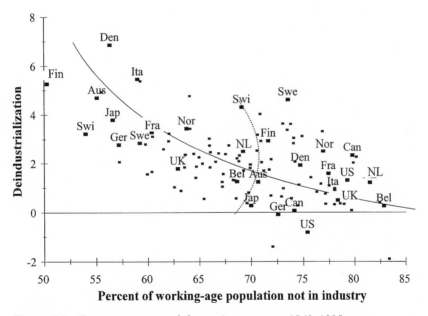

Figure 5.7 Convergence toward the service economy, 1960–1995.

Notes: Labeled dots are the first (1960–3) and last (1992–5) observations in the data set. Early observations fall to the left of the dotted line, except in the cases of Canada and the United States, where both observations are to the right of the line. The unlabeled dots represent the observations of intervening years.

215

become too dependent on the welfare state to want its dismantlement (Pierson 1994, 1996). However, the slowdown is likely to be accompanied by more intense distributive battles between those in secure and those in insecure labor market positions. If people in secure positions know that they are highly unlikely to end up in insecure ones (i.e., face low labor market risks), they have less reason to be solidaristic with those in insecure positions. This general conclusion stands in sharp contrast to the postmaterialism thesis advanced by Inglehart (1987, 1990) and others, and it will be subject to more intense analysis in Chapter 6.

6

New Tradeoffs, New Policies

CHALLENGES OF THE SERVICE
ECONOMY

This chapter applies the welfare production regime argument to the case of service employment and tests its economic and political implications. Because job growth in high-skilled, better-paid services is limited by the size of the domestic market, whereas growth in low-skilled, low-paid service jobs is hampered by wage compression and high social costs, the transition toward a more sheltered postindustrial economy has produced a difficult tradeoff between equality and employment, mediated only by the willingness of the government to increase public employment or subsidize private employment at a cost to tax payers.

As Anne Wren and I have argued (Iversen and Wren 1998), governments initially responded to this "trilemma" in a manner that clearly reflected partisan preferences and broader institutional conditions. Thus, right governments in liberal market economies sought to further deregulate labor markets, whereas governments in coordinated market economies embarked on policies to either ration work (primarily in countries with independent central banks and strong Christian democratic parties) or to increase spending on public employment (primarily in countries with highly centralized wage bargaining and strong social democratic parties). The division between varieties of capitalism described in Part I has thus been overlaid by new divisions that are the result of different political responses to deindustrialization.

This chapter takes a fresh look at the tradeoffs and how governments in different parts of the world have adapted to them. After a period of intensely partisan responses, governments are increasingly embarking on strategies – including deregulation of part-time employment, new educational initiatives aimed at upskilling, service trade liberalization, and tax reforms – that are designed to supplant the trilemma and return to a more virtuous cycle between social protection, equality, and private sector employment.

In the final section of this chapter, I discuss the nature of these new policy initiatives, including their underlying coalitional dynamics, their record of success so far, and their prospects for success in the future – in particular the possibilities for recreating the linkage between generous social protection, high wages, and open trade that existed in the golden era of the industrial economy (outlined in Chapter 2).

6.1. A New Set of Tradeoffs

At the crux of the regime argument applied to services is the notion that wage structure affects relative prices and employment. High labor costs for low-skilled labor raise relative prices in low productivity services and are therefore not conducive to the rise of low-cost, labor-intensive services (Esping-Andersen 1990; Iversen and Wren 1998). This section examines the empirical basis for this thesis in detail, focusing first on prices and then on employment. While the main aim is to establish the economic tradeoffs faced by governments in a deindustrializing economy, I note that the analysis provides a solution to one of the most enduring puzzles in international economics, namely why domestic price levels vary systematically across countries – what is known as the purchasing power parity puzzle.

6.1.1. Prices

It is very difficult to compare prices on particular services directly across countries. Detailed international classifications of services do not exist, and even very similar services, such as long-distance phone rates, typically exhibit so many subtle product differences that systematic cross-country comparisons are all but impossible. The approach I adopt here relies instead on international comparisons of the prices on comparable baskets of goods and services, called purchasing power parities (PPP).[1] Although these comparisons are based on the domestic prices of both manufactures and services, because prices are likely to diverge more on sparsely traded services than on highly traded manufactures, lasting price differentials are likely to primarily reflect differences in prices on services. Another advantage of using these data is that I can plug into an well-established theoretical and empirical tradition in economics, purchasing power parity theory, with a clear methodology and an agreed set of empirical puzzles.

---

[1] The baskets are not identical, but the OECD encourages countries to follow the same standards, and the measures are widely considered reasonably reliable for comparison.

The PPP approach to international price comparisons is to first determine the exchange rate, usually in dollars, that would buy the same basket of products in different countries. This PPP exchange rate can then be compared to the actual exchange rate. If the latter is higher, in dollars, than the PPP exchange rate, the domestic price level is above the price level in the comparison country. A simple measure of the degree of over- or undervaluation at time t is the *real exchange rate q*:

$$q_t = e_t \frac{p_t^*}{p_t} \tag{6.1}$$

where e is the nominal (dollar) exchange rate, p is the domestic consumer price index, and p^* is the U.S. consumer price index. The fraction p/p^* is the PPP exchange rate.

According to the *law of one price*, identical products that can costlessly be transported from one location to another should have the same price in all localities. If not, goods-market arbitrage would quickly eliminate any price discrepancies. Hence, at least over a period of time sufficiently long to allow for price adjustments to shocks, q should equal 1. This is the fundamental null hypothesis in PPP theory. In the strong version of the theory, q is always equal to 1. But if prices are sticky, short-term price or exchange rate shocks will not be immediately eliminated. In the weaker version, therefore, PPP theory predicts parity only after the period of time it takes for prices to adapt. Most crucially, perhaps, if nominal wages are set through collective wage bargaining, price adjustments will be delayed by the frequency with which wages are renegotiated.

There is a wealth of empirical studies seeking to test the PPP thesis against data on real exchange rates. The results are mixed. Early studies found no evidence that deviations from PPP were *ever* corrected, implying that real exchange rates could be treated as random walks (Krugman 1978; Adler and Lehmann 1983; Meese and Rogoff 1988). This finding was disconcerting, if not outright embarrassing, for economists. Subsequent evidence, however, suggests that real exchange rates do eventually revert to their mean value. Estimates of the time it takes for disturbances to decay vary, but most imply half-life ranges of 3–6 years (a half-life is the time it takes for a PPP deviation to decay by 50 percent). Recent examples of this research include Frankel and Rose (1996), Lothian and Taylor (1996), Oh (1996), and Papell (1997).

The findings of mean reversion are comforting for PPP theory, but, as noted by Rogoff, "a half-life of three to five years [is] seemingly too long to be explained by nominal rigidities" (1996, p. 648). A related, and potentially more serious, problem is that many of the empirical results leave open the possibility that real exchange rates revert to means that are persistently different from PPP, or a real exchange rate of one. Indeed, this is what the empirical results in this section clearly imply. I argue that these deviations from parity, the purchasing power parity puzzle, are in large measure the result of cross-national differences in the level of social protection – in particular differences in the politically mediated wage structure.

To see this, first express Equation (6.1) in natural logarithms:

$$\ln q_t = \ln e_t + \ln p_t^* - \ln p_t \tag{6.2}$$

If PPP holds in the long run, the right-hand side must revert to zero over time (the real exchange rate is unity). By implication, deviations from zero must be temporary, and any disturbance must be followed by a decay process. This decay process can be estimated using the following regression equation:

$$\ln q_t = \rho \ln q_{t-1} + \varepsilon_t \tag{6.3}$$

where ρ must be between 0 and 1 for disturbances to decay over time. Alternatively, by subtracting $\ln q_{t-1}$ on both sides, (6.3) can be written as

$$\Delta \ln q_t = \delta \ln q_{t-1} + \varepsilon_t \tag{6.4}$$

where $\delta = (\rho - 1)$ is each period's decay in the initial deviation from PPP. For example, if $\delta = -.25$ it means that disturbances are damped out at 25 percent in each period.

Tests of this model on single currencies in the post–Bretton Woods era all tend to fail to reject the null hypothesis of a random walk. As Wu summarizes the evidence, "while results obtained by employing long-horizon data (century plus) offer limited support for the validity of PPP in the long run, those obtained by using the post–Bretton Woods data remain largely negative" (Wu 1996, p. 55). To overcome these problems, a number of recent studies use pooled data for several countries. This method is particularly relevant to our purposes because it allows us to detect cross-national differences in deviations from PPP.

If real exchange rates are measured against the same base currency, here the U.S. dollar, the model to be estimated is simply

$$\Delta \ln q_{i,t} = \delta \ln q_{i,t-1} + \varepsilon_{i,t} \tag{6.5}$$

where i indexes countries. Because there is leftover first-order serial correlation, it is common practice in this literature to include a lagged difference
term.[2] With this refinement, Table 6.1, column 1, shows the results of estimating this equation on annual data for eighteen OECD countries in the
post-Bretton Woods era.

Note that the parameter on the lagged dependent level variable is negative so that deviations from PPP dampen over time. This process of mean
reversion, however, is rather slow with a half-life of almost 4 years. This
is at the higher end of the range of existing estimates, and it is significantly above the estimates in some studies of OECD currencies for the
post–Bretton Woods period where the half-life tends to be much shorter.
For example, Wu (1996) finds a half-life of 2.3 years, Papell (1997) one of
2.5 years, and Oh (1996) one of between 1 and 2 years. However, this
discrepancy turns out to be the result of a simple difference in model specification. Whereas I have used absolute PPP levels, the practice in the literature is to measure real exchange rates as *deviations from their national means*.
This procedure is equivalent to controlling for country-specific effects:

$$\Delta \ln q_{i,t} = \delta \ln q_{i,t-1} + \sum_{i=1}^{N} b_i d_i + \varepsilon_{i,t} \tag{6.6}$$

where d_i is the dummy variable for country i. Column 2 in Table 6.1 shows
the results of estimating this fixed effect model.

Note that there is a notable increase in the explained variance from
the model without dummies, and an F-test unambiguously shows that the
dummies belong in the model. Moreover, the half-life of deviations from
parity is now significantly reduced to only 1.7 years. This is more consistent
with a sticky price hypothesis than the 4-year half-life in Equation (6.6). It
may still be too long to be fully explained by slowly adjusting wages and
prices, and it is possible that trade costs at the consumer level provide an
important reason for slow price adjustments (see Rogoff 1996; Obstfeld and
Rogoff 2000). But it is quite in agreement with existing results.

The key issue for our purposes, however, is not the speed of price adjustments but the fact that real exchange rates in many countries *never* converge to PPP, as implied by the significant effects of the country dummies.
To find out how much, on average, the real exchange rate of a country
is overvalued, we take the inverse of the log value of the parameter for

---

[2] Higher order lags show no significant effects.

Table 6.1. *Real Exchange Rates for Eighteen OECD Countries, 1973–1997[a]*

	(1)	(2)	(3)	(4)	(5)
Intercept	0.02	0.00	−0.66**	−1.65***	−0.97**
	(3.67)	(0.00)	(−2.18)	(−3.39)	(−2.80)
ln(Real exchange rate)$_{t-1}$	−0.17***	−0.32***	−0.34***	−0.36***	−0.25***
	(−8.12)	(−11.62)	(−11.73)	(−9.87)	(−8.48)
ln(GDP per capita)$_t$	–	–	0.07**	0.18***	0.11***
			(2.19)	(3.66)	(3.06)
d5/d1 ratio$_{t-1}$	–	–	–	−0.15	−0.16***
				(−0.73)	(−4.00)
Australia	–	0.02	0.03	0.01	–
Austria	–	0.02	0.05	0.07	–
Belgium	–	0.02	0.04	0.04	–
Canada	–	0.01	0.02	0.06	–
Denmark	–	0.08	0.10	0.06	–
Finland	–	0.07	0.09	0.09	–
France	–	0.02	0.04	0.05	–
Germany	–	0.05	0.07	0.06	–
Ireland	–	−0.01	0.04	0.11	–
Italy	–	−0.04	−0.01	0.03	–
Japan	–	0.07	0.09	0.12	–
Netherlands	–	0.03	0.06	0.07	–
New Zealand	–	−0.05	−0.03	−0.01	–
Norway	–	0.11	0.13	0.09	–
Sweden	–	0.09	0.11	0.09	–
Switzerland	–	0.09	0.10	0.13	–
United Kingdom	–	−0.02	−0.00	0.02	–
Lagged difference term	0.37***	0.42***	0.43***	0.41***	0.37***
	(8.60)	(10.03)	(10.24)	(7.64)	(6.99)
R-squared	.208	.310	.317	.340	.265
Number of observations	450	450	445	284	284

Significance levels: *** <.01; ** <.05 (t-scores in parenthesis).
[a] Exchange rates are measured against the U.S. dollar and expressed in logged differences. The reference country for the country dummies is the United States.

Sources: Exchange rates: OECD (1999c); GDP per capita: World Bank's Global Development Network Growth Database at *www.worldbank.org/research/growth/GDNdata.htm* (this variable is constructed from Penn World Table label="5.6", Global Development Finance and World Development Indicators); d5/d1 ratios: *OECD Electronic Data Base on Wage Dispersion*, undated.

that country's dummy and subtract 1 (parity) from the result. The long-run equilibrium value is determined by dividing by $-\delta$. Using this formula, the Swedish real exchange rate, for example, turns out to be an average of 31 percent overvalued compared to the U.S. dollar. Hence, a dollar would on average buy 31 percent less in Sweden than in the United States during the period 1973–97. For comparison, the Swedish real GDP per capita grew by a mere 9 percent in this period, implying that an elimination of the price gap between Sweden and the United States would add three times more to the Swedish GDP than what real economic growth accomplished during this period.[3] Deviations from PPP are clearly not trivial by any reasonable economic yardstick. But how do we explain them?

In a classic formulation of PPP theory, Balassa and Samuelson propose one possible solution (Balassa 1964; Samuelson 1964). They hypothesize that because productivity in traded sectors rises faster than productivity in nontraded sectors – in accordance with the Baumol hypothesis – rich countries will have higher real exchange rates than poor countries insofar as competitive labor markets eliminate wage differentials between sectors. The logic is that lower productivity growth in one sector will result in higher real labor costs, and therefore higher relative prices. High per capita GDP, which equals high relative productivity in the traded sector, will therefore be associated with a high real exchange rate.

Rogoff (1996) shows that this proposition is supported by data covering both rich and poor countries, but he also shows that per capita income fails to explain most of the variance among developed countries. The same conclusion follows if GDP per capita is included in our previous regression (see column 3 of Table 6.1). A 1 percent increase in per capita income raises the long-term real exchange rate by about 0.2 of a percentage point, although this estimate is not very accurate (the effect is statistically different from zero only at a .05 significance level). More importantly, the country-specific effects are not much affected by the inclusion of per capita income. The correlation coefficient between the parameters on the country dummies before and after inclusion of per capita income is 0.98, and the mean predicted currency overvaluation in fact *rises* from 11 to 17 percent (in the case of Sweden it is now 36 percent).

To explain the variance among developed countries, we need to drop the assumption of perfectly competitive labor markets. If skills are partly firm, industry, or sector specific, or if there are market imperfections, then wages for workers at similar skill levels can vary considerably between traded and nontraded sectors (as well as within these). Yet, such productivity-based wage differentials do not necessarily affect workers in the same sector to the

---

[3] In fairness, though, it should be mentioned that 1993 was a terrible year for the Swedish economy. Using 1994 instead shows a 23 percent increase in real per capita.

same extent. Some may be more unionized than others, while some will be in product market segments with price-inelastic demands that make it easier to externalize higher wage costs. Still others will enjoy monopoly power through accreditation, certification, and other measures that may restrict labor supply. In any of these scenarios the most important determinant of the price effects of differential productivity growth is the extent of intra- and inter-industry wage-coordination. And we know that coordinated wage-setting institutions tend to raise relative wages for low-paid workers, which tend to be concentrated in certain nontraded services.

It should be noted that this logic does not require wages to be institution-ally coordinated across sectors. The relative price effect will occur whenever the wage leaders in low-productivity, nontraded industries, based on their labor market power, are able to keep up with wages in traded sectors, *and* wages within the sector are tightly coupled as a result of intra-industry wage coordination. Under these conditions, the relative prices of services pro-duced with low-paid, low-productivity labor will be higher. That said, it is generally true that the higher the level of coordination, the more wage com-pression across sectors there is, and the greater the relative price effect is.

The effect of wage compression is illustrated in Figure 6.1, which shows the relationship between earnings dispersion and the percentage overval-uation of countries' real exchange rates (using the procedure described previously in the Swedish example), controlling for per capita income. The dispersion measure is OECD's figures for the earnings of a worker with the median earnings relative to a worker with earnings in the bottom decile (d5/d1 ratios).[4]

Note that the relationship is in the predicted direction and moderately strong ($r = .56$). For example, the three egalitarian Scandinavian coun-tries have significantly "overvalued" real exchange rates, whereas three inegalitarian countries – Britain, Canada, and the United States – have rel-atively undervalued currencies. Italy is clearly an outlier, exhibiting a com-pressed wage structure but also a relatively "cheap" currency. Unlike other figures, however, OECD's estimate of Italian wage compression varies. In the 1997 OECD *Employment Outlook*, the average d5/d1 ratio reported for Italy is 1.8, whereas the average in OECD's Electronic Data Base on

---

[4] The numbers are averages for the period from 1979, when data starts in most countries, to the early 1990s. I used d5/d1 rather than d10/d1 ratios because dispersion at the lower end of the earnings distribution is more pertinent to the argument than earnings for high-income people.

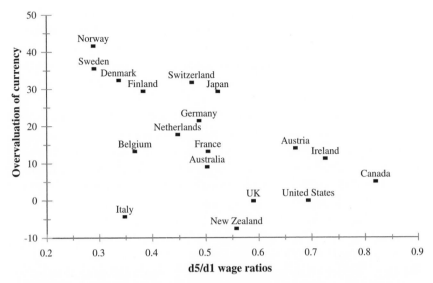

Figure 6.1 Wage dispersion and average currency overvaluation, 1993–1997.
Note: Figures for overvaluation are based on the estimated parameters for the country dummies model, Table 6.1, column 3.
Source: OECD, *Electronic Data Base on Wage Dispersion*, undated.

Wage Dispersion (undated) is 1.4. Using the number in the printed version eliminates Italy as an outlier and raises the correlation coefficient between dispersion and real exchange rates to .70. If the electronic figure is more accurate, a plausible explanation may center on the many and large devaluations of the Italian Lira in the post-Bretton Woods period.

If we include d5/d1 ratios directly in the regression equation (column 4 in Table 6.1), we can get a more precise estimate of the price effects of the wage structure.[5] Because we only have dispersion data for a subset of the original period from 1973 to 1997, the number of observations is significantly reduced. In some cases, data are only available for part of the 1980s, and in one case, Ireland, there is only a single observation (for 1993). Another problem is multicollinearity: The country dummies explain nearly 97 percent of the variance in wage dispersion, making it difficult to obtain statistically significant results for the dispersion variable. This is evident if we take the dummies out of the equation (column 5) since the parameter for wage dispersion then becomes highly significant.

---

[5] I am using the electronic data here and throughout the rest of this chapter.

Removing the dummies also slightly increases the effect of dispersion, but the parameters are very similar in both regressions. Because we are confident about the relationship between wage structure and real exchange rates, we can therefore get a good sense of the substantive impact from either estimate. It turns out that the immediate (one year) effect of a 1 percent increase in dispersion is to reduce prices by 0.15 percent (using the fixed effect model). After 2 years, the effect is 0.21 percent, and in the long run it approaches 0.41 percent. If we converted the dependent variable into percentage over- or undervaluation, the long-term parameter on the dispersion variable would be −52, which is nearly identical to the slope on the regression line in Figure 6.1 (−53). The results of the multivariate pooled times-series analysis thus confirm the simple bivariate cross-sectional analysis.

A nice check on these results is to make use of the so-called Big Mac Index developed by *The Economist*. The Big Mac PPP is the exchange rate that would mean that a McDonald Big Mac hamburger, presumably an almost identical product wherever it is sold, costs the same in that country as in the United States. Comparing actual exchange rates with PPPs indicates whether a currency is under- or overvalued, or, alternatively, whether a Big Mac is cheap or expensive. And because Big Macs are not internationally traded, we have a direct measure of prices in a nontraded industry.

The index is available only for a subset of the OECD countries, and only for 14 years. Still, relating d5/d1 ratios to average currency overvaluation by this measure (Figure 6.2) produces a very similar pattern to that in Figure 6.1. The most notable difference is that the range of under- and overvaluation is almost twice that for the basket of goods and services used to calculate regular PPP ratios. The likely reason is that the price of a Big Mac is determined primarily by the cost of nontraded inputs, especially low-skilled labor, whereas the regular PPP basket of goods and services contain both traded and nontraded components as well as labor inputs across the wage scale.

To take an illustrative example on the regression line, the average overvaluation of the Swedish currency compared to the Big Mac PPP is 50 percent, whereas the overvaluation of the currency compared to the basket PPP is about 35 percent in the same period. We can explain the Big Mac overvaluation directly in terms of differential wages. Assuming that McDonald's workers' wages are on average in the bottom twentieth percentile of the earnings distribution in both countries, which seems reasonable, OECD wage data show that a Swedish worker is earning 52 percent more than an American worker during the period for which both wage and Big Mac

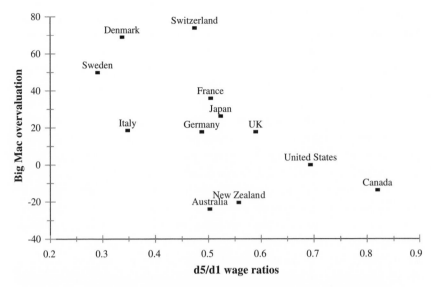

Figure 6.2 Wage dispersion and the relative price of Big Macs, 1988–2000.
Sources: Big Mac Index: *The Economist*, 6.9.86, 17.1.87, 2.4.88, 15.4.89, 8.5.90, 13.4.91, 18.4.92, 17.4.93, 9.4.94, 15.4.95, 27.4.96, 12.4.97, 11.4.98, 3.4.99, 29.4.00. d5/d1 ratios: OECD, *Electronic Data Base on Wage Dispersion*, undated.

price data are available (at the bottom tenth percentile of the distribution, the figure is 73 percent). This is almost exactly equivalent to the surcharge for a Big Mac in Sweden compared to that in the United States. Moreover, this gap in the wages of low-paid workers is not simply a reflection of higher average Swedish wages (which is essentially the Balassa-Samuelson hypothesis) – the mean wage in Sweden is almost equivalent to that in the United States during this period (in fact it is 6 percent higher). Swedes pay more for their Big Macs than Americans primarily because Swedish wages are more compressed.[6]

From this analysis, it seems safe to conclude that permanent differences in the price level of different countries – or deviations from PPP – are in large measure attributable to a combination of lower productivity in nontraded services and institutionally mediated wage compression. After these effects have been taken into account, the real exchange rate data are fully compatible with the thesis that prices on traded goods converge to PPP

---

[6] Of course, there are inputs other than labor that matter for hamburger prices. But many of these are traded and therefore less likely to account for cross-national differences, and about three quarters of all costs in the hotel and restaurant business are due to labor costs.

after a lag that can be explained by a combination of sticky prices/wages and trade imperfections.

6.1.2. Employment

When relative prices of an industry rise, all else being equal, production and employment fall – assuming, of course, that prices and employment are market determined.[7] The second effect of wage compression is, therefore, an employment effect. The magnitude of this effect, however, varies across sectors. As discussed previously, intraoccupational compression in the heavily traded manufacturing sector primarily has the effect of shifting the comparative advantage of countries toward higher value added and skill-intensive activities without reducing employment. As long as unions are fairly encompassing, they have an incentive to set general wages at a level consistent with maintaining international competitiveness.

In nontraded sectors, by contrast, because specialization has not evolved to the same extent, wage and other forms of social protection lead to rising relative prices and reduced employment growth if services are market supplied (Iversen and Wren 1998; Scharpf 2000; Manow 2002). The magnitude of this effect, however, is conditioned by several factors. First, and rather obviously, the greater the capacity of an industry to increase productivity is, the smaller the relative price effect is, and the smaller the employment effect is. Second, the lower the price elasticity of demand is, the easier it is for firms to externalize the costs of higher real wages and not cut employment. This tends to be true in skill-intensive services such as consulting and medicine. Conversely, the more an industry relies on low-skilled labor to produce easily substitutable products, and the higher the proportion of total costs is that goes to wages, the more sensitive the industry will be to wage compression. Consequently, companies in an industry that is lagging in productivity, faces price-elastic demand, relies heavily on low-paid labor, and engages in production where labor costs constitute a high share of total costs will be particularly vulnerable to wage compression.

With these distinctions in mind, Table 6.2 compares three private service sectors in terms of productivity growth, share of labor costs in total costs, and relative wages. Together these services account for the entire

---

[7] I consider the possibility of nonmarket provision of services later in this chapter, where the cost of provision is covered through taxation.

Table 6.2. *Productivity, Relative Earnings, Labor Shares, and Private Employment in Four Sectors*

	Productivity[a]	Relative Wages[b]	Labor Shares[c]	Change in Employment[d]
Manufacturing (Isic 3)	3.1	100	0.70	−5.9
Business services (Isic 8)	0.0	106	0.41	2.7
Wholesale and retail trade (Isic 6)	1.2	82	0.73	2.6
Social and personal services (Isic 9)	−0.3	70	0.69	4.7

[a] Average growth in total factor productivity 1970–95.
[b] Average sector wages as a percent of manufacturing wages.
[c] Average share of labor compensation in value added.
[d] Change in employment as a share of the working-age population (population-weighted).
Source: Calculated from OECD (1999a).

rise in private employment between 1970 and 1995.[8] Manufacturing employment, which has everywhere declined, is used as a reference for the comparison.

It is apparent from these data that business services (Isic 8) are quite different from other services. Although productivity is stagnant, relative wages are much higher than in other services – presumably a result of more skill-intensive production – and the factor share of labor in total output is notably smaller than in other sectors. The latter is likely a reflection of the importance of proprietary standards and intellectual capital that simultaneously raise capital intensity and the level of wages. The wholesale and retail sector (Isic 6), and social and personal services (Isic 9), by contrast, are both relatively low-pay sectors with high labor shares and low productivity. Social and personal services are particularly dependent on low-paid labor and record the lowest capacity for productivity growth. On the other hand, wholesale and retail trade is the most labor-intensive sector. Unfortunately it is not possible to get any systematically comparable indicators for price elasticity. Yet, one would expect that the more knowledge-intensive character of business services makes demand less price elastic than in the other two sectors where price competition tends to be fierce.

To explore the linkage between wage structure and private employment, the four panels in Figure 6.3 show the relationship between dispersion of industry earnings and annual change in private employment (as a percent

[8] I ignore a small sector of transport and storage services where employment has declined slightly (0.14 percent of the working-age population).

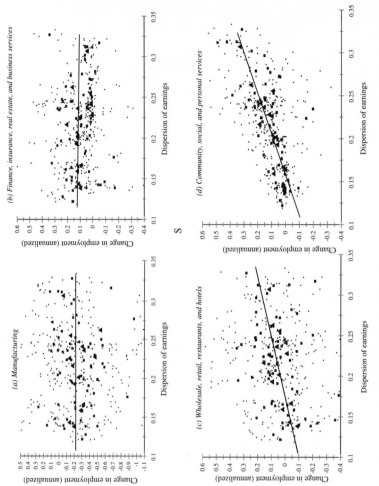

Figure 6.3 Dispersion of earnings and employment growth in four economic sectors.

of the working-age population) by sector. As in Iversen and Wren (1998), I use figures for industry dispersion in wages, rather than d5/d1 ratios, because these are available for the same countries and years as the employment data. Yet, as I show in the subsequent statistical analysis, the pattern is similar using d5/d1 ratios.

Because the yearly changes (small dots) are very volatile, the graphs also use 5-year averages (squares) as well as whole-period averages (triangles). Note that for two sectors, manufacturing and business services, there is virtually no relationship between wage dispersion and employment growth. The only difference between these sectors is that manufacturing has experienced a dramatic drop in employment, while producer services have been a net gainer (as indicated by the averages on the y-axis). Yet, while the growth in the number of jobs in business services has been rapid, in no country except the United States has the gain in employment in business services been sufficient to compensate for the loss in manufacturing.

The sectors that account for most of the divergence in private sector employment performance across countries are wholesale and retail trade (Isic 6), and especially social and personal services (Isic 9). In both sectors, greater dispersion is associated with more rapid growth in employment. This is particularly notable in social and personal services, which has been the main engine of employment across the OECD area during the past three decades. The pattern is consistent with the expectations first explained in Iversen and Wren (1998). Thus, employment in the slow-productivity and low-wage sectors exhibits a close association with wage compression, while in other sectors it does not.

Table 6.3 shows the magnitudes of the differences in the relationships between wage structure and private employment performance, using slopes of the regression lines in Figure 6.3 and correlation coefficients at different levels of aggregation as statistics.[9] Confirming a visual inspection of the graphs, there is no relationship between dispersion and employment in manufacturing or in business services – the latter might even be slightly negative – whereas there is a clear positive relationship in the wholesale and retail sector and especially in social and personal services.

The relationship between dispersion and employment is likewise strong if we combine the latter two sectors (Isic 6 and 9), which we may simply call *consumer services*. At the level of whole-period averages, the bivariate

[9] One large outlier, Canada in 1989, is left out here and in the subsequent analysis. The reasons for this one outlier (out of 331) is unclear.

Table 6.3. *The Bivariate Relationship between Dispersion of Earnings and Employment Growth in Three Service Sectors*

Periodization	Sector	Slope	Correlation Coefficient
Annual (14 × 25 obs.)	(1) Manufacturing	0.31	0.04
	(2) Finance, insurance, and business services	−0.21	0.07
	(3) Wholesale, retail, restaurants, and hotels	0.82	0.18
	(4) Social and personal services	1.84	0.48
	(5) Consumer services (3+4)	2.66	0.40
5-year averages (14 × 5 obs.)	(1) Manufacturing	0.32	0.06
	(2) Finance, insurance, and business services	−0.18	0.08
	(3) Wholesale, retail, restaurants, and hotels	0.92	0.28
	(4) Social and personal services	1.88	0.67
	(5) Consumer services (3+4)	2.80	0.56
Whole period (14 obs.)	(1) Manufacturing	0.07	0.03
	(2) Finance, insurance, and business services	−0.27	0.24
	(3) Wholesale, retail, restaurants, and hotels	1.00*	0.74
	(4) Social and personal services	1.73*	0.90
	(5) Consumer services (3+4)	2.73*	0.90

* Statistically significant at a .01 level (only pertains to whole period slopes since the observations in the time series data are not statistically independent).
Source: Calculated from OECD (1999a).

relationship is almost perfect ($r = .9$) whether we consider social and personal services separately or look at consumer services as a whole.

But bivariate correlations can be misleading, especially in data that exhibit both cross-sectional and cross-time variance, and other factors surely play a role. First, it has been argued that restrictive macroeconomic conditions in many European countries during the 1980s and early 1990s hurt employment performance in those countries (Scharpf 1991; Soskice 2000; Hall and Soskice 2001; Manow 2002). Furthermore, as argued by Scharpf

(1991), Hall and Franzese (1998), Iversen (1999) and others, equilibrium unemployment can vary across countries depending on the particular setup of macroeconomic institutions. We should therefore expect better unemployment performance to be associated with better employment performance. However, this *does not* explain why cross-national employment performance varies *across sectors*, as is clearly the case.

This intersectoral variance may potentially be explained with reference to the effects of trade with less-developed countries. As argued by Wood (1994) and Leamer (1996), LDC trade puts downward pressure on wages in those industries with the highest concentration of low-skilled workers. If low-wage competition simultaneously causes deindustrialization and migration of workers to services, then LDC trade would confound the relationship between earnings dispersion and employment. In particular, we should expect LDC trade to be positively related to employment in low-paid services. Recall, however, that we found no evidence in Chapter 5 that LDC trade leads to deindustrialization, so there is reason for some ex ante skepticism about the empirical importance of this argument.

In contrast to the purportedly strong effect of LDC trade, the analysis in Chapter 5 found clear evidence that per capita income affects service employment, and for good reasons. Because demand for services, in accordance with Engel's law, tends to be income elastic (the higher the level of income is, the greater the demand is for services), we should expect higher levels of service employment in high-income countries, and rising levels of employment in countries experiencing growth in incomes. As with the macroeconomic argument, however, it is less clear that this helps us explain cross-national differences in the performance of particular service sectors.

An argument that points both to the supply and demand side concerns the influx of women into the labor market. Female labor force participation increases the supply of labor; at the same time, it raises demand for social and personal services such as daycare and food services (see Huber and Stephens 2000). The effect is dissipated, however, to the extent that these services (most obviously daycare) are provided through the public sector. Indeed, if such services are paid for through higher taxes that raise the costs of privately provided services, the net effect of female labor force participation on private sector employment would not be clear.

This leads us to an argument about taxation that has been recently proposed by Fritz Scharpf (Scharpf 2000). Scharpf points out that the tax wedge, which is the added costs of labor attributable to taxation, can hurt employment in cost-sensitive services if the tax code does not make exemptions for low-paid workers. In particular, taxes raised through employer social security contributions and taxation on consumption tend to be regressive compared to taxes on income, and regressive taxes place a particularly high burden on low-wage sectors. Note that this argument is a subspecies of the general wage structure argument, since what ultimately matters to employers is the total wage bill. Yet it important because it pinpoints a mechanism, the structure of taxation, that can be manipulated politically without raising inequality.[10]

A related issue concerns the use of tax revenues. While some revenues are returned to the private sector in the form of reimbursements for, say, medical expenses, other revenues are used to employ people to provide the services directly. Government provision of services varies greatly across countries, and such provision may have crowded out private services in some countries, while privatization of public services in other countries may have "inflated" private employment performance. This argument is only unambiguously relevant for social and personal services because the government is not involved to any significant degree in the provision of other services, but it is precisely in social and personal services that we find the strongest relationship between earnings structure and employment.

To test these alternative hypotheses, I carried out a regression analysis using changes in (private sector) consumer service employment as a percentage of the working age population, e, as the dependent variable. These services account for between 67 percent (country weighted) and 72 percent (population weighted) of the growth in total service employment between 1970 and 1996, and they account for almost the entire cross-national variance in private service employment performance (because employment growth varies more across countries in consumer services than in producer services).

In addition to the wage dispersion variable, I included the following set of controls designed to capture the preceding arguments:

1. Standardized unemployment rates to control for macroeconomic conditions (OECD, *Economic Outlook*, various years)

---

[10] Yet, one has to be careful in predicting the effects of altering the tax structure because a shift in the tax burden from employer contribution to income taxation may be accompanied by higher wage demands by low-paid unions. Lower social security contributions raise the capacity of employers to pay higher wages, which indirectly confers more bargaining power on unions.

2. Per capita income to capture income elasticity effects (Heston, Summers, and Aten, 2002, Penn World Table 5.6).
3. Trade with less-developed countries as a percentage of GDP to control for the effect of low wage competition (IMF, *Direction of Trade Statistics Yearbook*, various years),
4. Female labor force participation as a percentage of the working-age population to control for the supply-and-demand side effects of such participation (OECD, *Labour Force Statistics*, various years),
5. Consumption taxes and social security contributions as a percentage of GDP to control for the tax wedge thesis (OECD 2002).
6. Government employment as a percentage of the working-age population to control for the possible crowding-out effects of public employment (OECD, *Labour Force Statistics*, various years)

In addition, to hedge against arguments about country-specific conditions that are not captured by these variables, the regression includes a full set of country dummies.[11] Using the same error correction setup as in the case of prices, the model is

$$\Delta e_{i,t} = \delta e_{i,t-1} + \sum_{i=1}^{N} b_i d_i + \sum_{v=1}^{M} b_v x_{i,t-1,v} + \sum_{v=1}^{M} b_v^{\Delta} \Delta x_{i,t,v} + \varepsilon_{i,t} \qquad (6.7)$$

where d_i refers to the dummy variable for country i, and $x_{t,v}$ is the vth independent variable at time t (entered both as changes and as lagged levels), and Δ is the first difference operator.

The results of the analysis are shown in Table 6.4, which, for purposes of comparison, also includes the results for business services (the first column). Supporting the findings in Iversen and Wren (1998), wage dispersion is strongly positively related to employment in consumer services, but not in business services (compare the first two columns). The precision of the parameter estimate for consumer services is high and statistically different from zero.[12] In substantive terms, the first-year effect of a 1-standard-deviation increase in wage dispersion is to increase employment by 0.15 percent of the working-age population. After 3 years, the effect is 0.45

---

[11] An F-test also indicates that these dummies belong in the model.

[12] The setup with a full set of dummies in fact gives a very conservative estimate of the statistical significance level. As in the price equations, we have a fairly severe case of multicollinearity between wage dispersion and the country dummies – the latter account for 86 percent of the variance in the former – and if the dummies are removed, the significance level of the wage dispersion variable improves notably.

Table 6.4. *The Determinants of Private Service Sector Employment Growth*

	Business Services (Isic 8)[a]	Consumer Services (Isic 6 + Isic 9)[a]		
Intercept	−0.14	−0.85***	−0.92***	−0.34
	(−1.01)	(−3.95)	(−3.34)	(−1.11)
Earnings dispersion$_{t-1}$	0.40	3.07***	3.08***	2.22***
	(1.29)	(3.93)	(3.96)	(3.00)
Δ Earnings dispersion$_t$	−0.66	2.89	3.03	2.48
	(−0.79)	(1.47)	(1.55)	(1.33)
Unemployment$_{t-1}$	−0.01***	−0.03***	−0.03***	−0.04***
	(−3.21)	(−5.77)	(−5.03)	(−6.14)
Δ Unemployment$_t$	−0.06***	−0.12***	−0.12***	−0.12***
	(−6.18)	(−7.57)	(−7.52)	(−7.18)
GDP per capita$_{t-1}$	0.00	0.07***	0.06***	0.10***
	(0.20)	(2.88)	(2.73)	(4.21)
Δ GDP per capita$_t$	0.11***	0.36***	0.37***	0.41***
	(3.33)	(5.34)	(5.43)	(6.03)
LDC trade$_{t-1}$	0.00	0.03***	0.03***	0.03***
	(0.99)	(3.55)	(3.87)	(3.51)
Δ LDC trade$_t$	−0.00	0.01	0.01	0.00
	(−0.54)	(0.68)	(1.18)	(0.42)
Female LF participation$_{t-1}$	0.01***	0.00	0.00	0.01*
	(3.50)	(0.54)	(0.71)	(1.94)
Δ Female LF participation$_t$	0.02***	0.05***	0.05***	0.05***
	(3.82)	(4.52)	(4.19)	(3.75)
Taxation$_{t-1}$	–	–	0.03	0.02*
			(0.73)	(1.96)
Δ Taxation$_{t-1}$	–	–	0.01*	0.04**
			(1.78)	(2.28)
Public employment$_{t-1}$	–	–	–	−0.06***
				(−4.32)
Δ Public employment$_t$	–	–	–	−0.10*
				(−1.98)
Lagged dependent level	−0.03**	−0.04**	−0.04**	−0.07***
	(−2.18)	(−2.12)	(−2.09)	(−3.81)
Adjusted R-squared	.42	.57	.57	.59
Number of observations	331	331	331	331

Significance levels: *** < .01; ** < .05; * < .10 (t-scores in parentheses).
[a] All regressions were estimated with a full set of country dummies using panel corrected standard errors.

percent or about 0.1 standard deviation, and in the long run a 1-standard-deviation increase in dispersion is associated with a 0.8-standard-deviation increase in employment, or 4.3 percent of the working-age population.[13]

These estimates, however, must be treated with caution. The data exhibit strong path dependency, and that makes long-term equilibrium predictions unreliable. I am capturing a process, service sector expansion, as it unfolds, and it is risky business to extrapolate the exact long-term equilibrium conditions.[14] I return to this issue later. Suffice it to say here that the dispersion variable exhibits a statistically significant positive effect on employment. The long-run magnitude of the effect appears to be large, but the exact size is difficult to pin down.

Turning to the effect of per capita income, it is as unambiguous as it is unsurprising. Just as rising income during the latter part of the nineteenth century fueled demand for manufactured goods, so does rising income today spur demand for, and employment in, services. As we saw in Chapter 5, the combined effect of productivity growth in manufacturing and shifts in consumption patterns led to deindustrialization and simultaneously created the structural conditions for the rise of services.

Unemployment also has the expected effect on employment, where the permanent effect can be interpreted as an impact of institutions while the transitory effect can be interpreted as either the result of the business cycle or of countercyclical macroeconomic policies. Of course, one cannot cleanly separate out what is the cause and effect here, because both employment and unemployment are determined by the same underlying institutions and policies, but it seems safe to conclude that macroeconomic conditions *do* significantly affect employment performance – a result that is anticipated by Scharpf (1991), Hall and Franzese (1998), Iversen (1999), Soskice (2000), Manow (2002), and others. This is important to keep in mind when interpreting the performance of particular countries because some have benefited significantly from propitious macroeconomic conditions.

LDC trade appears to have a positive effect on service employment as expected. However, because there are off-setting indirect effects, LDC trade

---

[13] The results are substantively similar if we run the regressions on Isic 6 and Isic 9 separately (somewhat weaker for the former and somewhat stronger for the latter). I keep the two together for presentational economy.

[14] The task is a bit like predicting the cruising altitude of an airplane from data on speed and altitude during the first few minutes of flight. We know that the plane is increasing altitude at a decreasing rate, and this makes it possible to project the ultimate cruising altitude, but there are no actual observations of the steady state.

does not in fact have any net effect on employment, and without the other variables in the model, it exhibits only a small and insignificant relationship with employment. It is unclear exactly how to interpret these results – especially why LDC trade is associated with a *less* dispersed wage structure – but one is well advised not to draw strong conclusions about the effects of LDC trade from the direct effect. As I show later in this chapter, there is also no cross-national evidence that countries more exposed to LDC trade have higher service employment rates than other countries.

Female labor force participation does not appear to have a significant effect on private sector service employment. But, as argued previously, this may in part be because many of the services most directly associated with the demand side of female labor force participation, in particular daycare, are often provided through the state. Correspondingly, when public sector employment is controlled for (last column of Table 6.4), the effect of female labor force participation increases (though it is still only borderline significant). Another part of the story is that much of the demand effect of female labor force participation goes through per capita income (the relationship between participation and income is positive). The high income elasticity of services is therefore partly a result of the fact that a substantial portion of the new demand for services has come from women entering into the labor market (Huber and Stephens 2000).

As expected, government employment has a statistically significant and permanent effect on private consumer service employment.[15] A 1 percent rise in public employment is associated with about an 0.8 percent decline in long-term private employment. It is not clear, however, how to interpret this effect because it is likely that a substantial portion results from reversed causation. If private service employment is growing slowly, governments will be under greater pressure to employ people in the public sector. As I argue at length in the next section, this direction of causality is likely to have been particularly important in countries where the political left is strong, and these countries also tend to be the ones with the most compressed wage structures.[16] In addition, it is not the case that those countries with relatively compressed wage structures, but *without* large public sectors, exhibit better private employment performance than those with larger public sectors.

[15] As one would have expected, it does not have an effect if added to the equation for business service employment ($b = 0.0007$ for the lagged government employment variable).

[16] In principle, it is possible to deal with this problem by using recursive models. In practice, it is very hard to develop good instrumental variables, and it is impossible to get people to agree on their interpretation.

This suggests that public employment is not an important determinant of private employment, and that the causality therefore runs in the opposite direction.[17]

Regardless of how much of the effect of government employment can be attributed to reverse causation, the positive effect of the wage dispersion remains, although the parameter for the permanent effect is now reduced from 3.1 to 2.2. Perhaps tellingly, the bivariate regression reported in Table 6.3 implies a parameter of 2.6, which is right in the middle of these values. In addition to reducing the parameter of the dispersion variable, the inclusion of government employment increases the speed with which private service employment reaches its equilibrium, and this also reduces the long-term impact of the independent variables. Thus, the equilibrium effect of a 1-standard-deviation increase in dispersion is now 1.6 percent of the working-age population compared to 4.3 percent before. This result, however, almost certainly underestimates the true effect for the reasons just outlined.

To get a better idea of the likely range of effects, Table 6.5 shows the estimated impact on employment of a 1-standard-deviation increase in dispersion, using a range of different model specifications. The short-term effect is the rise in employment after 5 years; the long-term effect is the estimated increase in equilibrium employment. Moving down in the table implies that more variables are being added to the model. Thus, the numbers in the first line are the estimates when only per capita income is used as a control variable. The last line is the fully specified model corresponding to the last column in Table 6.4. I have estimated the effects both with and without controls for time periods (i.e., with and without $t - 1$ time dummies).

Note that the short-term effect is fairly stable around 0.4–0.7 percent, regardless of specification. The long-term predictions are also within a fairly narrow range of 4–7 percent, except when public sector employment is included as a control. Then the effect drops to between 1.4 and 1.6 percent. As noted earlier, a plausible explanation for this drop is that governments

---

[17] One reviewer also suggested that there might be bias in the results because some private services are publicly subsidized and therfore not really "private" (exactly where the OECD draws the line between public and private employment is unclear). Yet, if that were true, it would cut in the opposite direction of my hypothesis: egalitarian welfare states have more subsidization, which should *weaken* the relationship between equality and employment. Also, in the equations using public employment on the right-hand side, this variable is probably a good proxy for subsidization.

Table 6.5. *The Effect of Earnings Dispersion under Different Model Specifications*

| | Effect of Earnings Dispersion[a] | | | |
| | With Country Dummies | | With Country and Time Dummies | |
With Control for	Short Term[b]	Long Term[c]	Short Term[b]	Long Term[c]
GDP per capita *and*	0.39	n.a.[d]	0.46	6.22
Unemployment *and*	0.52	7.13	0.46	6.10
LDC trade *and*	0.70	5.64	0.61	5.71
Female LF participation *and*	0.72	4.26	0.61	3.99
Taxation *and*	0.73	4.39	0.63	4.16
Public employment	0.49	1.60	0.41	1.37
	(1.01)	(3.14)	(0.70)	(2.12)

[a] The effect of a 1-standard-deviation increase in earnings dispersion.
[b] Percentage increase in employment as a percentage of the working-age population after 5 years.
[c] Percentage increase in employment as a percentage of the working-age population in the long run.
[d] Equilibrium cannot be calculated because coefficient on lagged dependent level variable is indistinguishable from 0.

in countries with a flexible, and hence dispersed, wage structure are under less pressure to increase public employment. Putting public sector employment on the left-hand side supports this interpretation because wage dispersion is negatively related to public employment. There are therefore two interpretations: The first is that causality runs from wage dispersion to public employment, in which case the latter should not be included on the right-hand side. Alternatively, public employment does reduce private sector employment, in which case some of the effect of wage dispersion on private sector employment goes through public sector employment. If we take this indirect effect into account, the total long-term effect of a 1-standard-deviation increase in dispersion is to increase private service employment by 2.1–3.1 percent (noted in parentheses in the last line of Table 6.5). Based on these results, it seems safe to conclude that about 2.5 percent is the lower bound on the long-term effect of wage dispersion, which corresponds to 0.5 standard deviation on the dependent employment variable.

I have saved the discussion of taxation for last because the effects of this variable are in some respects the most intriguing. As noted previously,

Scharpf (2000) has argued persuasively for the importance of the variable, and he can point to a strong negative cross-national correlation between service employment and social security and consumption taxes. Yet, in the error correction model, the effect of the variable is *reversed*, although it is only borderline significant. The issue is not simply that the effect of this variable goes through wage dispersion, although there *is* a negative and statistically significant effect, but that taxation does not have the expected effect in *any* specification of the model.

This phenomenon (i.e., that a strong and theoretically sensible cross-sectional correlation disappears in a dynamic model with a lagged dependent variable, or in an error correction model) is well known to statistical practitioners. In the past, it has been taken to mean that the theoretical intuition must be wrong, but recently it has become an issue of contention among methodologists. In a recent paper, Chris Achen argues that a perfectly sensible relationship in a simple regression on levels can completely disappear in a dynamic model *even though the relationship does in fact exist* (see Achen 2000). The problem arises when there is strong trending in the data between the dependent and independent variables, and the lagged dependent variable soaks up most of the cross-sectional variance. In our case, there is no doubt that the variables are trending; therefore, this is a potential problem.

The issue applied to taxation is illustrated in Table 6.6. The variables in this table are the same as before except that only contemporaneous levels (not lagged levels plus changes) are used in the regression. Column 1 shows the bivariate relationship between taxation and employment, which is strong and negative, as in Scharpf's analysis. The effect is reduced, but still strong, in the multivariate model in column 2, which includes all the variables from Table 6.5. The problem, of course, is that the errors in the model are highly serially correlated, so the t-statistics are meaningless.

One standard method to deal with serial correlation is to add a lagged dependent variable as in column 3 (Beck and Katz 1995). This regression, which also controls for country-specific effects, immediately reveals the problem. While all the other variables retain at least some of their original effect, the parameter estimate for the taxation variable not only loses significance but turns positive. This is precisely the situation we had in the original model, and although the present model is not fully specified (because we cannot assume that the parameters on the lagged independent

Table 6.6. *The Effect of Taxation under Different Model Specifications*

	Employment in Consumer Services			(4) Long-Term Parameters[b]
	(1)[a]	(2)[a]	(3)[a]	
Intercept	4.66	2.66	0.25***	–
	(39.33)	(1.62)	(3.67)	
Earnings dispersion	–	15.38	2.65***	16.68
		(4.77)	(3.67)	
Unemployment	–	−0.38	−0.06***	−0.36
		(−9.00)	(−7.74)	
GDP per capita	–	1.26	0.22***	1.39
		(14.48)	(8.11)	
LDC trade	–	0.05	0.03***	0.17
		(0.77)	(2.84)	
Female LF participation	–	0.08	0.01*	0.04
		(3.83)	(1.88)	
Taxation	−0.48	−0.21	0.01	0.04
	(−16.11)	(−7.94)	(0.70)	
Public employment	–	−0.39	−0.10***	
		(−9.55)	(−6.50)	−0.65
Lagged dependent level	–	–	0.84***	
			(45.50)	
Adjusted R-squared	0.419	0.789	0.997	
Number of observations	359	343	331	

Significance levels: *** < .01; * < .10 (t-scores in parentheses).
[a] Estimated with a full set of country dummies using panel corrected standard errors.
[b] Estimated from the results of LDV regression in column 3.

variables are zero), this is a widely used setup that highlights the problem at hand.[18]

The last column of Table 6.6 shows the long-term parameters (b/ (1 − .84)) of each variable, and it is instructive to compare these results to the simple regression on levels in column 2. One would hope that the long-term parameters, which suggest the levels of employment expected in equilibrium, are not completely out of whack with the results for the nondynamic regression on the levels themselves. And such rough correspondence does indeed hold for wage dispersion, unemployment, and GDP per capita.

[18] The assumption of zero effects of lagged variables is not always appropriate; therefore, one should not, in my view, reduce a fully specified error correction model to the form in Table 6.5 unless the results are consistent. In our case, the results *are* broadly consistent.

On the other hand, the dynamic model (static model) appears to overestimate (underestimate) the effect of female labor force participation and underestimate (overestimate) the effect of LDC trade. But again, the result that is most inconsistent with the simple regression is the one for taxation. Here there is not simply a lack of correspondence, but a contradiction.

On the basis of these results, it is tempting to conclude that tax structure, despite the theoretical arguments to the contrary, really does not matter for employment. This is the conclusion many methodologists, including Nathaniel Beck who advocates use of lagged dependent variable (LDV) models, are inclined to draw.[19] Chris Achen, on the other hand, suggests that the simple regression without a lagged dependent variable may tell an important substantive story, even if the t-statistics are meaningless. This controversy will have to be resolved among methodologists, and that will take time. Here I simply conclude that the effect of tax structure on employment performance is potentially important, but inconclusive. For the time being, we need to retain a potential role for the tax wedge in understanding developments in specific countries.

As a final check on the robustness of the results for wage dispersion, I reran the error correction model using d5/d1 ratios in place of the industry dispersion measure (Table 6.7). The drawback is a 43 percent loss of observations since d5/d1 ratios are only available for a subset of years – in several cases only for the 1980s, and in one case (Norway) only for 2 years. To avoid the elimination of single observations as a result of differencing, I interpolated values whenever the gap between two values in a series was 3 years or less. This is identical to the procedure followed by Rueda and Pontusson (2000), who analyze the same earnings data. Out of the total of 202 observations, 14 were added in this manner. Because there was almost no change in the d5/d1 ratio in the cases of interpolation, and given the short period of time, the procedure does not appear to be problematic.[20]

The results are broadly in agreement with the previous findings, although the effects of wage dispersion are somewhat stronger (and always statistically significant at a .01 level or better). A 1-standard-deviation increase in dispersion is associated with an increase in employment (as a percent of the working-age population) of between 1.1 percent (with control for government employment) and 1.5 percent (without control for

---

[19] Private communication with Neal Beck.
[20] The results stand without interpolation, but Norway drops out since there are only two stand-alone observations that get eliminated when differencing.

Table 6.7. *Replication of Regression Results Using d5/d1 Ratios*

	Business Services (Isic 8)[a]	Consumer Services (Isic 6 + Isic 9)[a]		
Intercept	−1.64***	−3.67***	−3.75***	−2.58***
	(−2.71)	(−4.59)	(−4.59)	(−2.58)
d5/d1 ratio$_{t-1}$	0.73***	1.56***	1.59***	1.30***
	(2.69)	(3.96)	(4.02)	(3.14)
Δ d5/d1 ratio$_t$	0.07	0.27	0.30	0.04
	(0.18)	(0.37)	(0.40)	(0.05)
Unemployment$_{t-1}$	0.00	−0.00	−0.00	−0.01
	(0.21)	(−0.47)	(−0.27)	(−0.70)
Δ Unemployment$_t$	−0.06***	−0.12***	−0.12***	−0.12***
	(−5.47)	(−6.32)	(−6.15)	(−6.03)
GDP per capita$_{t-1}$	0.03***	0.08**	0.08**	0.11**
	(2.93)	(2.29)	(2.14)	(2.44)
Δ GDP per capita$_t$	0.13***	0.32***	0.33***	0.34***
	(2.79)	(3.59)	(3.59)	(3.75)
LDC trade$_{t-1}$	−0.01	−0.00	−0.00	0.00
	(−1.20)	(−0.29)	(−0.21)	(0.12)
Δ LDC trade$_t$	−0.02***	0.01	0.01	0.00
	(−2.53)	(0.58)	(0.73)	(0.26)
Female LF participation$_{t-1}$	0.01**	0.00	0.01	0.00
	(1.97)	(0.81)	(0.87)	(0.45)
Δ Female LF participation$_t$	0.01	0.04***	0.04**	0.04**
	(0.76)	(2.61)	(2.35)	(2.28)
Taxation$_{t-1}$	–	–	−0.00	0.00
			(−0.03)	(0.25)
Δ taxation$_{t-1}$	–	–	0.02	0.02
			(0.68)	(0.94)
Public employment$_{t-1}$	–	–	–	−0.06*
				(−1.84)
Δ public employment$_t$	–	–	–	−0.09
				(−1.50)
Lagged dependent level	−0.08	−0.03	−0.03	−0.05
	(−3.33)	(−1.12)	(−1.12)	(−1.50)
Adjusted R-squared	.61	.69	.70	.70
Number of observations	202	202	202	202

Significance levels: *** < .01; ** < .05; * < .10 (t-scores in parentheses).
[a] All regressions were estimated with a full set of country dummies using panel corrected standard errors.

government employment) after 5 years. That is about twice the effect that we found for the industry dispersion variable. We also note that the results do not change as much as we go from a model that excludes government employment to one that includes this variable. Moreover, there is now a statistically significant effect of dispersion on business service employment, although the effect is less than half of the effect on consumer services.

There is, however, a problem with these results insofar as the long-run predictions are very uncertain as suggested by the small and imprecise parameter estimate for the lagged level variable. It turns out that this problem is mainly caused by Canada, which has a much more dispersed wage structure when measured by $d5/d1$ ratios than when measured by the industry dispersion variable. In fact, Canada has by far the highest $d5/d1$ ratios among all countries in the sample, which seems too high compared to the independent dispersion estimates by Card and Freeman (1993 Chapter 1). If we remove Canada from the regression, the effects of dispersion are somewhat reduced, and the precision with which we can estimate the long-run effects is greatly improved. In this regression, the predicted long-term effect of a 1-standard-deviation increase in dispersion is 3.4 percent of the working-age population, which is almost exactly in the middle of the 1.6–4.4 percent range of estimates for the industry dispersion variable. The 3.6 percent corresponds to two thirds of standard deviation in employment.

Turning to the controls, the tax variable again has no discernable effect on employment, and LDC trade no longer registers an impact. The most notable difference in the results is the reduction in the long-term effect of unemployment. This, however, may be an artifact of differences in measurement. Because the $d5/d1$ ratios rely on wage data for employed workers, and because unemployment is concentrated among low-paid workers, when unemployment goes up, wage dispersion declines, and dispersion is associated with lower employment. Some of the negative effect of unemployment therefore goes through the dispersion measure, for purely accounting reasons. The same is not true for the industry dispersion measure because although unemployment is disproportionately drawn from low-wage sectors, this does not change the weight of these sectors in the calculation of dispersion.[21]

---

[21] To a lesser extent, the differences may also reflect that the period coverage in the $d5/d1$ regression is tilted toward the 1980s and 1990s where macroeconomic autonomy was arguably lower in many countries than during the 1970s (see Iversen and Soskice 1999). Reestimating the model for industry earnings on the restricted data available for $d5/d1$

Taken as a whole, the price and employment evidence is very clear. During the transition toward a more service-based economy, wage compression raises the relative prices of services, as reflected in long-term real exchange rates, and puts a damper on employment creation in low-wage and labor-intensive service industries where productivity lags that of manufacturing. The emerging tradeoff between wage equality and employment is central to understanding policy choices in the 1980s and 1990s because it jeopardized the virtuous circle between wage solidarism, wage restraint, and rising private sector employment that had existed during the golden age (as spelled out in Chapter 2).

6.2. Political Responses: The Service Economy Trilemma

In assessing the short- and longer-term responses by governments to the equality-employment tradeoff, it is useful to employ Peter Hall's distinction between changes in the levels of the settings of existing policy instruments and the adoption of new instruments (Hall 1993). In the short to medium term, politicians are constrained by the policy instruments that are readily available and tend to fall back on inherited ideological commitments to make choices over the tradeoffs they face. In the longer run the adoption of new instruments, and in some cases a redefinition of goals, may transform the original tradeoffs. In this section, I focus on short- to medium-term responses. The next will consider longer term adaptation.

As Anne Wren and I have argued (Iversen and Wren 1998), governments had available to them three immediate responses to the equality-employment tradeoff. One strategy was to deregulate labor markets to reduce the power of unions and increase wage flexibility. This, in a nutshell, is the strategy recommended by the OECD in their 1994 Jobs Study (OECD 1994b). It is exemplified by the neoliberal policies of governments in the United States, Britain, New Zealand, and, to a lesser extent, Australia during the 1980s. An alternative strategy was to accept sluggish employment growth in private services but simultaneously pursue an aggressive employment strategy through expansion of public sector services. This, by and large, was the option chosen by social democratic governments in Scandinavia, who essentially financed higher prices on a range of social

ratios, however, indicates that this is a minor cause. Thus, the parameter for the unemployment variable only declines marginally. Other parameters are also fairly stable, although the one for the lagged dispersion variable increases from 2.2 to 3.1.

services by increasing taxes.[22] The final option was to accept the employment consequences of a compressed wage structure but to seek to limit the disruptive effects by discouraging the labor market entry of women and by facilitating labor market exit, primarily among older workers through early retirement.[23] This is the pattern we find in some continental European countries, particularly those that have historically been strongly influenced by Christian democracy.

The policy choices can be represented as a trilemma (Iversen and Wren 1998; Wren 2000) where wage equality and private service employment represent two of the policy goals, while budgetary or fiscal restraint represents a third. By fiscal restraint, I have in mind whether or not the government responds to nonmarket-clearing wages by expanding public consumption and employment. The use of the macroeconomic concept of fiscal restraint is intentional because it is in fact closely related to the notion of a nonaccommodating fiscal policy.[24] Because fiscal policies are constrained by international and institutional constraints, the relationship between government consumption and fiscal policy matters.

The trilemma is illustrated in Figure 6.4 which links the three economic goals of equality, employment and fiscal restraint to three distinct partisan choices. The basic idea is that it is difficult to successfully pursue all three goals simultaneously as long as there is a tradeoff between wage equality and employment. Governments therefore tend to compromise the goal that is least dear to them in order to maximize the others.

For social democrats, this typically meant abandoning fiscal restraint and replacing private markets with publicly provided social services. Christian democrats shied away from such a solution because they feared that it would strengthen the state at the expense of private service providers and the family. In the Catholic countries of Europe, social and educational services have historically been provided to a considerable extent by the church or inside the family, and Christian democrats did not want to see these functions taken over by the state. Instead, the supply of labor was

---

[22] Because public services are very labor intensive, it is easy to show that there is a tight relationship between public employment and public consumption spending. Just how tight depends on the ability of governments to hold back average wage costs for public sector employees.

[23] A range of disability pensions that effectively removed marginalized workers from the labor market has also been used, especially in Italy and The Netherlands.

[24] A number of people have commented that fiscal restraint here has nothing to do with the macroeconomic concept, which is simply incorrect.

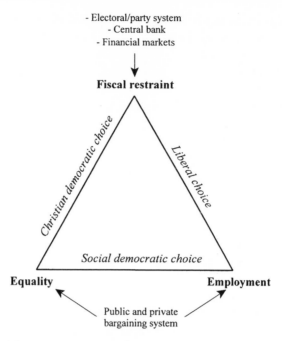

- Electoral/party system
- Central bank
- Financial markets

Fiscal restraint

Christian democratic choice

Liberal choice

Social democratic choice

Equality

Employment

Public and private
bargaining system

Figure 6.4 The service economy trilemma.

kept down by tax incentives that dissuaded women from entering the labor market and by early retirement to facilitate the exit of older workers. For liberal and conservative parties of the free market right, by contrast, the problem was rather seen as one of market clearing. Wage equality and social protection had gone too far, preventing firms and workers from taking advantage of opportunities that the market would naturally offer. The solution was deregulation and measures that would reduce the monopoly power of unions. Equality had to give way for what neoliberals believed was greater efficiency.[25]

Although this is obviously a simplification, to a considerable extent the initial adjustment of countries can be understood as the interaction of partisan politics and the structural constraints defined by the trilemma. But choices are also subject to institutional and international constraints

---

[25] Anne Wren (2000) has conducted a much more nuanced analysis of the role of partisanship and traces the differences between the three party families to ideological cleavages over the role of the family and women, the clash during the nineteenth century between the church and the rising secular state, and the historical relationship between parties, unions, employer associations, and the church.

(as indicated in Figure 6.4) and reflect, at least to some extent, underlying class alliances. The historical and institutional factors that led to the division of countries into liberal and coordinated market economies now shape the costs and benefits of particular courses of action (Wren 2001). Thus, in the specific skills countries of northern Europe, the traditionally dominant employer associations and unions in the export-oriented sector have opposed radical deregulation of labor markets because such reforms would undermine the incentives of firms and workers to invest in specific skills and possibly jeopardize the cooperative relationships between firms and skilled workers (Wood 1997; Manow 2002, Chapter 6). Though highly critical of interoccupational wage compression and inefficiencies in the public sector, firms and skilled workers recognized an important insurance function for social protection. This function has, to a considerable extent, been performed through the centralized collective bargaining system, over which the government has limited control (Wren 2000).

There are some salient differences, however, in the bargaining system between Scandinavia and continental Europe. In Scandinavia, the importance of national peak-level bargaining in densely unionized labor markets gave low-paid workers a degree of influence over wage-setting that they lacked in the rest of Europe (Iversen 1999). Also, because Scandinavian unions, unlike unions in countries like Austria and Germany, were sharply divided between blue- and white-collar workers, the influence of professionals in the main bargaining area was limited. These differences go some ways in explaining the exceptional egalitarianism of the Scandinavian labor markets, although we need to take account of government ideology to explain the starkly different labor-market positions of women, especially why the public service sector expanded to the degree it did in Scandinavia (Huber and Stephen 2000).

In addition to affecting the wage structure, the bargaining system also affects employment by inducing more or less overall wage restraint. This is also important in the public sector because it affects the tradeoff between employment and fiscal restraint. Where governments are better able to control the wage bill in the public sector, the costs of expanding public sector employment will be lower. Correspondingly, we find that the correlation between increases in public sector employment and increases in the total wage bill is less than perfect (around .8), presumably reflecting differences in the labor cost of public sector employees.

In general skills countries such as Britain, New Zealand, and the United States, the political support for social spending is more tenuous because

249

it rarely enhances economic efficiency and because it is not usually supported by strong organized interests. Support for employment and income protection does not extend very far into the middle classes because protection is less important to general skills workers and because such protection undermines wage and employment flexibility, which is in high demand among employers. Unions and collective bargaining also tend to be less well developed. In electoral politics, majoritarian electoral systems and leader-dominated parties also provide a weak bulwark against cutbacks, as argued in detail in Chapter 4. Compared to specific skills countries, where skilled unions in manufacturing have always played a pivotal role, policies and labor market conditions in general skills countries tend to be much more influenced by the preferences of professionals.

Another important institutional variable is the degree of central bank independence. Because expansion of public spending in response to private sector employment problems is an accommodating fiscal policy, independent central banks keen to control prices will have an incentive to meet such policies with monetary contraction (Scharpf 1991; Manow 2002, Chapter 5). This raises the costs of fiscal accommodation, signified by a rising real interest rate, and reduces the incentives of governments to pursue accommodating policies. Monetary integration into a system of fixed but adjustable exchange rates has very similar effects (Iversen and Soskice 1999), and it has significantly affected the ability of governments to respond to employment problems with expansionary fiscal policies (Manow 2002, Chapter 5).

Finally, it is necessary to recognize that macroeconomic conditions are in some measure exogenous to the argument that has been made in this chapter. Nothing prevents countries from running current account surpluses, even at high levels of unemployment. As shown by Carlin and Soskice (2000), when countries are specialized in highly differentiated product markets ("Ricardian trade"), it is possible for governments to have some control over domestic levels of employment. As we saw in the statistical analysis in the previous section, this can have significant effects on employment performance, and needs to be taken into account as we examine the experience of particular countries.

6.3. National Variations

As in Iversen and Wren (1998), the differences in national paths of adjustments can be readily illustrated with some comparative data (see Table 6.8).

250

Table 6.8. *Wage Equality, Service Employment, and Institutions in Eight OECD Countries, 1970–1996 (percentage of adult population)*

	Denmark			Sweden			Britain			United States			Netherlands			Germany		
	1	2	3	1	2	3	1	2	3	1	2	3	1	2	3	1	2	3
1970–73	–	14	16	–	17	17	.29	13	17	.27	10	22	–	7	17	–	8	13
1974–77	–	17	16	.45	20	18	.33	15	18	.27	10	24	.39	7	18	–	9	14
1978–81	.46	20	16	.49	24	18	.34	15	19	.26	10	26	.39	7	18	–	10	15
1982–85	.46	22	16	.50	26	18	.32	14	20	.25	9	28	.41	7	18	.34	10	15
1986–89	.46	22	18	.48	26	20	.30	14	23	.24	10	31	.39	7	19	.36	10	16
1990–93	.47	22	17	.48	25	20	.29	13	26	.23	10	33	.38	7	21	.37	9	16
1994–96	–	22	18	.45	–	–	.29	–	–	.22	10	36	.37	6	22	.35	–	–
Change	.01	8	1	0	8	3	0	0	9	-.05	0	14	-.02	-1	5	.01	1	3
El. sys.	PR			PR			Maj			Maj			PR			PR		
CBI[a]	0.40			0.22			0.21			0.72			0.45			0.99		
Centralized[b]	0.46			0.48			0.16			0.07			0.40			0.33		
Social democrats[c]	0.43			0.64			0.23			0.00			0.21			0.43		
Christian democrats	0.02			0.02			0.00			0.00			0.56			0.41		
Liberal	0.33			0.11			0.77			0.76			0.19			0.00		

Notes on columns: Column 1: d9/d1 earnings ratios (Source: OECD, *Electronic Data Base on Wage dispersion*, undated); column 2: public sector employment as a percentage of working-age population (Sources: Cusack 1991; OECD, *Labour Force Statistics*, various years); column 3: private service employment as a percentage of working-age population (Sources: Cusack 1991; OECD, *Labour Force Statistics*, various years).

[a] Average (after standardization) of three widely used central bank independence indexes by Cukierman (1992), Bade and Parkin (1982), and Grilli, Masciandaro, and Tabellini (1991).

[b] Index of centralization of wage bargaining (Source: Iversen 1999).

[c] The percentage of total government seats held by (i) social democratic parties, (ii) Christian democratic parties, and (iii) Liberal–conservative secular parties (Liberal) (Source: Huber et al. 1997).

251

For each of the six countries in the top part of the table, there are three columns of data: one for wage equality, one for public sector employment, and one for private service sector employment. It is immediately obvious that all three variables differ sharply among countries. The social-democratic-dominated Scandinavian countries have the most egalitarian wage structures, but private services employment has been stagnant in these countries. Public sector employment, by contrast, rose rapidly during the 1970s and early 1980s, causing a substantial increase in public spending (more than 70 percent of all government consumption goes to paying wages).

Compare this to that of the United States and Britain where neoliberal policies of privatization and deregulation dominated during the 1980s. Employment in private services grew rapidly in these countries, while public sector employment and consumption remained largely unchanged. Not surprisingly, these are also the countries in the table with the most inegalitarian wage structures, and they are the only countries that display an increase in inequality during the 1980s.

Finally, in two countries where Christian democratic parties have been dominant, Germany and The Netherlands, service employment has been stagnant in *both* the public sector (as in the neoliberal countries) *and* in the private sector (as in the social democratic countries). These countries have instead performed well in terms of holding back public consumption and taxes ("budgetary restraint") and maintaining a relatively egalitarian earnings structure. In looking at changes over time, it should be noted that private service employment in The Netherlands may suggest an important change in direction during the 1990s. I will discuss this change in the next section.

The bottom half of Table 6.8 compares the six countries on a set of institutional and partisan variables that are relevant in distinguishing the three clusters. Sweden, the United States, and Germany come closest to each of the three ideal types. Sweden with centralized wage bargaining, a dependent central bank, PR electoral institutions, and social democratic dominance in government stands in sharp contrast to the United States with decentralized bargaining, a relatively independent central bank, a majoritarian electoral system, and right dominance of government. Germany is similar to Sweden in terms of having a relatively centralized bargaining system and PR, but the central bank in Germany, before European Monetary Union (EMU), was much more independent and in fact exceeded the U.S. Federal Reserve in this respect. Finally, Germany differs from both Sweden and the

United States by having a much stronger Christian democratic party with a dominant position in government in much of the period since 1982.

Based on this comparison, it is clear that the 1970s and 1980s were characterized by politically distinct responses to the trilemma. Continental European countries used labor market exit, and restrictions on entry, to cope with poor employment performance; liberal Anglo-Saxon countries cut social benefits and deregulated labor and product markets with little regard for the inequalizing consequences; while social democratic countries in Scandinavia vastly expanded their public service sectors, and paid for it through higher taxes.

But partisan strategies were constrained by new economic and political realities. Restricting labor force participation limited the tax base for the welfare state and ran counter to the desire of many women to acquire financial independence from men; deregulation and growing inequality created growing social problems of crime, inner city decay, and a growing pool of working poor; further public sector expansion ran counter to the need for fiscal discipline in an integrating international monetary system and pitted private and public sector interests against each other. During the 1990s, governments have therefore striven to relax the tradeoffs between different goals and permit the pursuit of employment without jeopardizing fiscal discipline or exacerbating economic inequalities. In many countries, these policy experiments came with the return of a reformed left to government power in the 1990s. In the next section, I discuss the nature and effectiveness of these experiments.

6.4. Pathways Out of the Trilemma

6.4.1. New Social Liberalism: Workfare

When Tony Blair won the British parliamentary election in a landslide in 1997, it was on a very different political platform than advocated by the Labour Party in the past. Gone was the traditional emphasis on Keynesian full-employment policies, nationalization of industry, and negotiated incomes policies. In their place, the new government pledged commitment to fiscal (and monetary) conservatism, competitive product and labor markets, public investment in education, and work-based welfare.

The most novel aspect of Labour's strategy is the attempt to use social policies to stimulate private sector employment while simultaneously reducing inequality. Young long-term unemployed must accept offers of work or education, while the state subsidizes the wage of workers if regular employment cannot be found (Undy 1999). For families, the government has created a tax credit program, the Working Families Tax Credit (WFTC) that guarantees a minimum income (currently £200 per week) when at least one family member works full time. In addition, daycare subsidies have been raised, and tax schedules lowered, for low-income workers (Glyn and Wood 2000). One study estimates that these measures have raised the income of the lowest 20 percent of households by about 8 percent (Immervoll et al. 1999 cited in Glyn and Wood 2000).

The principle for all social policy reforms is to raise the income of the lowest paid while preventing healthy working-age people from receiving benefits while not working. There is no attempt to alter the wage structure itself, or to otherwise limit the incidence of low-paid work. Indeed, subsidies to employers can be seen as expanding the range of low-paid jobs that can profitably be created. Yet, the biggest employment effect is not supposed to come from stretching the postsubsidy wage structure but by increasing labor market competition from those who would otherwise not search actively for employment, thereby putting greater downward pressure on overall wages in the economy (Glyn and Wood 2000). Lower wage pressure is a means to reducing the equilibrium level of unemployment.

A potential medium- to long-term problem with this strategy is that since those nonemployed who are likely to respond to the new tax and in-work benefits – mostly long-term unemployed and people at the margin of the labor market, especially young mothers – have few qualifications, effective wage competition will only occur in the low-pay segment of the labor market, and therefore potentially increase pretax wage dispersion without much of an effect on average wages.[26] This in turn raises the costs of the tax credit program and the in-work benefits as more workers qualify. If there is not political will to shoulder the financial burden, the result could be an increase in posttax inequality over the longer run despite the government's assurances to the contrary.

Better access to education is supposed to deal with this problem. Individual Learning Accounts (ILA) give workers a small amount of money in an account that can be used to pay for training courses throughout a person's career. The scheme is supported by tax deductions for employer and individual contributions, as well as discounts for training courses (Glyn

---

[26] The problem is exacerbated by regionally concentrated unemployment because it increases the supply of labor most where the demand is lowest (Glyn and Wood 2000).

and Wood 2000). For young people, policies are being initiated that will increase the financial incentives to stay in education or return to the school system in order to complete a degree. The hope is that people at the lower end of the wage distribution will acquire a basic education as well as some subsequent practical skills, such as computer literacy. It remains to be seen, however, whether employers and low-wage workers will make extensive use of these opportunities and whether, relatedly, it will significantly improve their income. Cathie Jo Martin, in a survey of fifty-two large British firms, found little evidence that employers are engaging in upskilling of their low-paid employees, and to the extent that they participate in the government's active labor market program, they do so as a means to gain access to cheap labor (Martin 2003).

British social policies are in some measure built upon the American experience. As in Britain, there have been few attempts in the United States to change the incidence of low-paid work, or to alter the pretax wage structure. Nor has there been any rise in public sector employment. But there has been a massive reorientation of the welfare system away from "passive" benefits to benefits that are closely tied to work.

Welfare reform in the United States started at the state level in the late 1980s and early 1990s when the federal government replaced open-ended support for poor families (Aid to Families with Dependent Children, AFDC) with block grants (Temporary Assistance to Needy Families, TANF) and reduced the maximum duration of benefits for families with nonworking parents. The response by states varied, but benefits, or the duration of benefits, for nonworking individuals were cut everywhere. Millions of poor Americans were pushed off welfare as a consequence. At the same time, however, these cuts were matched by massive increases in support for low-income working families, especially through the Earned Income Tax Credit (EITC) program. The system gives people up to 40 percent in tax credits for every dollar up to a maximum after which the credit is gradually phased out (in 1997 the maximum credit was $3,656). In addition, Medicaid – the medical assistance program for the poor – was extended to children with working parents under the poverty line, and some states also started to subsidize child care.

In some respects, these reforms are reminiscent of nineteenth-century liberalism in the insistence on healthy people working in order to receive help. There is no attempt to interfere with the market mechanism of wage setting, and the whole system is based on the assumption that there is work for all who want to work. Compared to the British system, it also has no guaranteed income level. This said, there is little doubt about the effectiveness of the reforms. David Ellwood (2000) has documented the dramatic effect on the incidence of work among the poor. For example, the percent of working single mothers increased from about 30 percent to about 50 percent between 1992 and 1997, and as much as 80 percent of this rise can be attributed to the combined effects of welfare reform and EITC (see also Meyer and Rosenbaum 1999).[27]

Workfare reforms have some political advantages because it is generally easier to get higher-income people to accept support for working than nonworking healthy adults, and because businesses hiring in the low-skilled labor market benefit from the increased labor supply. Tax credits rather than outright welfare benefits also shift the attention away from highly visible spending programs to obscure technical changes in an immensely complicated tax code (Myles and Pierson 1997). However, the reforms carry costs and potential dangers that need to be weighted against the benefits. First, by making it very difficult to be out of employment for any sustained period of time, there is an added disincentive for workers to acquire specific skills. Such skills typically mean that workers need to spend more time searching for jobs when they are out of work, and that is prohibitively expensive in a welfare model where benefits are tied to being in work. The British and American reforms may therefore have little to offer the specific skills countries of continental Europe.

Second, and perhaps more worrisome for general skills countries, work-related benefits may discourage low-skilled workers from improving their skills through additional formal education. Not only is it difficult to finance such upskilling in a system that ties benefits to income, but limited improvements in skills typically qualify workers for jobs where the income is just high enough for work-related benefits to be phased out. The tax credit system could thus act as an indirect tax on basic education, which bodes ill for the longer-term effects on reducing poverty.

Third, by raising the effective supply of unskilled labor, workfare may increase pretax inequality and require more subsidies in order to prevent an erosion of posttax inequality. Governments committed to fiscal restraint are not necessarily in a position to cope effectively with this second-order effect. Tying benefits so closely to work also raises some unpleasant questions about the effects of the next sustained economic recession. Overt poverty could

---

[27] The incentives for poor married mothers are biased against work, however, and this is evident in a much smaller rise in employment among these women.

quickly return to the streets of British and American cities, and there is a risk that the crisis may be deepened by procyclical cuts in spending as low-wage workers simultaneously lose their jobs and benefits. What appears to be an optimal policy in a healthy economy may therefore not be optimal if evaluated across an entire business cycle.

6.4.2. Selective and Shielded Deregulation: A Continental European Experiment

The key dilemma for the high-protection countries of Western Europe is that while flexibilization of labor markets may be the only route to a sustained reversal of the deterioration of employment performance, governments cannot significantly trim the social protection system without triggering strong political opposition from entrenched groups, and without endangering the complementarities between the social protection system and the successful production system in the export-oriented sector of the economy. In Paul Pierson's fitting metaphor, the European welfare model is an immovable object meeting an irresistible force (Pierson 1998). In the clash of these forces, a new strategy, which I tentatively call *selective and shielded deregulation*, is being attempted.

The essence of the strategy is very simple: (i) keep the full set of protections in place for workers in the internationally oriented manufacturing sector, (ii) allow flexibilization of product and labor markets in the domestically oriented service sector, while (iii) compensating low-wage workers through tax-benefit subsidies and opportunities to acquire skills. Deregulating only part of the labor market is not as impossible as it sounds because the incidence of part-time and temporary employment is much higher in services than in manufacturing. Deregulating the labor market for temporary and part-time employment therefore does not necessarily interfere with the protection system that underpins most employment in the international sector. Thelen and Kume (1999) have made a related argument from the perspective of employers. In addition, changes in the tax and social transfer system can cushion the inequalizing effects of deregulation.

The political logic for selective and shielded deregulation is also quite compelling. Private employers in low-paid services are in the best position to take advantage of more flexible labor markets and have long favored deregulation (Schwartz 2001). Workers with a peripheral relation to the labor market, especially among women, often prefer the flexibility of temporary or part-time jobs and see selective deregulation as a welcome opportunity to enter the labor market. Shielding, however, may encounter opposition among better-paid workers who must accept a shift in the tax burden to make it possible to reduce the pretax wages of low-paid part-time and temporary workers without altering their take-home pay. On the other hand, there may be significant savings on benefits for the long-term unemployed, and presumably it will allow prices on services to fall as implied by the analysis in Section 6.1.1.

For full-time workers, especially in manufacturing, a principal concern is that insurance against loss of skills remains high, in particular that employment and unemployment protection is not being undermined for skilled workers. The former entails that an existing full-time job cannot be replaced by temporary or part-time contracts, while the latter requires that workers who lose their jobs are not forced to accept temporary or part-time employment. With such guarantees, full-time workers benefit from more flexible markets in services including longer opening hours, a more diversified choice of services, and possibly lower prices. Employers and unions in the exposed sectors have long been critical of cross-sector coordination of wages and working conditions, especially with the public sector, precisely because such coordination raises the relative price of services and may undermine competitiveness (Swenson 1991b; Iversen 1999). Selective deregulation, by creating a second-tier labor market in low-end services could address some of those problems.

The trend toward selective deregulation is picked up in OECD data on employment protection for full-time regular employment, and for temporary and part-time employment. Figure 6.5 compares the stringency of employment protection for full-time workers in the late 1990s to the mid-1980s. Assuming that the OECD methodology, which relies heavily on legal regulations, accurately reflects practice, there is practically no change. With the exception of Finland, all points lie on the 45° status quo line. Compare this pattern to changes in the stringency of regulations of temporary and part-time employment during the same period (Figure 6.6). In the majority of high-protection countries (France is a notable exception), the possibilities for temporary employment, which comes with no employment protection, and part-time employment, which sometimes comes with little protection, have been expanded. Indeed, it is reasonable here to talk about convergence to a more deregulated model. The mean for the protection index has dropped from 2.2 to 1.5, and the standard deviation has dropped from 1.7 to 1.1.

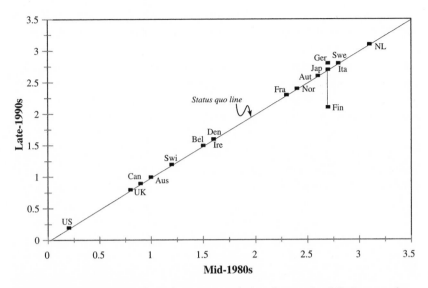

Figure 6.5 Stringency of employment regulation for regular full-time employment, 1980s versus 1990s.
Source: OECD (1999b).

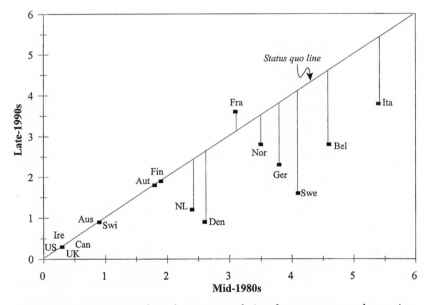

Figure 6.6 Stringency of employment regulation for temporary and part-time employment, 1980s versus 1990s.
Source: OECD (1999b).

259

Table 6.9. *Employment and Unemployment in Denmark, the Netherlands, and Europe, 1990–1999*

	Denmark			Netherlands			OECD-Europe		
	Unemployment Rate[a]	Employment/Government Ratio[b]	Government/Unemployment Consumption[c]	Employment Rate[a]	Government Ratio[b]	Unemployment Consumption[c]	Employment Rate[a]	Government Ratio[b]	Consumption[c]
1990	7.7	75.4	23.1	6.2	61.1	12.1	8.0	61.2	16.1
1995	7.3	73.9	23.4	6.9	64.2	12.3	10.5	59.6	16.5
1996	6.8	74.0	23.5	6.3	65.4	11.9	10.5	59.7	16.6
1997	5.6	75.4	23.0	5.2	67.5	11.8	10.3	59.6	16.2
1998	5.2	75.3	23.0	4.0	69.4	11.8	9.7	60.3	16.0
1999	5.2	76.5	n.a.	3.3	70.9	n.a.	9.2	61.5	n.a.
Change	-2.5	1.1	-0.1	-2.9	9.8	-0.3	1.2	0.3	-0.1

[a] Standardized unemployment rates.
[b] Total employment as a percentage of the working-age population.
[c] Government consumption as a percentage of GDP.

Source: OECD (2000).

If we look closer at the development in particular countries, two stand out: Denmark and The Netherlands. Under governments with social democratic participation, both have experienced a significant improvement in employment during the 1990s (see Table 6.9) *without* resorting to increased government spending and without significantly increasing the inequality of take-home pay. Unemployment rates have also fallen significantly below the European average, and The Netherlands has seen employment as a share of the adult population rise from 61 to 71 percent during the 1990s, an impressive increase of 16 percent in the total number of employed people.

The Dutch efforts to deregulate temporary and part-time work during the 1980s and early 1990s have gone further in recent years, with notable effects on performance. Replacement rates for workers under 50 on disability pensions have been cut, while eligibility rules have been significantly tightened, and more of the burden on financing has now been placed on employers (Becker 2001; Green-Pedersen, van Kersbergen, and Hemerijck 2001). Single parents with children over 5 years of age lose benefits if they do not accept a part-time job, and the definition of suitable jobs for unemployed has been notably broadened, now including employment with lower pay than in a worker's previous job. As noted, the minimum wage has also been significantly cut as a result of a more restrictive indexation (Salverda 1996).

Because most long-term unemployed and disability recipients are low skilled, one would expect these reforms to cause considerable downward pressure on wages at the lower end of the distribution. There is some evidence to this effect. Hemerijck, Unger, and Visser report that hourly wages for part-time employees is a modest 7 percent lower in the private sector than for similar workers in full-time jobs (2000, p. 227), but documentation is not very good on this issue.[28] That said, industry wage dispersion data appear to tell a rather clear story. As noted previously, there seems to be a trend break in wage dispersion in 1983, and the coefficient of variation in wages has increased by about 25 percent since then (the last data point is 1995). Because these data are based on all wages divided by the number of "man years" (or full-time equivalents), they pick up the effects of declining hourly wages for part-time jobs as well as any other changes in pretax earnings.

---

[28] They offer no data on temporary employees. Temporary and part-time employed are excluded from OECD's dispersion statistics, so this source cannot be used.

A closer scrutiny of the data by industry shows that relative wages decline in all services except finance (measured as the average wage in an industry divided by the average wage for the economy), whereas wages have been rising in all manufacturing industries (see Figure 6.7). At the same time, nearly all gains in employment – shown at the end of each bar as the change in employment as a percentage of the working-age population – have come in services with declining relative wages. From the perspective of these

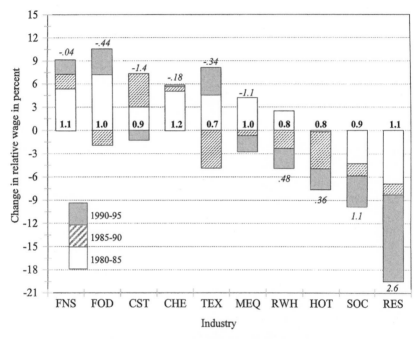

Figure 6.7   Relative wages in The Netherlands, 1980–1995.

Key: FNS: financial institutions and insurance (Isic-81/2); FOD: food, beverages, and tobacco (Isic-31); CST: construction (Isic-5); CHE: chemicals and chemical petroleum, coal, rubber, and plastic products (Isic-35); TEX: textile, apparel and leather industries; MEQ: fabricated metal products, machinery, and equipment (Isic-38); RWH: wholesale trade and retail trade (Isic-61/2); HOT: restaurants and hotels (Isic-63); SOC: community, social, and personal services (Isic-9); RES: real estate and business services (Isic-83).

Notes: The bolded number at the base of each bar is the average wage in that industry divided by the average wage in the economy. The italicized number at the end of each bar is the change in employment as a percentage of the working-age population between 1980 and 1995 (in sectors where relative wages have been falling the number is below the bar).

Source: Calculated from OECD (1999a).

data, growth in private service employment can scarcely be characterized as a "miracle" (cf. Visser and Hemerijck 1997). Rather, it looks suspiciously similar to a neoliberal choice in the trilemma, and Becker (2001) suggests that deregulation is in fact the main source of new employment in The Netherlands.

There is, however, an important departure from a traditional neoliberal strategy that recalls Scharpf's tax wedge argument. Thus, there has been a deliberate effort to change the tax burden to maintain the income of low-wage workers and reduce the costs to employers of hiring low-skill workers. Social security contributions have been lowered for all jobs paying 115 percent of the minimum wage or less. New tax reforms will also lower value-added taxes for employers in labor-intensive services (Hemerijck et al. 2000). There is little doubt that such reforms shield some of the inequalizing effects of lower wages for part-time employees, but the strategy is perhaps not as clearly distinguished from the workfare reforms in Britain and the United States as some of its advocates would like to have it. There is, as several scholars have noted, a trend toward mixing policies from different welfare models (Green-Pedersen et al. 2001; Manow 2001). Yet, even though there is some convergence in policy reforms, most would agree that fundamental differences remain. It is this pattern of lasting divergence and convergence at the margin that the regime argument in a deindustrializing world captures.

Politically, selective deregulation works up to the point where the savings on transfers to the nonworking population are exceeded by the costs to the pivotal voter of shifting the tax burden away from the low-skilled, low-productivity occupations toward the rest of the economy. Beyond that point, additional subsidization requires either a shift in political power or in the preferences for redistribution. There is no way to know with certainty where this point lies, but enough time has elapsed from the onset of the employment crisis and the initiation of new policies to get some sense of the scope for improvement in employment performance through these "shielded" policies.

For the sake of argument, assume that reforms have not increased posttax and posttransfer inequality. To address the question of impact, we then need to look at whether the volume of work (as opposed to the number of people working) has changed, and by how much. If most of the employment gains have come through reducing hours, adopting work sharing, and splitting full-time jobs into part-time ones, it may signify an important change in

Table 6.10. *The Volume of Work in Twelve OECD Countries, 1990–1999*

	Social Democratic			Liberal			Christian Democratic	
Year		Hours	1990		Hours	1990		Hours	1990
1990	Finland	1,306	100	Australia	1,269	100	Germany	1,021	100
1995		1,081	83		1,266	100		992	97
1999		1,165	89		1,271	100		996	98
1990	Norway	1,047	100	New Zealand	1,225	100	Italy	902	100
1995		1,039	99		1,290	105		826	92
1999		1,088	104		1,289	105		854[b]	95
1990	Sweden	1,285	100	United Kingdom	1,279	100	France	993	100
1995		1,165	91		1,206	94		952	96
1999		1,176	92		1,233	96		953[b]	96
1990	Denmark	1,192	100	United States	1,403	100	**Netherlands**	**876**	**100**
1995		1,182	99		1,415	101		**889**	**101**
1999		1,222	103		1,460	104		**921[c]**	**105**
1990	*Average*	1,207	100	*Average*	1,294	100	*Average*	948	100
1995		1,117	93		1,294	100		915	97
1999		**1,163**	**97**		**1,314**	**101**		**931**	**98**

[a] Average annual hours worked per person in the working-age population.
[b] 1998.
[c] 1997.

Source: OECD (2000).

264

the distribution of work, but that would merely be a movement within the trilemma. We thus need numbers for the volume of work, not the number of workers.

In Table 6.10, I have used OECD's measures of the number of hours actually worked by employed workers, and then multiplied this number by the employment ratio to get a measure of the volume of work available. The number is similar to the employment ratio, *except* that the unit of analysis is hours worked instead of number of people working. Table 6.10 shows the results for The Netherlands (bold faced) as well as for eleven other OECD countries for which more or less complete data are available (organized into social democratic, liberal, and Christian democratic clusters). Note that The Netherlands does indeed experience an increase in the volume of work between 1990 and 1997, but the gain is considerably smaller than the increase in the number of employees. During this period, the number of employed persons increased by 16 percent, while the volume of work increased by only 5.2 percent. About two thirds of the increase in employment is, therefore, accounted for by a greater spread in the distribution of available work, not by an increase in the volume of work.

Whether a 5 percent increase in the volume of work during the 1990s is a lot depends on your perspective. If one compares The Netherlands to the other Christian democratic countries, it appears that The Netherlands has simply been catching up to the average level in that cluster. In 1990, the hours worked were significantly below the other countries in the cluster, whereas in 1997 they were similar. The main reason that The Netherlands outperforms the other countries in terms of the employment ratio, as we saw earlier, is that the Dutch have accepted a much larger proportion of part-time employees than other countries, either inside or outside the Christian democratic cluster (see Table 6.11). In 1998, part-time employment accounted for a remarkable 30 percent of total employment, which is roughly twice as high as the other countries in the cluster (which range from 17 percent in Germany to 12 percent in Italy). It is also significantly higher than in any other country in Table 6.11, including the most deregulated market economies. Note also that during the 1990s the part-time workforce became increasingly feminized, with the share of women in part-time employment rising from 70 to 76 percent.[29] In other words, selective deregulation in The Netherlands has created a dual labor market of part- and full-time employment, divided along gender

---

[29] Data are from *OECD Employment Outlook* (1999b, p. 240).

Table 6.11. *Part-Time Employment in Twelve OECD Countries, 1990–1999*

	Social Democratic			Liberal			Christian Democratic		
Year		Part-Time Employment	Women's Share[b]		Part-Time Employment	Women's Share[b]		Part-Time Employment	Women's Share[b]
1990	Finland	7.6	66.8	Australia	22.6	70.8	Germany	13.4	89.7
1998		9.7	63.1		25.9	68.8		16.6	84.1
1990	Norway	21.3	82.7	New Zealand	19.6	77.1	Italy	8.8	70.8
1998		21.0	79.1		22.8	74.3		11.8	70.4
1990	Sweden	14.5	81.1	United Kingdom	20.1	85.1	France	12.2	79.8
1998		13.5	97.3		23.0	80.4		14.8	79.3
1990	Denmark	19.2	71.5	United States	13.8	68.2	**Netherlands**	**28.2**	**70.4**
1998		17.0	68.5		13.4	68.0		**30.0**	**75.8**
1990	*Average*	15.7	75.5	*Average*	19.0	75.3	*Average*	15.7	77.7
1998		15.3	77.0		21.3	72.9		18.3	77.4

[a] Part-time employment as a share of total employment.

[b] Women's share in part-time employment.

Source: OECD (1999b, p. 240).

lines.[30] This may not be an unambiguously bad thing because many women prefer to work part-time, but the low volume of work continues to be a distinctly Christian democratic pattern.

Denmark is the country that stands out in the social democratic cluster because it exhibits significant gains in the volume of work during the 1990s, despite starting from a relatively high level in 1990. As in the case of The Netherlands, these gains, which occurred under social democratic governments, have partly been achieved through a combination of more flexible work-time and opening hours, and significant tightening of eligibility requirements for unemployment benefits among long-term unemployed and unemployed workers under 25 without a qualifying education.[31] As in Britain, a series of tax reforms has reduced income taxation, especially for low-income people, while tax deductions, especially for home owners, have been scaled back. To alleviate some of the pressures on the low-skilled labor market, wage subsidies and upskilling among young and low-paid workers have been promoted ("Handlingsplan for Beskaeftigelse"). The wage subsidies to employers hiring unemployed workers amount to about 50 percent of wages (Martin 2003), and expanded training opportunities have allowed firms to hire long-term unemployed while their core workers receive training (Torfing 1999). The fall in vacancy rates during the 1990s can at least in part be seen as a result of better matching of skills to jobs, and the reforms have met with support among employers (Martin 2003). Finally, an element of the reforms that clearly distinguishes the reforms under the social democrats from those in the Christian democratic model is the significant scale-back of the early retirement scheme, which had induced a large number of workers to leave the labor market.

In the Danish case, however, one also needs to control for changes in the macroeconomic conditions. Open economies can sustain several different equilibrium rates of unemployment at the cost of a deterioration in the trade balance. Soskice (2000) suggests that, as a rule of thumb, a 1 percent change in the external current account is equivalent to about a 1 percent change in the rate of unemployment. Because Denmark went from a 0.9

---

[30] This association between part-time employment and gender segmentation is a general phenomenon across the OECD, as can clearly be seen by comparing across regime clusters in Table 6.11.

[31] But the improvements are clearly not coming from an expansion of part-time employment, which is an important contrast to The Netherlands.

surplus to a 1.2 percent deficit on the current account between 1990 and 1998[32] – with most of this change resulting from the tax reforms – some of the 2.5 percent reduction in unemployment is accounted for by fiscal policy.

If we look beyond the Danish and Dutch cases, the data on the volume of work in Table 6.10 show that there has been no overall gain in the volume of work in Europe during the 1990s, and the employment gaps between clusters of countries persist and have in fact widened. While bearing in mind that the numbers are not necessarily fully comparable across countries, the variance across clusters is much greater than within clusters, and the differences across clusters are entirely consistent with the differences in employment ratios that were apparent by the early 1980s. Specifically, the volume of work in the liberal cluster in 1999 was 41 percent higher than in the Christian democratic cluster and 16 percent greater than in the social democratic cluster. These numbers were up from 37 and 7 percent, respectively, in 1990, and 25 and 5 percent in 1979. Concerning the gap between social democratic and Christian democratic countries (25 percent in favor of the Nordic countries in 1999), this can largely be accounted for by higher levels of public employment in the former countries, which is a familiar story by now.

So while the Danish and Dutch cases point to the potential for real employment gains through selective deregulation, the big picture presented in Table 6.10 hardly suggests that the tradeoffs captured by the trilemma are a thing of the past. Indeed, it is hard to escape the conclusion that selective deregulation of labor markets, as it has been practiced up to now at least, has had little effect on the employment gap with liberal countries. In the case of The Netherlands, at least part of the employment gain, which is less impressive when measured in hours than in workers, has been accomplished at the expense of a somewhat more dispersed wage structure. On the other hand, shielding low-wage workers through tax incentives, wage subsidies, and training opportunities – especially in the Danish case – has prevented the inequality to rise nearly as sharply as in the Anglo-Saxon cases.

---

[32] The trade balance went from a 5.9 percent surplus to a 2.9 percent surplus in the same period. The figures are calculated by dividing the trade balance in dollars with the GDP in dollars. Both current account and trade balances are from *OECD Employment Outlook* (1999b).

6.4.3. The Coalitional Dynamics of Labor Market Reforms

The national experiences discussed in the previous two sections suggest systematic differences in the politics of reform in specific as opposed to general skills countries. As I have suggested, these differences reflect structural, institutional, and partisan influences on political processes. But they also reflect differences in the logic of political coalition building, and in this section I briefly outline what these logics might look like, building on the theoretical framework developed in Part II.

A useful starting point is to imagine a two-dimensional policy space: One dimension is protection through redistributive transfers; the other is protection through labor-market regulation, especially legislated job security. Now distinguish three economic classes: (i) low-skilled and low-income workers, (ii) high specific skill and middle-income workers, and (iii) general skills, and high-income, professionals. These are similar to the classes identified in Chapter 4, except that they here combine both skill specificity and income (similar to the model in Chapter 3.)

In terms of preferences, low-skilled workers unambiguously benefit from redistributive transfers. They may or may not benefit from labor-market regulation because although such regulation can improve their security in the labor market, they may have significant costs in terms of job opportunities. The latter depends on the extent to which low-skilled workers are complements to high-skilled workers in production. If skilled workers benefit from regulation, as I will assume, and skilled and unskilled workers are close complements, unskilled workers may also benefit from, and therefore prefer, regulation.

Because it serves as a protection of their skill investments, specific skill workers will prefer high job security, but they may or may not benefit from redistributive spending. The latter depends on the progressivity of such spending as explained in Chapter 4. Finally, professionals are unambiguously hurt by both redistributive transfers (because they are net contributors), as well as by high job security (because it restricts mobility and efficiency).

Assume further that specific skills countries have PR electoral systems, whereas general skills countries have majoritarian systems. As discussed in Chapter 4, this is a good approximation to the empirical reality. If the former are dominated by center-left governments, it corresponds to an alliance between low skilled and skilled workers. As long as these workers are strong complements in production, and such production is facilitated by job protection (owing to the effects on skill investments), both will have an interest in a highly regulated labor market. As explained in Chapter 4, center-left coalitions can also use a combination of flat-rate and targeted transfers to produce relatively high levels of redistribution. By contrast, in general skills countries, the two-dimensional space essentially collapses into a single dimension where the median income voter will tend to vote for the center-right party.

Now introduce an economic shock that undermines the complementarity of skilled and unskilled workers in production. Empirically, this corresponds to the rise of low-productivity and low-skilled services, replacing "good" manufacturing jobs. The tradeoff between employment regulation and jobs now becomes steeper, and low-skilled workers will prefer less regulation. Because professionals and skilled workers are consumers of services, and also pay the bill for long-term unemployed workers, they both prefer lower protection for unskilled workers. In general skills countries with majoritarian electoral systems, this unambiguously leads to labor market reforms designed to maximize the flexibility of low-skilled labor markets. Insofar as such reforms cause significant increases in inequality, they may be accompanied by some redistribution (e.g., negative income taxes), but such redistribution ultimately depends on middle-class altruism.

The dynamic in special skill countries with PR is more complicated, but distinct. On the one hand, center-left governments have an incentive to endorse selective deregulation of low-skilled labor markets (especially part-time and temporary employment) because the tradeoff between regulation and employment is now steeper. On the other hand, unskilled workers will be worse off than before the shock, and the question is therefore whether deregulation will be accompanied by agreements to increase transfers ("shielding" as I have called it).

The answer turns on whether skilled workers (M in terms of the model in Chapter 4), will be willing to accede to more redistribution. And this, it seems to me, depends on whether low-skilled workers (L in the model) can credibly threaten to ally with professionals (H in the model). Because their preferences on employment protection are similar to the preferences of professionals, an alliance between L and M could undermine the entire employment protection system, which would serve as a strong incentive for skilled workers to agree to "compensating" unskilled workers when part-time and temporary job markets are deregulated. The idea is not far-fetched. As documented by Kitschelt (1994), many unskilled workers in Europe have turned to the New Right, thereby abandoning social democracy. The incentive to limit such exit is an important source of support for redistribution among skilled workers.

What this analysis provides is some theoretical pieces to the puzzle of explaining deregulation. But it certainly does not offer a complete picture. The reason is that the coalition game is occurring in at least four dimensions simultaneously: Redistribution can be divided into flat-rate and targeted transfers, and regulation can be divided into regulation for L and regulation for M. Because there are also multiple players (and I have not even considered the role of employers), this is an inherently very complicated, and potentially intractable, game. What I have done here is to combine some theoretical building blocks from Part II with the empirical discussion in this chapter to suggest how the game may be played out. I suspect that ideology plays a critical role as focal point for the outcome, but I leave this as an open-ended question.

6.4.4. Service Trade Liberalization as a Long-Term Solution?

Adam Smith's famous dictum that the division of labor is limited by the size of the market is as applicable to services as it is to manufactures.[33] What has become painfully clear to many European governments is that you cannot have high social protection with a compressed wage structure while simultaneously cultivating a vibrant private service sector *unless* you are able to specialize in high value-added services through international trade. Specialization in product markets that require an intensive use of workers with good vocational skills raises the relative price on these skills and makes them more attractive to invest in. But specialization requires trade, and services have traditionally been shielded from trade.

This is one of the most important reasons for the concerted effort in recent years by many European governments to liberalize service trade. There are contributing factors, of course. Technological change, especially in telecommunications and the internet, has opened up possibilities for trade where previously they did not exist (Vogel 1996). Lower costs of setting up foreign branches have also increased competition in domestic

---

[33] It is interesting to note that Smith had little regard for the value of services. He claimed that service workers were "unproductive of any value" and included in this category "churchmen, lawyers, physicians, men of letters of all kinds, players, buffoons, musicians, and opera singers" (quoted in Knudsen 2000).

markets and provided firms with stronger incentives to sell their products in international markets. In addition, liberalization of telecommunication and air transport in the United States has intensified competitive pressures on European firms and demonstrated the possibility of cheap, privately provided services (Vogel 1996). The notion that many services, especially telecommunications, were natural monopolies was simply unsustainable in the face of technological change and the emergence of fierce competition in the American market.

But as Knudsen persuasively shows, liberalization would have been very unlikely had it not been for a reinforcing change in the policy outlook of governments (Knudsen 2000). In the cases of the United States under Reagan and Britain under Thatcher, change was not simply driven by ideological zeal but also by a pragmatic drive to exploit and deepen comparative advantages in a world that was only just waking up to the realities of two decades of postindustrialization. Opening up to international competition came early in Britain and applied to services across the board. British firms had strong competitive positions in insurance and many financial services owing to decades of more liberal policies, and the government aimed at creating new ones in air transport, telecommunications, and postal services. Britain had been falling behind continental Europe in telecommunications, and the reforms seem to have greatly increased the competitiveness of former monopolies such as British Telecom, which now command a significant share of the European and North American markets. Likewise, Britain developed an early competitive advantage in the airline industry (Lehrer 2000).

It is important to point out that the change in government policy was not limited to right-leaning governments of the neoliberal variety. In Britain, the new Labour government under Blair came to power with a firm commitment to competition and free trade in services (Knudsen 2000, Chapter 6). Likewise, Christian democratic governments in Germany have made the *Dienstleistungswueste* – the "service desert" – a major target of policy reforms by inducing competition and by opening up world markets for German telecommunication and insurance companies. The German Social Democratic Party eventually came to the same view, and this was a critical change since some deregulation required changes in German Basic Law (*Grundgesetz*) that could only be passed with social democratic support (Knudsen 2000, Chapter 3).

Liberalization in Germany has led to a rapid expansion in exports of telecommunications and insurance services, with leading German firms establishing strong positions in integrated and customized communication services, some branches of business consulting, and specialized business insurance. On the other hand, German service producers have been losing out to British and American firms in some markets such as personal insurance, advertising, corporate finance, and entertainment (Hall and Soskice 2001). A trade pattern that is not unlike that in manufacturing seems to be developing here, although the data are woefully inadequate.[34]

Not surprisingly, the initial business preferences for and against trade liberalization depended on actors' perceptions of their ability to thrive in a global marketplace. Small firms in highly protected market segments typically opposed liberalization, and so did many unions fearing rationalizations, more job insecurity, and downward pressures on wages. Large internationally oriented firms with strong core competencies, on the other hand, were eager to expand their markets and to assist their clients in foreign markets. Likewise, large corporate consumers benefited from better products and lower prices, and although mass consumer groups often worried about lack of transparency, inequality of service provision (especially across regions), and nonuniform standards, they were often swayed by the reality of lower prices, greater choice, and improved quality and efficiency.

However, it was only after governments turned their backs on old protectionist policies that sustained coalitions of domestic interests emerged to push for further liberalization. As noted by Vogel (1996), interest groups that eventually benefited from reforms often play no role in advocating the policy. This shift in policy was significant because services, as noted earlier, have traditionally been viewed by left-leaning governments as a buffer against swings in the business cycle, as public goods or natural monopolies, and even as a social policy instrument where gross inefficiencies could be justified by the need to provide jobs or equalize access to services. But with deindustrialization gaining steam, and more women entering the labor market, this strategy had unacceptable fiscal consequences. Precisely when European monetary integration demanded fiscal austerity, the protected sector approach to services required more spending in order to deal with the growing employment problem. The tension between these opposing

---

[34] Knudsen quotes Mike Moore, Director-General of the World Trade Organization, as saying that "we are still surprisingly ignorant about services trade flows. Compare the material published on services trade with the abundance of information available on merchandise trade! It is certainly easier to find data on pork filets in EC intervention stocks, by year and origin (and, possibly, by name of the pig), than on the Community's external trade in computer or accountancy services" (Knudsen 2000, footnote 8, pp. 23–4).

forces gave way to a shift in thinking toward the view that efficiency and trade are prerequisites for sustainable growth in employment. In Hall's terminology (Hall 1993), this is a potentially paradigmatic change in ideas.

Was this shift in thinking justified? That is to say, is international trade truly a long-term avenue out of the trilemma? The answer has to be very tentative because we have yet to see the full impact of trade liberalization, and research in the area is very limited. Theoretically, however, the trade liberalization strategy strikes at the two key problems that gave rise to the trilemma: an incomplete division of labor and low productivity. In that sense, I am inclined to view trade liberalization in services as a profound and important step in the right direction. However, one must be cognizant of the limitations of the strategy. Trade liberalization has occurred primarily in insurance, telecommunications, financial services, and air transport. These services all fall into either the Isic-4 (transportation) or the Isic-8 (business services) industrial classes, and these constitute only about one quarter of the growth in service employment between 1970 and 1995. Moreover, they explain little of the variance in employment performance among countries (especially between the United States and continental Europe). Also, services continue to make up only a small portion of total trade. Of course, being a very recent phenomenon, this fact could change significantly over the next decade as the rate of growth in services trade is much faster than in manufacturing (Paemen and Bensch 1995). Changes in the retail trade sector by such companies as Amazon promise to add to this change, as do business-to-business transactions and other services that can be done over the internet.

That said, the employment heavy sectors of social and personal services are inherently less susceptible to trade. In these areas, workfare, selective deregulation, and continued government provision will likely play a much more important role. Nor should it be forgotten that trade liberalization is accompanied by significant short- and medium-term pain as greater efficiency is accomplished primarily by laying off workers. The long-term dynamic gains may be very significant, but in the short term there could be significant losses. Ironically, it is precisely these losses that may be the best bet for social democracy to remain in power.

6.5. Conclusion

While deindustrialization spurred much of the rise in the level of social protection during the 1970s and 1980s, it also gave rise to new tradeoffs and political conflict. In particular, the virtuous circle between employment and high levels of protection and wage compression became harder to sustain. The initial political response was to either (i) limit labor market entry (e.g., through tax disincentives for women to work) and maximize exit (e.g., through long maternity leave and early retirement), (ii) vastly expand employment in the public sector, or (iii) deregulate the labor market and undermine the power of the unions. These responses in many respects deepened the division between high- and low-protection countries, but they also sharpened the distinction between countries dominated by Christian democratic and social democratic ideas and governments.

As the costs of each strategy became increasingly apparent, governments embarked on reforms that sought to limit the severity of the tradeoffs of potentially overcoming trilemma altogether. Liberal countries have sought to restrict the opportunities to opt out of an unattractive labor market for the low-skilled by tying benefits to employment (workfare instead of welfare), while governments have used tax subsidies to somewhat improve the plight of the working poor. The result has been labor markets with stark income inequalities but ample employment opportunities and a thriving service economy. Workfare has done little to improve the skills of low-paid workers, but the fluidity of the labor market, a good post-secondary educational system, and the availability of low-paid social and personal services have limited gender-based inequalities, which tend to rise with high job protection and specificity of skills.

In the high-protection, specific skills countries, recent efforts have concentrated on expanding employment in the private sector while maintaining fiscal discipline. Governments have sought to accomplish this through some measures of deregulation and privatization of services (longer opening hours, private daycare, hospitals, etc.) combined with flexibilization of especially part-time and temporary employment. As in the liberal countries, benefits have become more closely tied to work, but governments have generally gone farther in ensuring that greater dispersion in pretax income is offset by tax subsidies and transfers benefiting low-paid workers. The generous social protection system for a core, skilled full-time labor force has largely been retained, creating a pattern of selective and shielded deregulation. This has preserved many of the key differences between the high-protection European welfare states and the low-protection Anglo-Saxon ones described in Chapter 2. In addition, although countries like Denmark and The Netherlands share many new policies, differences in the influence of Christian democracy and social democracy continue to shine through, especially in terms of the position of women in the labor market and the role of the public sector.

It is not difficult to see that the character of reforms is closely tied to the nature of politics in different countries. In the liberal cases, reforms cater to an increasingly well-educated and professionalized middle and upper-middle class who face little risk of poverty but benefit from inexpensive services and relatively low taxes. Poverty in this system is limited by the desire of pivotal voters to ensure that the low-skilled choose regular jobs instead of "careers" on the streets or in crime. In high-protection countries, reforms require the consent of organized labor and business, and coalitions that exclude the left from political influence are more difficult to sustain in multiparty PR electoral systems. Even though skilled workers and employers in the exposed sector benefit from deregulation of services and flexibilization of low-skilled labor markets, they want to retain most protections for full-time core workers but need to compromise with unions representing service sector and the low-skilled workers. Again, selective and shielded deregulation is a descriptive term that captures this political reality, as well as a plausible representation of the underlying coalitional game.

The differences between market-based general skills systems and protective specific skills systems are likely to endure because of (*not* in spite of) the international division of labor. Social protection is a complement to different types of production, and specialization on international markets makes convergence unlikely. The pressure for convergence has instead come in sectors of the economy and the labor market where trade and division of labor have traditionally been limited. This places governments under pressure to adopt similar policies, and the rise in direct or indirect subsidization of low-skilled labor in many countries is an expression of this pressure. It can only be relieved in a permanent way by increasing trade and specialization in services, but precisely because the scope for such trade is limited, chances are that we will continue to observe tendencies toward dualism in labor and product markets.

The resilience of existing differences between social democratic and Christian democratic varieties of this dualism seems less certain. In particular, countries dominated in the past by Christian democracy are bound to come under greater pressure to provide job opportunities for women, both because many young women increasingly prefer an active life outside the family and because paid work is a source of independence and therefore an insurance against the adverse effects of divorce. It is not inconceivable, in my view, that governments will respond by expanding public employment as happened in the Scandinavian countries. This may even be facilitated by the greater fiscal autonomy afforded by EMU and the single currency. If this does not happen, the dualistic tendencies in the private labor market will be exacerbated, producing a large second tier of part-time and temporary jobs primarily occupied by women. To some extent, as discussed earlier, the Dutch case already exemplifies this possibility.

Bibliography

Acemoglu, Daron and James Robinson. 2005. *Political Origins of Dictatorship and Democracy*. Cambridge, MA: MIT Press.

Achen, Chris. 2000. "Why Lagged Dependent Variables Can Suppress the Explanatory Power of Other Independent Variables." Paper presented at the Annual Meeting of the Methodology Section of the American Political Association Meeting, UCLA, July 20–22.

Adler, Michael and B. Lehmann. 1983. "Deviations from Purchasing Power Parity in the Long Run." *Journal of Finance* 38 (5): 1471–87.

Aldrich, John. 1993. "Rational Choice and Turnout." *American Journal of Political Science* 37: 246–78.

1995. *Why Parties? The Origin and Transformation of Political Parties in America*. Chicago: University of Chicago Press.

Alesina, Alberto and Roberto Perotti. 1997. "The Welfare State and Competitiveness." *American Economic Review* 87 (5): 921–39.

Alesina, Alberto and Dani Rodrik. 1994. "Distributive Politics and Economic Growth." *Quarterly Journal of Economics* 109: 465–90.

Allsopp, Christopher. 1983. "Inflation," in Andrea Boltho (ed.): 72–103. *The European Economy: Growth and Crisis*. Oxford: Oxford University Press.

Alt, James, Jeffry Frieden, Michael J. Gilligan, Dani Rodrik, and Ronald Rogowski. 1996. "The Political Economy of International Trade – Enduring Puzzles and an Agenda for Inquiry." *Comparative Political Studies* 29 (6): 689–717.

Alt, James E., Fredrik Carlsen, Per Heum, and Kåre Johansen. 1999. "Asset Specificity and the Political Behavior of Firms: Lobbying for Subsidies in Norway." *International Organization* 53 (1): 99–116.

Aoki, Masahiko. 1994. "The Japanese Firm as a System of Attributes," in Masahiko Aoki and Ronald Dore (eds.), 11–40. *The Japanese Firm: Sources of Competitive Strength*. Oxford: Clarendon.

Appelbaum, Eileen and Ronald Schettkat. 1994. "The End of Full Employment? On Economic Development in Industrialized Countries." *Intereconomics* 29 (May/June): 122–30.

1995. "Employment and Productivity in Industrialized Countries." *International Labour Review* 134 (4–5): 605–23.

Bacon, Robert and Walter Eltis. 1976. *Britain's Economic Problem: Too Few Producers*. London: Macmillan Press.

Bade, Robin and Michael Parkin. 1982. "Central Bank Laws and Monetary Policy." Mimeo, Department of Economics, University of Western Ontario.

Balassa, Bela. 1964. "The Purchasing Power Parity Doctrine – A Reappraisal." *Journal of Political Economy* 72 (6): 584–96.

Baldwin, Peter. 1990. *The Politics of Social Solidarity*: Class Bases of the European Welfare State 1875–1975. Cambridge: Cambridge University Press.

Barlett, Donald N. and James B. Steele 1992. *America: What Went Wrong?* Kansas City, MO: Andrews and McMeel.

Bates, Robert H., P. Brock, and J. Tiefenthaler. 1991. "Risk and Trade Regimes – Another Exploration." *International Organization* 45 (1): 1–18.

Baumol, William J. 1967. "The Macroeconomics of Unbalanced Growth." *American Economic Review* 57 (3): 415–26.

Bawn, Kathleen. 1999. "Constructing 'Us'": Ideology, Coalition Politics, and False Consciousness." *American Journal of Political Science* 43 (2): 303–34.

Beck, Nathaniel. 1992. "Comparing Dynamic Specifications: The Case of Presidential Approval," in James Stimson (ed.), *Political Analysis*, pp. 51–87. Ann Arbor: University of Michigan Press.

Beck, Nathaniel and Jonathan Katz. 1995. "What to Do (and Not to Do) with Time-Series Cross-Section Data." *American Political Science Review* 89 (September): 634–48.

1996. "Nuisance vs. Substance: Specifying and Estimating Time-Series-Cross-Section Models," in John R. Freeman (ed.), *Political Analysis*, Vol. 6: 1–36. Ann Arbor: University of Michigan.

Becker, Gary. 1964. *Human Capital: A Theoretical and Empirical Analysis with Special Reference to Education*. Chicago: The University of Chicago Press and the National Bureau of Economic Research.

Becker, Uwe. 2001. "A 'Dutch Model': Employment Growth by Corporatist Consensus and Wage Restraint? A Critical Account of an Idyllic View." *New Political Economy* 6 (1): 19–43.

Bénabou, Roland. 1996. "Inequality and Growth." *National Bureau of Economic Research Macro Annual*, 11: 11–74.

Berton, Fabienne, Gerard Podevin, and Eric Verdier. 1991. "Continual Vocational Training in France: Review and Perspectives." *Training & Employment: French Dimensions* 2 (winter). CEREQ (Centre d'Etudes et de Recherches sur les Qualifications).

Blanchard, Olivier and Justin Wolfers. 2000. "The Role of Shocks and Institutions in the Rise of European Unemployment: The Aggregate Evidence." *Economic Journal* 100: C1–33.

Block, Fred. 1994. "The Roles of the State in the Economy," in Neil Semlser and Richard Swedberg (eds.), *The Handbook of Economic Sociology*, pp. 691–710. Princeton, NJ: Princeton University Press.

Bibliography

Boix, Carles. 1998. *Political Parties, Growth and Equality.* New York: Cambridge University Press.

———. 1999. "Setting the Rules of the Game: The Choice of Electoral Systems in Advanced Democracies." *American Political Science Review* 93: 609–24.

Bradley, David, Evelyne Huber, Stephanie Moller, François Nielsen, and John Stephens. 2003. "Distribution and Redistribution in Post-Industrial Democracies." *World Politics* 55 (2): 193–228.

Brady, David. 2003. "Rethinking the Sociological Measure of Poverty." *Social Forces* 81 (3): 715–52.

Breen, Richard and Cecilia Garcia-Penalosa. 2002. "Bayesian Learning and Gender Segregation." *Journal of Labor Economics* 20 (4): 899–922.

Broadway, Robin W. and David E. Wildasin. 1989. "A Median Voter Model of Social Security." *International Economic Review* 30 (2): 307–28.

Brown, William. 1994. "Incomes Policy in Britain: Lessons from Experience," in Ronald Dore, Robert Boyer, and Zoe Mars (eds.), *The Return to Incomes Policy*: 31–46. London: Pinter Publishers.

Browning, Edgar K. 1975. "Why the Social Insurance Budget is Too Large in a Democratic Society." *Economic Inquiry* 13 (3): 373–88.

Cameron, David. 1978. "The Expansion of the Public Economy: A Comparative Analysis." *American Political Science Review* 72: 1243–61.

Card, David and Richard B. Freeman, eds. 1993. *Small Differences That Matter: Labor Markets and Income Maintenance in Canada and the United States.* National Bureau of Economic Research. Chicago: Chicago University Press.

Carey John M. and M. S. Shugart. 1995. "Incentives to Cultivate a Personal Vote: A Rank Ordering of Electoral Formulas" *Electoral Studies* 14 (4): 417–39.

Carlin, Wendy and David Soskice. 2000. "Modern Theories of Trade and the Political Economy of Macroeconomics." Typescript, Wissenschaftszentrum Berlin für Sozialforschung.

Castles, Francis and Peter Mair. 1984. "Left-Right Political Scales: Some 'Expert' Judgments." *European Journal of Political Research* 12: 73–88.

Chang, Mariko. 2000. "The Evolution of Sex Segregation Regimes." *American Journal of Sociology* 105 (6): 1658–1701.

Cooper, Russell W. 1999. *Coordination Games: Complementarities and Macroeconomics.* Cambridge: Cambridge University Press.

Cox, Gary. 1997. *Making Votes Count. Strategic Coordination in the World's Electoral Systems.* Cambridge: Cambridge University Press.

Crouch, Colin, David Finegold, and Mari Sako. 1999. *Are Skills the Answer? The Political Economy of Skill Creation in Advanced Industrial Countries.* Oxford: Oxford University Press.

Cukierman, Alex. 1992. *Central Bank Strategy, Credibility, and Independence: Theory and Evidence.* Cambridge, MA: MIT Press.

Cusack, Thomas. 1991. "The Changing Contours of Government." WZB Discussion Paper.

———. 1997. "Partisan Politics and Public Finance: Changes in Public Spending in the Industrialized Democracies, 1955–1989." *Public Choice* 91: 375–95.

Cusack, Thomas R. and Lutz Engelhardt. 2002. "The PGL File Collection: File Structures and Procedures." Wissenschaftszentrum Berlin für Sozialforschung.

Cusack, Thomas R. and Susanne Fuchs. 2002. "Documentation Notes for Parties, Governments, and Legislatures Data Set." Wissenschaftszentrum Berlin für Sozialforschung.

Daly, Mary. 1994. "A Matter of Dependency? The Gender Dimension of British Income-Maintenance Provision," *Sociology* 28 (3): 779–97.

Dansk Arbejdsgiverforening. *Lønstatistikken*. Copenhagen (various years).

Dertouzos, Michael L., Richard K. Lester, and Robert. M. Solow. 1989. *Made in America: Regaining the Productive Edge*. Cambridge, MA: MIT Press.

Dickson, Eric S. and Kenneth A. Shepsle. 2001. "Working and Shirking: Equilibrium in Public-Goods Games with Overlapping Generations of Players." *Journal of Law, Economics and Organization* 17 (2):285–318.

Downs, Anthony. 1957. *An Economic Theory of Democracy*. New York: Harper.

Duch, R. M. and M. A. Taylor. 1993. "Postmaterialism and the Economic Condition." *American Journal of Political Science* 37 (3): 747–79.

Due, Jesper and Jørgen Steen Madsen. 1988. *Når der Slås Søm i: Overenskomstforhandlinger og Organisationstruktur* (Sealing the Deal: Wage Bargaining and Organizational Structure). Copenhagen: Juristog Økonomforbundets Forlag.

Ebbinghaus, Bernhard and Jelle Visser. 2000. *Trade Unions in Western Europe since 1945*. CD-ROM. London: Macmillan.

Eichengreen, Barry. 1997. "Institutions and Economic Growth: Europe after World War II," in Nicholas Crafts and Gianni Toniolo (eds.), *Economic Growth in Europe since 1945*. Cambridge: Cambridge University Press.

Eichengreen, Barry and Torben Iversen. 1999. "Institutions and Economic Performance in the 20th Century: Evidence from the Labor Market." *Oxford Review of Economic Policy*, 15 (4): 121–38.

Elkin, Stephen L. 1985. "Pluralism in Its Place: State and Regime in Liberal Democracy," in Roger Benjamin and Stephen L. Elkin (eds.), *The Democratic State*: 179–212. Lawrence: University Press of Kansas.

Ellwood, David. 2000. "The Impact of the Earned Income Tax Credit and Social Policy Reforms on Work, Marriage, and Living Arrangements." Paper presented at the Inequality Summer Institute, Kennedy School of Government, June 2000.

Esping-Andersen, Gøsta. 1985. *Politics against Markets*. Princeton, NJ: Princeton University Press.

1990. *The Three Worlds of Welfare Capitalism*. Princeton, NJ: Princeton University Press.

1999a. *Social Foundations of Postindustrial Economies*. Oxford: Oxford University Press.

1999b. "Politics without Class; Postindustrial Cleavages in Europe and America," in Herbert Kitschelt, Peter Lange, Gary Marks, and John Stephens (eds.), *Continuity and Change in Contemporary Capitalism*: 293–345. Cambridge: Cambridge University Press.

Bibliography

Estevez-Abe, Margarita. 1999a. "Welfare and Capitalism in Contemporary Japan." Unpublished Ph.D. Dissertation, Harvard University.

1999b. "Comparative Political Economy of Female Labor Force Participation." Paper presented at the 95th American Political Science Association Meeting in Atlanta, September 1999.

2002. "Gendering Varieties of Capitalism." Paper prepared for a conference on The Political Economy of Family and Work, Yale University, July.

Estevez-Abe, Margarita, Torben Iversen, and David Soskice. 2001. "Social Protection and the Formation of Skills: A Reinterpretation of the Welfare State," in Peter A. Hall and David Soskice (eds.), *Varieties of Capitalism: The Institutional Foundations of Comparative Advantage*: 145–183. Oxford: Oxford University Press.

European Commission. Various years. *Employment in Europe*. Luxembourg: Office for Official Publications of the European Communities.

Falkner, Gerda and Emmerich Talos. 1994. "The Role of the State within Social Policy." In Wolfgang Muller and Vincent Wright (eds.), special issue, The State in Western Europe: Retreat or Redefinition? *Western European Politics* 17 (July): 53–76.

Ferner, Anthony and Richard Hyman, eds. 1992. *Industrial Relations in the New Europe*. Oxford: Blackwell.

Finegold, David, Keith W. Brendley, Robert Lempert, Donald Henry, Peter Cannon, Brent Boultinghouse, and Max Nelson. 1994. *The Decline of the U.S. Machine Tool Industry and Prospects for its Sustainable Recovery*, Vol. 1, RAND, MR-479/1-OSTP.

Finegold, David and David Soskice. 1988. "The Failure of Training in Britain: Analysis and Prescription." *Oxford Review of Economic Policy* 4 (Autumn): 21–53.

Flanagan, Robert J., David W. Soskice, and Lloyd Ulman. 1983. *Unionism, Economic Stabilization, and Incomes Policies: European Experience*. Washington, DC: The Brookings Institution.

Frankel, Jeffrey A. and Andrew K. Rose. 1996. "A Panel Project on Purchasing Power Parity: Mean Reversion within and between Countries." *Journal of International Economics* 40 (1–2): 209–24.

Franzese, Robert J. 1998. "Political Participation, Income Distribution, and Public Transfers in Developed Democracies." Unpublished paper, The University of Michigan, Ann Arbor.

2002. *Macroeconomics of Developed Democracies*. Cambridge: Cambridge University Press.

Freeman, Richard B. and Lawrence Katz. 1994. "Rising Wage Inequality: The United States vs. Other Advanced Countries," in Richard Freeman (ed.), *Working under Different Rules*: 29–62. New York: Russell Sage Foundation.

Frieden, Jeffry. 1991. "Invested Interests: The Politics of National Economic Policies in a World of Global Finance," *International Organization* 45 (Autumn): 425–51.

Ganzeboom, Harry B. G. and Donald J. Treiman. 1996. "Internationally Comparable Measures of Occupational Status for the 1988 International

Standard Classification of Occupations." *Social Science Research* 25 (3): 201–39.

Garrett, Geoffrey. 1993. "The Politics of Structural Change: Swedish Social Democracy and Thatcherism in Comparative Perspective." *Comparative Political Studies* 25 (4): 521–47.

1998. *Partisan Politics in the Global Economy*. Cambridge: Cambridge University Press.

Garrett, Geoffrey and Peter Lange. 1985. "The Politics of Growth: Strategic Interaction and Economic Performance, 1974–1980." *Journal of Politics* 47: 792–27.

Glyn, Andrew and Stewart Wood. 2000. "New Labour's Economic Policy: How Social-Democratic Is the Blair Government?" in Andrew Glyn (ed.), *Economic Policy and Social Democracy*. Oxford: Oxford University Press.

Gordon, Robert J. 1987. "Productivity, Wages and Prices Inside and Outside of Manufacturing in the U.S., Japan, and Europe." *European Economic Review* 31: 685–739.

Gottschalk, Peter and T. M. Smeeding. 2000. "Empirical Evidence on Income Inequality in Industrialized Countries," in A. B. Atkinson and F. Bourguignon (eds.), *The Handbook of Income Distribution*. London: North Holland Press.

Goul-Andersen, Jørgen. 1989. "Social Klasse og Parti," in Jørgen Elklit and Ole Tonsgaard (eds.), *To Folketingsvalg*: 176–207. Århus: Politica.

1992. "The Decline of Class Voting Revisited," in Peter Gundelach and Karen Siune (eds), *From Voters to Participants*: 91–107. Copenhagen: Politica.

Green-Pedersen, Christoffer, Kees van Kersbergen, and Anton Hemerijck. 2001. "Neo-Liberalism, the 'Third Way' or What? Recent Social Democratic Welfare Policies in Denmark and the Netherlands." *Journal of European Public Policy* 8 (April): 307–25.

Grilli, Vittorio, Donato Masciandaro, and Guido Tabellini. 1991."Political and Monetary Institutions and Public Financial Policies in the Industrial Countries." *Economic Policy* 13 (October): 341–92.

Grossman, Gene M. and Elhanan Helpman. 1998. "Intergenerational Redistribution with Short-Lived Governments." *Economic Journal* 108 (September): 1299–1329.

Hacker, Jacob and Pierson, Paul. 2000. "Business Power and Social Policy: Employers and the Formation of the American Welfare State." *Politics and Society* 30(2): 277–325.

Hall, Peter A. 1986. *Governing the Economy*. Oxford: Oxford University Press.

1993. "Policy Paradigms, Social Learning and the State." *Comparative Politics* 25 (3): 275–96.

Hall, Peter A. and Robert Franzese. 1998. "Central Bank Independence, Coordinated Wage-Bargaining, and European Monetary Union." *International Organization* 52 (summer): 505–35.

Hall, Peter A. and David Soskice. 2001. "An Introduction to Varieties of Capitalism," in Peter A. Hall and David Soskice (eds.), *Varieties of Capitalism: The Institutional Foundations of Comparative Advantage*, pp. 1–68. Oxford: Oxford University Press.

Bibliography

Hemerijck, Anton, Brigitte Unger, and Jelle Visser. 2000. "How Small Countries Negotiate Change: Twenty-Five Years of Policy Adjustment in Austria, the Netherlands, and Belgium" in Fritz W. Scharpf and Vivien A. Schmidt (eds.), *Welfare and Work in the Open Economy: Diverse Response to Common Challenges in Twelve Countries*, vol 2, pp. 175–263. Oxford: Oxford University Press.

Heston, Alan, Robert Summers, and Bettina Aten. 2002. Penn World Table Version 6.1, Center for International Comparisions at the University of Pennsylvania (CICUP), October 2002.

Hibbs, Douglas. 1977. "Political Parties and Macroeconomic Policy." *American Political Science Review*, 71 (December): 1467–87.

Hibbs Douglas A. and Håkan Locking. 2000. "Wage Dispersion and Productive Efficiency: Evidence for Sweden." *Journal of Labor Economics* 18 (4): 755–82.

Hoel, Michael. 1990. "Local Versus Central Wage Bargaining with Endogenous Investments." *Scandinavian Journal of Economics* 92: 453–69.

Hollingsworth, J. Rogers and Robert Boyer, eds. 1997. *Contemporary Capitalism: The Embeddedness of Institutions*. Cambridge: Cambridge University Press.

Honaker, James, Anne Joseph, Gary King, Kenneth Scheve, and Naunihal Singh. 1999. *AMELIA: A Program for Missing Data*. Department of Government, Harvard University. Free Software Program.

Hu, Sheng Cheng. 1982. "Social Security, Majority-Voting Equilibrium and Dynamic Efficiency." *Intentional Economic Review* 23: 269–87.

Huber, Evelyn, Charles Ragin, and John Stephens. 1993. "Social Democracy, Christian Democracy, Constitutional Structure and the Welfare State." *American Journal of Sociology* 99 (3): 711–49.

1997. *Comparative Welfare States Data Set*. Data set, Northwestern University and University of North Carolina.

Huber, Evelyn and John D. Stephens. 2000. "Partisan Governance, Women's Employment, and the Social Democratic Service State." *American Sociological Review* 65 (3): 323–342.

2001. *Development and Crisis of the Welfare State: Parties and Policies in Global Markets*. Chicago: University of Chicago Press.

Huber, John D. and Ronald Inglehart. 1995. "Expert Interpretations of Party Space and Party Locations in 42 Societies." *Party Politics* 1: 73–111.

Ibsen, Flemming and Jørgen Stamhus. 1993. *Fra Central til Decentral Lønfastsættelse* (From Centralized to Decentralized Wage Setting). Copenhagen: Jurist- og Økonomforbundets Forlag.

ILO (International Labour Organization). *Labour Statistics Database*: Segregat. ILO 1998–2004. *laborsta.ilo.org*.

ILO (International Labour Organization). 1999. "International Statistical Comparisons of Occupational and Social Structures: Problems, Possibilities and the Role of ISCO-88." ILO background paper written by Eivind Hoffmann.

IMF (International Monetary Fund). Various years. *Direction of Trade Statistics Yearbook*. Washington, DC: IMF.

IMF (International Monetary Fund). Various years. *Government Finance Statistics Yearbook*. Washington, DC: IMF.

Immervoll, H., L. Mitton, C. O'Donoghue, and H. Sutherland. 1999. "Budgeting for Fairness?" Microsimulation Unit MU/RN/32 Cambridge, March.

Income Data Services. 1996. *Industrial Relations and Collective Bargaining*. London: Institute of Personnel and Development.

Inglehart, Donald. 1987. "Value Change in Industrial Society." *American Political Science Review* 81: 1289–1303.

——— 1990. *Culture Shift in Advanced Industrial Society*. Princeton, NJ: Princeton University Press.

International Institute for Democracy and Electoral Assistance. 1997. *Voter Turnout from 1945 to 1997: A Global Report on Political Participation*. Stockholm: IDEA Information Services.

ISSP (International Social Survey Program). 1993. *International Social Survey Program: Role of Government II, 1990* [ICPSR computer file]. Cologne, Germany: Zentralarchiv fuer Empirische Sozialforschung (producer) and Ann Arbor, MI: Inter-university Consortium for Political and Social Research (distributors).

——— 1999. *International Social Survey Program: Role of Government III, 1996* [ICPSR computer file]. Cologne, Germany: Zentralarchiv fuer Empirische Sozialforschung (producer) and Ann Arbor, MI: Inter-university Consortium for Political and Social Research (distributors).

——— 2000. *International Social Survey Program: Work Orientations II, 1997* [ICPSR computer file]. Cologne, Germany: Zentralarchiv fuer Empirische Sozialforschung (producer) and Ann Arbor, MI: Inter-university Consortium for Political and Social Research (distributors).

Iversen, Torben. 1996. "Power, Flexibility and the Breakdown of Centralized Wage Bargaining: The Cases of Denmark and Sweden in Comparative Perspective." *Comparative Politics* 28: 399–436.

——— 1999. *Contested Economic Institutions: The Politics of Macroeconomics and Wage Bargaining in Advanced Democracies*. Cambridge: Cambridge University Press.

Iversen, Torben and Thomas Cusack. 2000. "The Causes of Welfare State Expansion: Deindustrialization or Globalization?" *World Politics* 52 (April): 313–49.

Iversen, Torben and Frances Rosenbluth. 2003. "The Political Economy of Gender: Explaining Cross-National Variation in Household Bargaining, Divorce, and the Gender Voting Gap." Paper presented at the Annual Meetings of the American Political Science Association, Philadelphia, Pennsylvania, August 28–31, 2003.

Iversen, Torben and David Soskice. 1999. "Monetary Integration, Partisanship, and Macroeconomic Policy." Paper presented at the 95th American Political Association Meeting in Atlanta, September 2–5, 1999.

——— 2001. "An Asset Theory of Social Policy Preferences." *American Political Science Review* 95 (4): 875–93.

——— 2002. "Political Parties and the Time Inconsistency Problem in Social Welfare Provision." Paper presented at 2002 Annual Meeting of the Public Choice Society, San Diego.

2004. "Electoral Systems and the Politics of Coalitions: Why Some Democracies Redistribute More Than Others." Paper presented at the Conference of Europeanists, Chicago.

Iversen, Torben and Niels Thygesen. 1998. "Denmark: From External to Internal Adjustment," in Erik Jones, Jeffry Frieden, and Francisco Torres (eds.), *Joining Europe's Monetary Club: The Challenge for Smaller Member States*: 61–81. New York: St. Martin's Press.

Iversen, Torben and Anne Wren. 1998. "Equality, Employment, and Budgetary Restraint: The Trilemma of the Service Economy." *World Politics* 50 (July): 507–46.

Johansen, Hans Christian. 1987. *The Danish Economy in the 20th Century*. London: Croom Helm.

Katzenstein, Peter. 1984. *Corporatism and Change*. Ithaca, NY: Cornell University Press.

1985. *Small States in World Markets*. Ithaca, NY: Cornell University Press.

King, Gary, James Honaker, Anne Joseph, and Kenneth Scheve. 2001. "Analyzing Incomplete Political Science Data: An Alternative Algorithm for Multiple Imputation." *American Political Science Review* 95 (1): 49–69.

Kitschelt, Herbert. 1994. *The Transformation of European Social Democracy*. Cambridge: Cambridge University Press.

Knudsen, Jette. 2000. "Liberalization of Services Trade." Ph.D. Dissertation, Department of Political Science, MIT.

Korpi, Walter. 1983. *The Democratic Class Struggle*. London: Routledge & Kegan Paul.

1989. "Power, Politics, and State Autonomy in the Development of Social Citizenship – Social Rights during Sickness in 18 OECD Countries Since 1930." *American Sociological Review* 54 (3): 309–28.

Korpi, Walter and Michael Shalev. 1979. "Strikes, Industrial Relations, and Class Conflict in Capitalist Societies." *British Journal of Sociology* 30 (2): 164–87.

Kotlikoff, Laurence, Torsten Persson, and Lars E. O. Svensson. 1988. "Social Contracts as Assets: A Possible Solution to the Time-Consistency Problem." *American Economic Review* 78 (4): 662–77.

Kreps, David M. 1990. *A Course in Microeconomic Theory*. Princeton: Princeton University Press.

Krugman, Paul. 1978. "Purchasing Power Parity and Exchange Rates – Another Look at the Evidence." *Journal of International Economics* 8 (3): 397–407.

1996. *Pop Internationalism*. Cambridge: MIT Press.

Laasko, Markku and Rein Taagepera. 1979. "Effective Number of Parties: A Measure with Applications to Western Europe." *Comparative Political Studies* 12 (3): 3–27.

Lane, Christel. 1989. "From 'Welfare Capitalism' to 'Market Capitalism': A Comparative Review of Trends towards Employment Flexibility in the Labour Markets of Three Major European Societies." *Sociology* 23 (4): 583–610.

Lange, Peter and Geoffrey Garrett. 1985. "The Politics of Growth: Strategic Interaction and Economic Performance, 1974–1980." *Journal of Politics* 47: 792–82.

Laver, Michael and W. Ben Hunt. 1992. *Policy and Party Competition*. New York: Routledge.

Leamer, Edward E. 1996. "A Trade Economists View of U.S. Wages and 'Globalization.'" Paper presented at the Political Economy of European Integration Study Group Meeting, University of California at Berkeley, January 1996.

Lehrer, Mark. 2000. "Macro- Varieties of Capitalism and Micro-Varieties of Strategic Management in European Airlines," in Peter A. Hall and David Soskice (eds.), *Varieties of Capitalism: The Institutional Foundations of Comparative Advantage*, pp. 361–86. Oxford: Oxford University Press.

Lijphart, Arend. 1994. *Electoral Systems and Party Systems: A Study of Twenty-Seven Democracies, 1945–90*. New York: Oxford University Press.

1997. "Unequal Participation: Democracy's Unresolved Dilemma." *American Political Science Review* 91: 1–14.

1999. *Patterns of Democracy. Government Forms and Performance in Thirty-Six Countries*. New Haven, CT: Yale University Press.

Lindblom, Charles E. 1980. *Politics and Markets: The World's Political Economic Systems*. New York: HarperCollins.

Lindert, Peter H. 1996. "What Limits Social Spending?" *Explorations in Economic History* 33 (1): 1–34.

Lipset, Seymour M. and Stein Rokkan. 1967. "Cleavage Structures, Party Systems, and Voter Alignments: An Introduction," in Lipset and Rokkan (eds.), *Party Systems and Voter Alignments: Cross-National Perspectives*, pp. 1–64. New York: Free Press.

Lothian James R. and Mark P. Taylor. 1996. "Real Exchange Rate Behavior: The Recent Float from the Perspective of the Past Two Centuries." *Journal of Political Economy* 104 (3): 488–509.

Luebbert, Gregory. 1991. *Liberalism, Fascism, or Social Democracy: Social Classes and the Political Origins of Regimes in Interwar Europe*. Oxford: Oxford University Press.

Mackie, Thomas T. and Richard Rose. 1991. *The International Almanac of Electoral History*, 3rd edition. London: Macmillan.

Madrick, Jeffrey G. 1995. *The End of Affluence: The Causes and Consequences of America's Economic Dilemma*. New York: Random House.

Maier, Charles. 1987. *In Search of Stability: Explorations in Historical Political Economy*. Cambridge: Cambridge University Press.

Manow, Philip. 2001. "Comparative Institutional Advantages of Welfare State Regimes and New Coalitions in Welfare State Reforms," in Paul Pierson (ed.), *The New Politics of the Welfare State*, pp. 146–64. New York: Oxford University Press.

2002. "Social Protection, Capitalist Production. The Bismarckian Welfare State and the German Political Economy from the 1880s to the 1990s." Habilitation thesis, Department of Politics and Management, Konstanz University, Germany.

Mares, Isabela, 1998. "Negotiated Risks: Employers' Role in Social Policy Development." Unpublished Ph.D. Dissertation, Harvard University.

Bibliography

2001. "Firms and the Welfare State: When, Why, and How Does Social Policy Matter to Employers?" in Peter A. Hall and David Soskice, *Varieties of Capitalism: The Institutional Foundations of Comparative Advantage*, pp. 184–212. Oxford: Oxford University Press.

2003. *The Politics of Social Risk: Business and Welfare State Development.* Cambridge: Cambridge University Press.

Marshall, Alfred. 1922. *Principles of Economics*, 4th edition. London: Macmillan.

Martin, Cathie J. 1995. "Nature or Nurture? Sources of Firm Preference for National Health Reform." *American Political Science Review* 89 (4): 898–913.

2003. "Active Social Policy and the Sorcerer's Stone: Firms' Preferences and Welfare Regimes in Denmark and Britain." Department of Government, Boston University.

Meese, Richard and Kenneth Rogoff. 1988. "Was it Real – The Exchange Rate Interest Differential Relation over the Modern Floating-Rate Period." *Journal of Finance* 43 (4): 933–48.

Melkas, Helinä and Richard Anker. 1997. "Occupational Segregation by Sex in Nordic Countries: An Empirical Investigation." *International Labour Review* 136 (3): 341–63.

Meltzer, Allan H. and Scott. F. Richards. 1981. "A Rational Theory of the Size of Government." *Journal of Political Economy* 89 (5): 914–27.

Meulders, Daniele, Olivier Plasman, and Robert Plasman. 1994. *Atypical Employment in the EC.* Brookfield, VT: Dartmouth Publishing Company.

Meyer, Bruce and Daniel Rosenbaum. 1999. "Welfare, the Earned Income Tax Credit, and the Labor Supply of Single Mothers." Mimeo, Northwestern University.

Moene, Karl Ove and Michael Wallerstein. 2001. "Inequality, Social Insurance and Redistribution." *American Political Science Review* 95 (4): 859–74.

Muthoo, Abhinay. 1999. *Bargaining Theory with Applications.* Cambridge: Cambridge University Press.

Myles, John and Paul Pierson. 1997. "Friedman's Revenge: The Reform of 'Liberal' Welfare States in Canada and the United States." *Politics and Society* 25 (4): 443–72.

Nannestad, Peter. 1991. *Danish Design or British Disease? Danish Economic Crisis Policy 1974–79 in Comparative Perspective.* Århus: Århus University Press.

North, Douglas. 1990. *Institutions, Institutional Change and Economic Performance.* Cambridge: Cambridge University Press.

Obstfeld, Maurice and Kenneth Rogoff. 2000. *The Six Major Puzzles in International Macroeconomics: Is There a Common Cause?* National Bureau of Economic Research Working Paper, July.

O'Connor, Julia, Ann Orloff, and Sheila Shaver. 1999. *States, Markets, Families: Gender, Liberalism and Social Policy in Australia, Canada, Great Britain, and the United States.* Cambridge: Cambridge University Press.

OECD (Organization for Economic Co-ordination and Development). Undated. *Electronic Data Base on Wage Dispersion.*

Undated. *Database on Unemployment Benefit Entitlements and Replacement Rates.* Electronic datafile.

Various years. *Economic Outlook.* Paris: OECD.

Various years. *Labour Force Statistics.* Paris: OECD.

National Accounts, Part II: Detailed Tables. Paris: OECD.

1991. *OECD Employment Outlook.* Paris: OECD.

1993. *OECD Employment Outlook.* Paris: OECD.

1994a. *OECD Employment Outlook.* Paris: OECD.

1994b. *The OECD Jobs Study.* Paris: OECD.

1995. "Income Distribution in OECD Countries: Evidence from the Luxembourg Income Study." Social Policy Studies No. 18. Paris: OECD.

1996. *International Sectoral Data Base.* Paris: OECD.

1997a. "Economic Performance and the Structure of Collective Bargaining." In OECD, OECD *Employment Outlook.* Paris: OECD.

1997b. *OECD Employment Outlook.* Paris: OECD.

1998. *OECD Employment Outlook.* Paris: OECD.

1999a. *International Sectoral Data Base.* Paris: OECD.

1999b. *OECD Employment Outlook.* Paris: OECD.

1999c. *Industrial Structure Statistics,* Vol. 1: Core Data. Paris: OECD.

2000. *OECD Employment Outlook.* Paris: OECD.

2002. *Revenue Statistics 1965–2001.* Paris: OECD.

OECD (Organization for Economic Co-ordination and Development). and Statistics Canada. 2000. *Literacy in the Information Age. Final Report of the International Adult Literacy Survey.* Paris: OECD.

Oh, Kevn-Yeob. 1996. "Purchasing Power Parity and Unit Root Tests Using Panel Data." *Journal of International Money and Finance* 15 (3): 405–18.

Orloff, Ann Shola. 1993. "Gender and the Social Rights of Citizenship: The Comparative Analysis of Gender Relations and Welfare States." *American Sociological Review* 58: 303–28.

Paemen, Hugo and Alexandra Bensch. 1995. *From the GATT to the WTO: The European Community in the Uruguay Round.* Leuven, Belgium: Leuven University Press.

Papell, David H. 1997. "Cointegration and Exchange Rate Dynamics." *Journal of International Money and Finance* 16 (3): 445–59.

Penn World Tables. *Global Development Finance and World Development Indicators.*

Perotti, Roberto. 1996. "Growth, Income Distribution and Democracy: What the Data Say." *Journal of Economic Growth* 1 (2): 149–87.

Persson, Torsten and Guido Tabellini. 1999. "The Size and Scope of Government: Comparative Politics with Rational Politicians." *European Economic Review* 43: 699–735.

2000. *Political Economics: Explaining Economic Policy.* Cambridge, MA: MIT Press.

2003. *The Economic Effects of Constitutions.* Cambridge, MA: MIT Press.

Piersson, Paul. 1994. *Dismantling the Welfare State? Reagan, Thatcher and the Politics of Retrenchment.* Cambridge: Cambridge University Press.

Bibliography

1996. "The New Politics of the Welfare State." *World Politics* 48 (2): 143–79.

1998. "Irresistible Forces, Immovable Objects; Post-Industrial Welfare States Confront Permanent Austerity." *Journal of European Public Policy* 5: 539–60.

2000. "Three Worlds of Welfare State Research." *Comparative Political Studies* 33 (6–7): 791–821.

Piven, Frances Fox. 1991. *Labor Parties in Postindustrial Societies.* New York: Oxford University Press.

Polanyi, Karl. 1944. *The Great Transformation.* New York: Rinehart & Co.

Pontusson, Jonas. 2002. "Doubts about Varieties of Capitalism: Labor-Market and Welfare-State Dynamics in OECD Countries." Mimeo, Department of Government, Cornell University.

Pontusson, Jonas and Hyeok Yong Kwon. 2004. "Welfare Spending, Government Partisanship, and Varieties of Capitalism." Prepared for delivery at the Conference of Europeanists, Chicago, IL, March 11–13, 2004.

Pontusson, Jonas and Peter Swenson. 1996. "Labor Markets, Production Strategies, and Wage Bargaining Institutions: The Swedish Employer Offensive in Comparative Perspective." *Comparative Political Studies* 29 (April): 223–50.

Porter, Michael E. 1990. *The Competitive Advantage of Nations.* New York: Free Press.

Porter, Stacy. 2002. "Production Systems, Skill Equilibria, and Family Policy: Understanding Women's Employment in the Advanced Economies." Honors Thesis, Harvard University.

Powell, Bingham. 2002. "PR, the Median Voter, and Economic Policy: An Exploration." Paper presented at the 2002 Meetings of the American Political Science Association, Boston.

Przeworski, Adam. 1986. *Capitalism and Social Democracy.* Cambridge: Cambridge University Press.

2003. *States and Markets.* Cambridge: Cambridge University Press.

Quinn, Denis P. and Carla Inclan. 1997. "The Origin of Financial Openness: A Study of Current and Capital Account Internationalization." *American Journal of Political Science* 41 (3): 771–813.

Rae, Douglas W. 1967. *The Political Consequences of Electoral Laws.* New Haven, CT: Yale University Press.

Rangel, Antonio. 2003. "Forward and Backward Intergenerational Goods: Why is Social Security Good for the Environment?" *American Economic Review* 93(3): 813–34.

Reich, Robert B. 1983. *The Next American Frontier.* New York: Times Books.

Rodrik, Dani. 1997. *Has Globalization Gone Too Far?* Washington, DC: Institute for International Economics.

1998. "Why Do More Open Economies Have Larger Governments," *Journal of Political Economy* 106 (5) (October): 997–1032.

Rogoff, Kenneth. 1996. "The Purchasing Power Parity Puzzle." *Journal of Economic Literature* 34 (2): 647–68.

Rogowski, Ronald and Mark Andreas Kayser. 2002. "Majoritarian Electoral Systems and Consumer Power: Price-level Evidence from the OECD Countries." *American Journal of Political Science* 46 (3): 526–39.

Rokkan, Stein. 1970. *Citizens, Elections, Parties. Approaches to the Comparative Study of the Processes of Development*. Oslo: Universitetsforlaget.

Rothstein, Bo. 1998. *Just Institutions Matter. The Moral and Political Logic of the Universal Welfare State*. Cambridge: Cambridge University Press.

Rowthorn, Robert. 1992. "Corporatism and Labour Market Performance," in Jukka Pekkarinen, Matti Pohjola, and Bob Rowthorn (eds.), *Social Corporatism: A Superior Economic System?*, pp. 44–81. Oxford: Clarendon Press.

Rowthorn, Robert and Ramana Ramaswamy. 1997. "Deindustrialization: Causes and Implications." International Monetary Fund, Working Paper 42.

1999. "Growth, Trade, and Deindustrialization," *International Monetary Fund Staff Papers* 46, no. 1 (March).

Rubery, Jill, Colette Fagan, and Friederike Maier. 1996. "Occupational Segregation, Discrimination and Equal Opportunity," in Gunther Schmid, Jacqueline O'Reilly, and Klaus Schomann (eds.), *International Handbook of Labour Market Policy and Evaluation*, pp. 431–61. Cheltenham, UK; Brookfield, US: Edward Elgar.

Rueda, David and Jonas Pontusson. 2000. "Wage Inequality and Varieties of Capitalism." *World Politics* 52 (3): 350–83.

Ruggie, John G. 1983. "International Regimes, Transactions and Change. Embedded Liberalism in the Post-War Economic Order," in Stephen D. Krasner (ed.), *International Regimes*: 195–231. Ithaca, NY: Cornell University Press.

Saeger, Steven S. 1996. "Globalization and Economic Structure in the OECD." Unpublished Ph.D. dissertation, Harvard University.

1997. "Globalization and Deindustrialization: Myth and Reality in the OECD." *Weltwirtschaftliches Archiv* 133 (4): 579–608.

Salverda, Wiemer. 1996. "Is the Dutch Economy Really Short of Low-Paid Jobs?" in C. H. A. Verhaar (ed.), *On the Challenges of Unemployment in a Regional Europe*, pp. 221–40. Aldershot: Avebury.

Samuelson, Paul. 1964. "Theoretical Notes on Trade Problems." *Review of Economics and Statistics* 46 (2): 145–54.

Scharpf, Fritz W. 1991. *Crisis and Choice in European Social Democracy*. Ithaca, NY: Cornell University Press.

2000. "Welfare and Work in the Open Economy. Constraints, Challenges and Vulnerabilities." Paper presented at the 96th American Political Association Meeting in Washington, DC, August 31–September 3, 2000.

Scheuer, Steen. 1992. "Denmark: Return to Decentralization," in Anthony Ferner and Richard Hyman (eds.), *Industrial Relations in the New Europe*: 298–322. Oxford: Basil Blackwell.

Scheve, Kenneth F. and Matthew J. Slaughter. 2001. "What Determines Individual Trade-Policy Preferences?" *Journal of International Economics* 54 (2): 267–92.

Schlesinger, James. 1984. "On the Theory of Party Organization." *Journal of Politics*, 46: 369–400.

Bibliography

Schmitter, Philippe. 1979. "Modes of Interest Intermediation and Models of Societal Change," in Philippe Schmitter and Gerhard Lehmbruch (eds.), *Trends toward Corporatist Intermediation*, pp. 43–94. Beverly Hills, CA: Sage.

Schwartz, Herman. 1994. "Small States in Big Trouble: State Reorganization in Australia, Denmark, New Zealand, and Sweden in the 1980s." *World Politics* 46 (July): 527–55.

2001. "Round of the Usual Suspects! Globalization, Domestic Politics, and Welfare State Change," in Paul Pierson (ed.), *The New Politics of the Welfare State*, pp. 17–44. Oxford: Oxford University Press.

Siaroff, Alan. 1999. "Corporatism in Twenty-Four Industrial Democracies: Meaning and Measurement." *European Journal of Political Research* 36: 175–205.

Sinn, Hans-Werner. 1995. "A Theory of the Welfare State." *Scandinavian Journal of Economics* 97 (4): 495–526.

Soskice, David. 1990. "Wage Determination: The Changing Role of Institutions in Advanced Industrialized Countries." *Oxford Review of Economic Policy* 6 (4): 36–61.

1999. "Divergent Production Regimes: Coordinated and Uncoordinated Market Economies in the 1980s and 1990s," in Herbert Kitschelt, Peter Lange, Gary Marks, and John D. Stepehens (eds.), *Continuity and Change in Contemporary Capitalism*, pp. 101–34. Cambridge: Cambridge University Press.

2000. "Macroeconomic Analysis and the Political Economy of Unemployment," in Torben Iversen, Jonas Pontusson, and David Soskice (eds.), *Unions, Employers and Central Banks: Macroeconomic Coordination and Institutional Change in Social Market Economies*. Cambridge: Cambridge University Press.

Stephens, John D. 1979. *The Transition from Capitalism to Socialism*. London: Macmillan.

Streeck, Wolfgang. 1991. "On the Institutional Conditions of Diversified Quality Production," in Egon Matzner and Wolfgang Streeck (eds.), *Beyond Keynesianism*, pp. 21–61. Aldershot: Edward Elgar.

1992. *Social Institutions and Economic Performance: Studies of Industrial Relations in Advanced Capitalist Economies*. London: Sage Publications.

1997. "German Capitalism: Does It Exist? Can It Survive?" in Colin Crouch and Wolfgang Streeck (eds.), *Political Economy of Modern Capitalism: Mapping Convergence and Diversity*: 33–54. London: Sage.

Swenson, Peter. 1989. *Fair Shares: Unions, Pay, and Politics in Sweden and West Germany*. Ithaca, NY: Cornell University Press.

1991a. "Bringing Capital Back in, or Social Democracy Reconsidered: Employer Power, Cross-Class Alliances, and Centralization of Industrial Relations in Denmark and Sweden." *World Politics* 43 (4): 513–45.

1991b. "Labor and the Limits of the Welfare State. The Politics of Intraclass Conflict and Cross-Class Alliances in Sweden and West-Germany" *Comparative Politics* 23 (4): 379–99.

1997. "Arranged Alliance: Business Interests in the New Deal." *Politics and Society* 25 (1): 66–116.

2002. *Employers against Markets*. Cambridge: Cambridge University Press.

Tabellini, Guido. 2000. "Constitutional Determinants of Government Spending." Mimeo, IGIER and Department of Economics, Bocconi University.

Thelen, Kathleen and Ikuo Kume. 1999. "The Effects of Globalization on Labor Revisited: Lessons from Germany and Japan." *Politics and Society* 27 (4): 477–505.

Toniolo, Gianni. 1996. "Europe's Golden Age (1950–73): A Long-Run Perspective," Tawney Memorial Lecture Delivered to the Annual Meetings of the Royal Economic Society.

Torfing, Jacob. 1999. "Workfare with Welfare: Recent Reforms of the Danish Welfare State." *Journal of European Social Policy* 9 (1): 5–28.

Undy, Roger. 1999. "New Labour's 'Industrial Relations Settlement': The Third Way?" *British Journal of Industrial Relations* 37 (2): 315–36.

UNESCO (United Nations Educational, Scientific, and Cultural Organization). 1999. *UNESCO Statistical Yearbook*. New York: UNESCO.

U.S. Census Bureau. 2000. *Current Population Survey*. http://www.bls.census.gov/cps.

Van Ark, Bart. 1996. "Sectoral Growth Accounting and Structural Change in Post-War Europe," in Bart Van Ark and Nicholas Crafts (eds.), *Quantitative Aspects of Post-War European Economic Growth*, pp. 84–164. Cambridge: Cambridge University Press.

Visser, Jelle. 1989. *European Trade Unions in Figures*. Deventer, Netherlands: Kluwer Law and Taxation Publishers.

1996. "Unionization Trends Revisited." Mimeo, University of Amsterdam.

Visser, Jelle and Anton Hemerijck. 1997. *A Dutch Miracle. Job Growth Welfare Reform and Corporatism in the Netherlands*. Amsterdam: Amsterdam University Press.

Vogel, Steven K. 1996. *Freer Markets, More Rules: Regulatory Reform in Advanced Industrialized Countries*. Ithaca, NY: Cornell University Press.

Wallerstein, Michael. 1999. "Wage-Setting Institutions and Pay Inequality in Advanced Industrial Societies." *American Journal of Political Science* 43 (3): 649–80.

Williamson, Oliver E. 1985. *The Economic Institutions of Capitalism: Firms, Markets, Relational Contracting*. New York: Free Press.

Windolf, Paul. 1989. "Productivity Coalitions and the Future of European Corporatism." *Industrial Relations* 28 (1): 1–20.

Wittman, Donald. 1973. "Parties as Utility Maximizers." *American Political Science Review* 67 (2): 490–8.

Wolff, E. N. 1998. "Recent Trends in the Size Distribution of Household Wealth." *Journal of Economic Perspectives* 12 (3): 131–50.

Wood, Andrian. 1994. *North-South Trade, Employment and Inequality: Changing Fortunes in a Skill-Driven World*. Oxford: Oxford University Press.

Wood, Stewart. 1997. "Capitalist Constitutions: Supply-Side Reforms in Britain and West Germany, 1960–1990." Dissertation, Department of Government, Harvard University.

Wren, Anne. 2000. "Distributional Tradeoffs and Partisan Politics in the Postindustrial Economy." Dissertation, Department of Government, Harvard University.

Bibliography

2001. (1) "The Challenge of De-Industrialization: Divergent Ideological Responses to Welfare State Reform" in Bernhard Ebbinghaus and Philip Manow (eds.), *Comparing Welfare Capitalism: Social Policy and Political Economy in Europe, Japan and the USA*: 239–269. New York and London: Routledge.

Wu, Yangru. 1996. "Are Real Exchange Rates Nonstationary? Evidence from a Panel-Data Test." *Journal of Money Credit and Banking* 28 (1): 54–63.

Zysman, John. 1983. *Governments, Markets, and Growth: Financial Systems and the Politics of Industrial Change*. Ithaca, NY: Cornell University Press.

Zysman, John and Stephen S. Cohen. 1987. *Manufacturing Matters: The Myth of the Post-Industrial Economy*. New York: Basic Books.

Index

Index

David D. Laitin, *Language Repertories and State Construction in Africa*

Fabrice E. Lehoucq and Ivan Molina, *Stuffing the Ballot Box: Fraud, Electoral Reform, and Democratization in Costa Rica*

Mark Irving Lichbach and Alan S. Zuckerman, eds., *Comparative Politics: Rationality, Culture, and Structure*

Evan Lieberman, *Race and Regionalism in the Politics of Taxation in Brazil and South Africa*

Pauline Jones Luong, *Institutional Change and Political Continuity in Post-Soviet Central Asia: Power, Perception, and Pacts*

Doug McAdam, John McCarthy, and Mayer Zald, eds., *Comparative Perspectives on Social Movements*

James Mahoney and Dietrich Rueschemeyer, eds., *Historical Analysis in the Social Sciences*

Scott Mainwaring and Matthew Soberg Shugart, eds., *Presidentialism and Democracy in Latin America*

Isabela Mares, *The Politics of Social Risk: Business and Welfare State Development*

Anthony W. Marx, *Making Race, Making Nations: A Comparison of South Africa, the United States and Brazil*

Joel S. Migdal, *State and Society: Studying How States and Societies Constitute One Another*

Joel S. Migdal, Atul Kohli, and Vivienne Shue, eds., *State Power and Social Forces: Domination and Transformation in the Third World*

Scott Morgenstern and Benito Nacif, eds., *Legislative Politics in Latin America*

Layna Mosley, *Global Capital and National Governments*

Wolfgang C. Muller and Kaare Strom, *Policy, Office, or Votes?*

Maria Victoria Murillo, *Labor Unions, Partisan Coalitions, and Market Reforms in Latin America*

Ton Notermans, *Money, Markets, and the State: Social Democratic Economic Policies since 1918*

Roger Petersen, *Understanding Ethnic Violence: Fear, Hatred, and Resentment in 20th-Century Eastern Europe*

Simona Piattoni, ed., *Clientelism, Interests, and Democratic Representation*

Paul Pierson, *Dismantling the Welfare State?: Reagan, Thatcher and the Politics of Retrenchment*

Marino Regini, *Uncertain Boundaries: The Social and Political Construction of European Economies*

Lyle Scruggs, *Sustaining Abundance: Environmental Performance in Industrial Democracies*

Jeffrey M. Sellers, *Governing from Below: Urban Regions and the Global Economy*

Yossi Shain and Juan Linz, eds., *Interim Governments and Democratic Transitions*

Beverly J. Silver, *Forces of Labor: Workers' Movements and Globalization since 1870*

Theda Skocpol, *Social Revolutions in the Modern World*

Richard Snyder, *Politics after Neoliberalism: Reregulation in Mexico*

David Stark and László Bruszt, *Postsocialist Pathways: Transforming Politics and Property in East Central Europe*

Sven Steinmo, Kathleen Thelen, and Frank Longstreth, eds., *Structuring Politics: Historical Institutionalism in Comparative Analysis*

Susan C. Stokes, *Mandates and Democracy: Neoliberalism by Surprise in Latin America*

Susan C. Stokes, ed., *Public Support for Market Reforms in New Democracies*

Duane Swank, *Global Capital, Political Institutions, and Policy Change in Developed Welfare States*

Sidney Tarrow, *Power in Movement: Social Movements and Contentious Politics*

Ashutosh Varshney, *Democracy, Development, and the Countryside*

Steven I. Wilkinson, *Votes and Violence: Electoral Competition and Ethnic Riots in India*

Elisabeth Jean Wood, *Forging Democracy from Below: Insurgent Transitions in South Africa and El Salvador*

Elisabeth Jean Wood, *Insurgent Collective Action in El Salvador*